3D PAPERCRAFT BUTTERFLIES & MOTHS

Bring Gorgeous Insects to Life
with Easy Color and Cut Projects

STACIA BALDWIN
Creator of Beastie and Bone

PAGE STREET PUBLISHING CO.

First published in 2026 by
Page Street Publishing Co.
27 Congress Street, Suite 1511
Salem, MA 01970
www.pagestreetpublishing.com

Distributed by Macmillan, sales in Canada by The Canadian Manda Group.

30 29 28 27 26 1 2 3 4 5

ISBN-13: 979-8-89003-483-0

Library of Congress Control Number: 2025949499

Edited by Alexandra Murphy
Cover and book design by Emma Hardy for Page Street Publishing Co.
Photography by Laurel Class

Printed and bound in China

Page Street Publishing protects our planet by donating to nonprofits like The Trustees, which focuses on local land conservation.

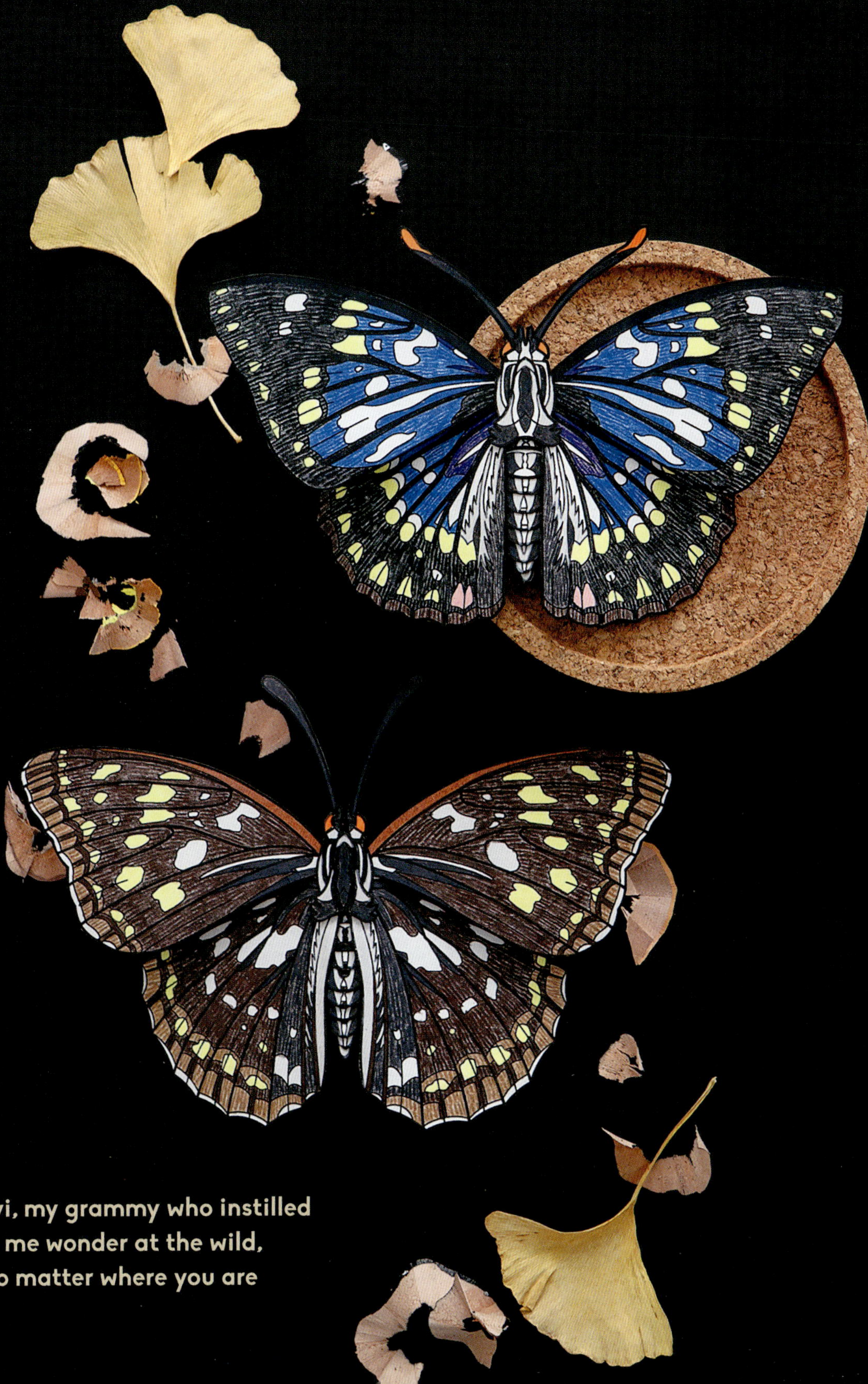

For Elvi, my grammy who instilled
in me wonder at the wild,
no matter where you are

CONTENTS

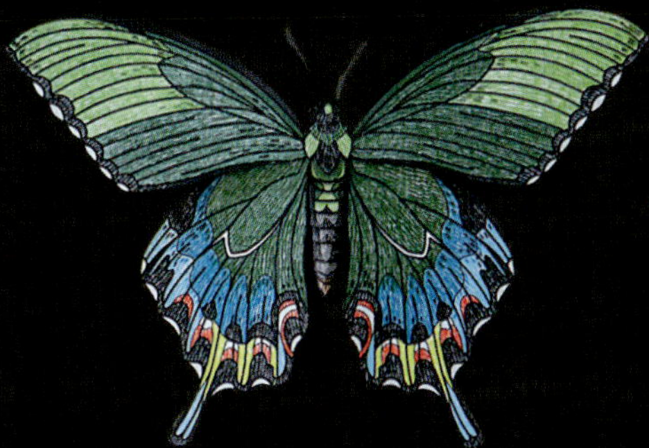

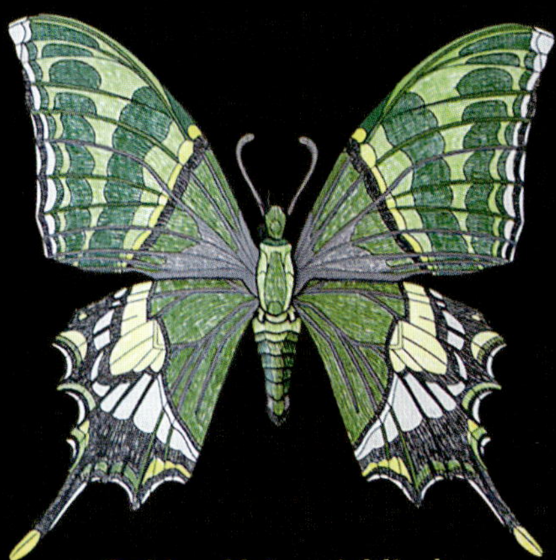

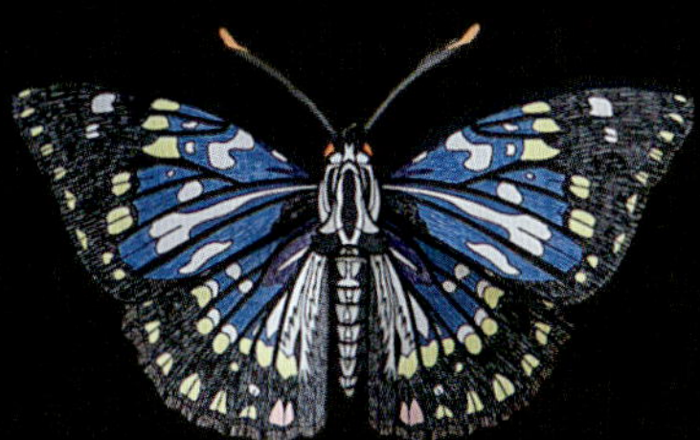

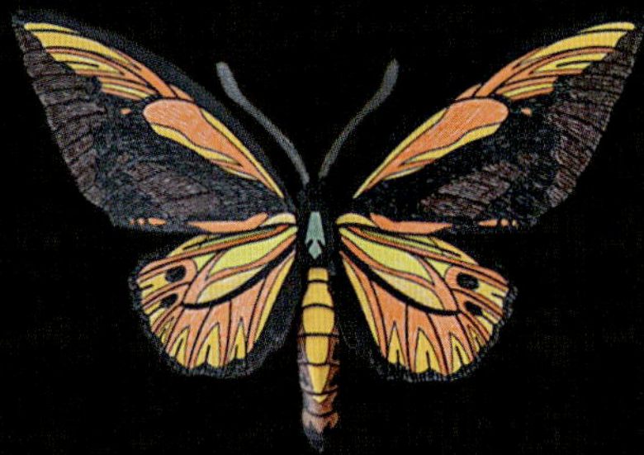

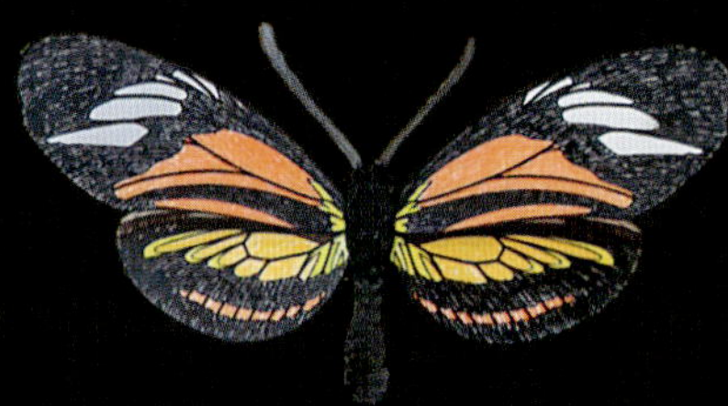

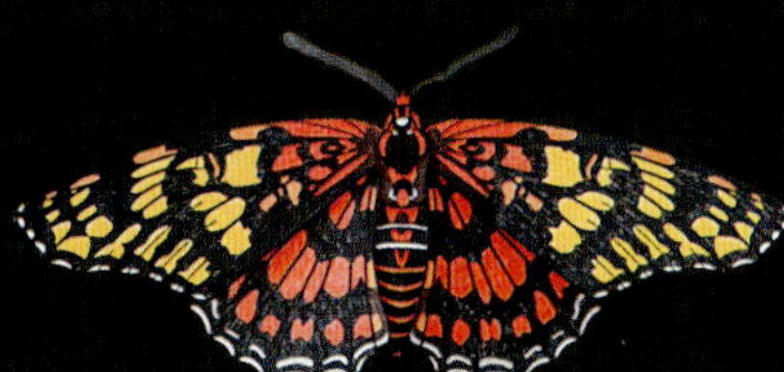

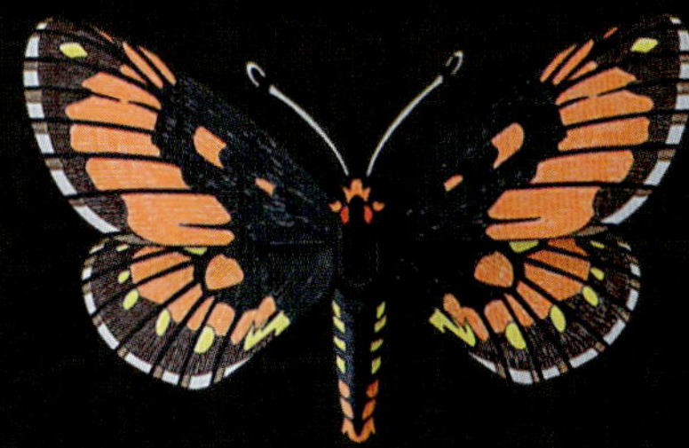

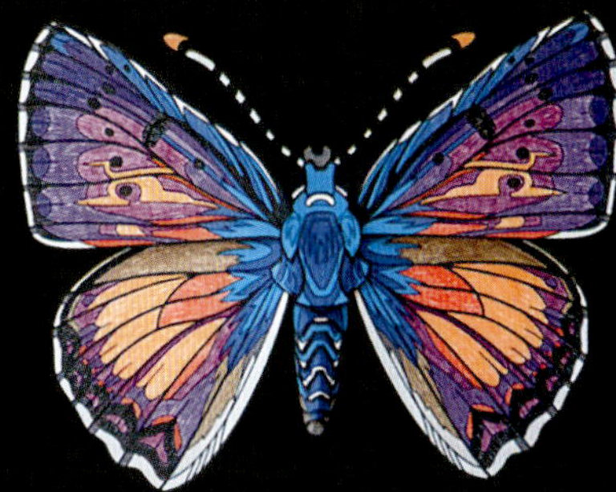

INTRODUCTION

One of the most common questions I get asked as a paper artist is, *Why bother making paper specimens of insects, when getting the real ones is becoming so easy?*

But I don't mind, because asking questions—curiosity—is how we should approach anything new. I wouldn't be a paper artist without asking questions.

See, I have a secret. I'm actually scared of butterflies touching me—have been since I was a kid. But as a child in a family of artists and scientists, my grandparents in particular encouraged me to slow down and simply observe that which was unfamiliar.

By pausing my fear reaction (run away, squish it, scream) I began to see the world as a shared space of lives, all making their own way, instead of a sea of strange potential threats to my own life. This is where my motto of "curiosity and compassion" springs from. It's also what, despite my lingering fear of having a butterfly land on me, inspired me to begin creating paper *entomology* artwork between assignments in art school. I was living in a city for the first time in my life, surrounded by so many lifestyles and experiences that were strange to me, and struggling for the first time with chronic health issues that left me feeling small, frail, and overwhelmed.

Entomology is the study of insects, and *lepidopterology* is the specialized study of order *Lepidoptera*, which contains all species of moths and butterflies. There are 6 families of butterflies and over *130* families of moths around the world.

This is also when I began to learn about wildlife conservation, and how the smaller and less human (non-mammalian) endangered creatures get less recognition, funding, and protection. Though, if you've ever been to a curiosity shop or alternative art market, the wide range of specimens available may have you think otherwise. In recent years, *insect pinning* has become increasingly popular among hobbyist insect and curio collectors, with the rise of the internet and social media increasing its visibility.

Insect pinning is the process of preserving and mounting specimens with specialized chemicals and tools that, yes, include long, delicate pins.

Plenty of collectors and artisans selling or sourcing specimens for display obtain the insects they use through *vulture culture*, using the motto "It was dead when I found it" as their guide. They only use insects found already deceased in the wild. Others breed and raise insects, gathering their captive insects to preserve and pin after they have bred, laid eggs, and passed naturally. These are called *farmed specimens*. Unfortunately, these renewable methods aren't always the ones used in this fast-growing field of insect interest.

Illegal collecting and selling of wild endangered lepidopterans occur all over the world, and, as increasingly more insect species veer toward endangered status, even collecting non-protected moths and butterflies can pose a risk to population health.

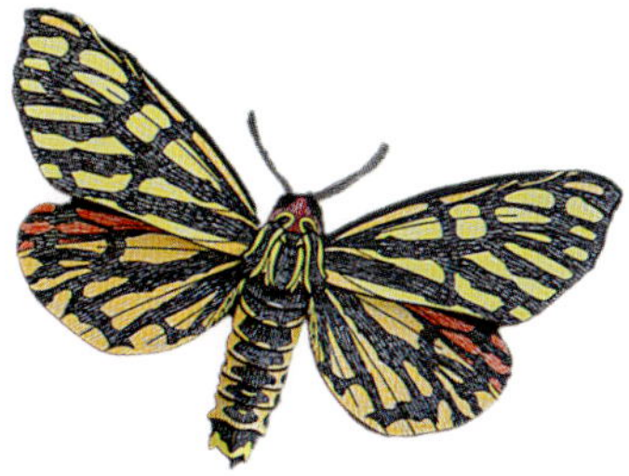

This is where alternative specimens like the ones you're about to create for yourself using this book come in.

The 15 species in these paper art projects represent endangered, rare, or threatened species of moths and butterflies from all over the world. Some are illegal to capture or sell worldwide (such as the Golden Kaiser-i-Hind [page 63]). Others are so rare or live in such remote areas (like the Menetries' Tiger Moth [page 27]), that we don't know how many of them are left in the wild. All are beautiful, and as you'll learn, have developed unique traits that have helped them survive and thrive.

So, let's slow down and observe through creating, together, and craft a whole collection of specimens to enjoy and display without ever harming one fuzzy hair or wing scale.

Be Well,
Stacia

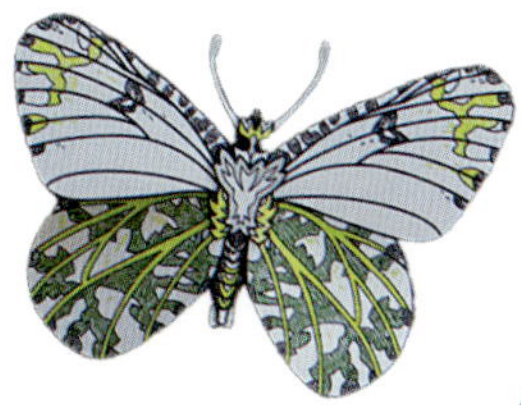

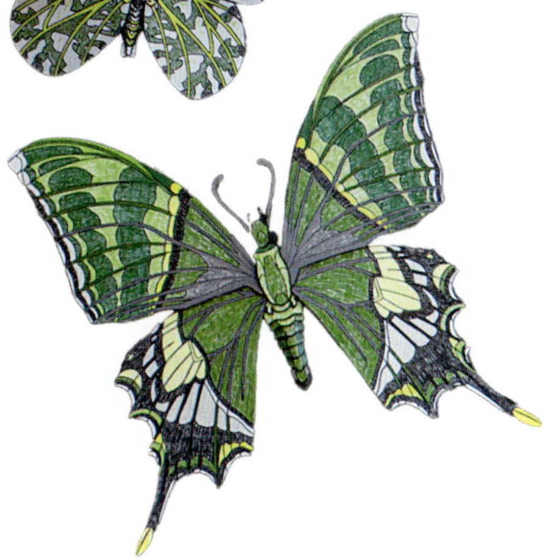

If you'd like to learn more about lepidopterology and endangered species, I've included a resource list at the end of this book that includes websites, articles, and other books that I've referred to in creating these projects, and other paper art specimens of moths and butterflies. You'll find that on page 114.

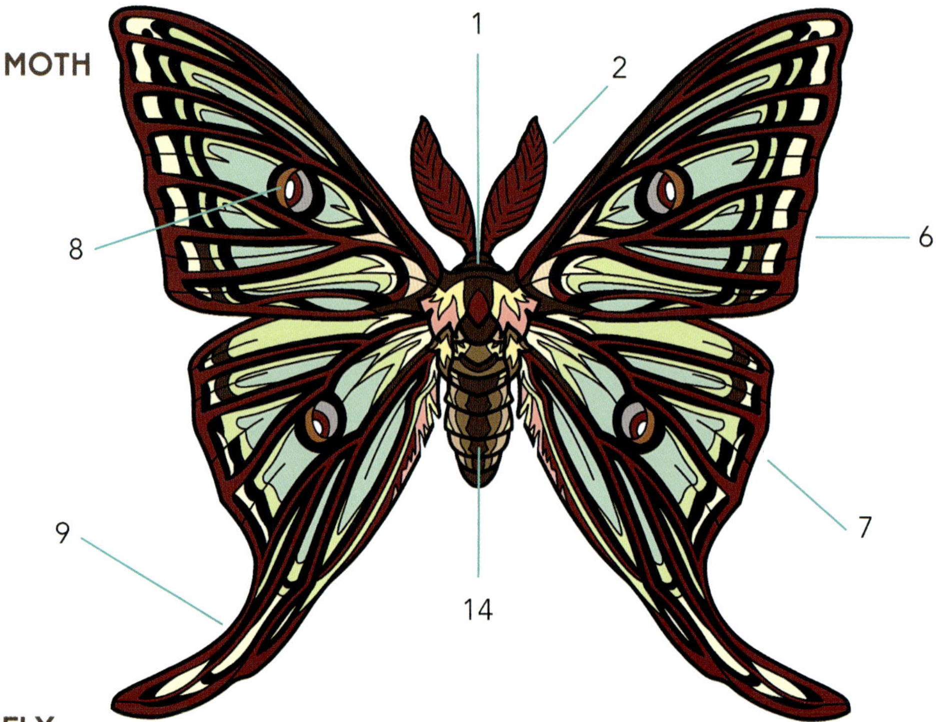

MOTH
1
2
6
7
8
9
14

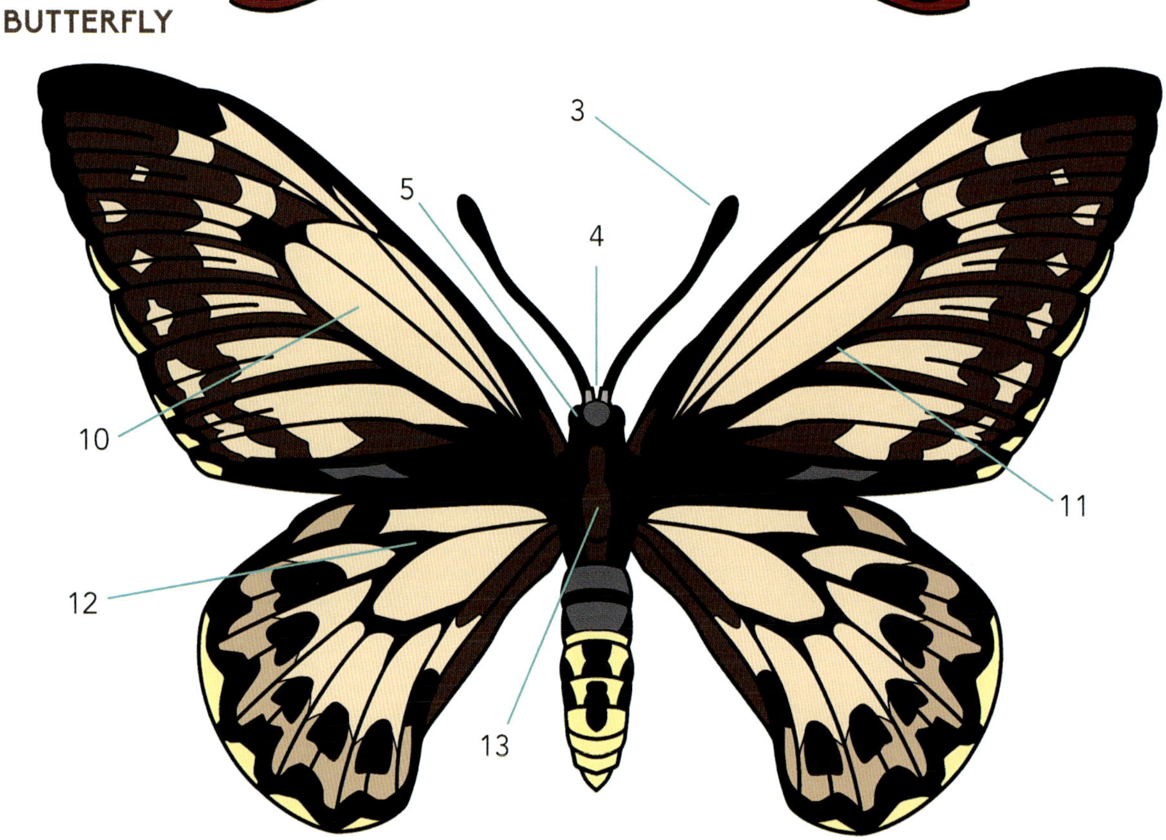

BUTTERFLY
3
4
5
10
11
12
13

LEPIDOPTERAN ANATOMY

Moths and butterflies belong to the same order of Lepidoptera since, in fact, butterflies are an offshoot of moths that evolved separately during the middle Eocene, approximately 40 to 50 million years ago. So, much of their anatomy is the same.

The projects in this book will reference anatomy of butterflies and moths as you work, but here is a full guide to many of the parts mentioned.

1. Head
2. Antennae
3. Club (distinctive feature of butterfly antennae)
4. Papillae
5. Eyes
6. Forewings
7. Hindwings
8. Eye patches/ocelli (not present on all species)
9. Hindwing extension/tail (not present on all species)
10. Scales
11. Wing veins
12. Costa (main wing vein)
13. Thorax
14. Abdomen

Like all true insects, lepidopterans are constructed of three main sections: the head, the thorax, and the abdomen, encased in a tough exoskeleton made of chitin. Their two sets of wings are made of two layers of membrane stretched over hollow veins. These wings, and the lepidopterans' six legs, all attach to the thorax.

The three main body sections and four wings are all present in the projects in this book, but you may notice that not all pieces of lepidopteran anatomy are. Several external lepidopteran body parts, such as the tube-like proboscis (long mouthpart) on the bottom front of the head, or the six slender legs, are typically not easily seen on real moth or butterfly specimens. That's because once the specimen is deceased, these body parts often curl up tight against the body. As these parts are also difficult to re-create in paper, even at the scaled-up size of many of the projects in this book, I've opted out of including them for the sake of ease and simplicity. They are not forgotten, however, as several of the species in this book possess unique qualities in these tiny body parts!

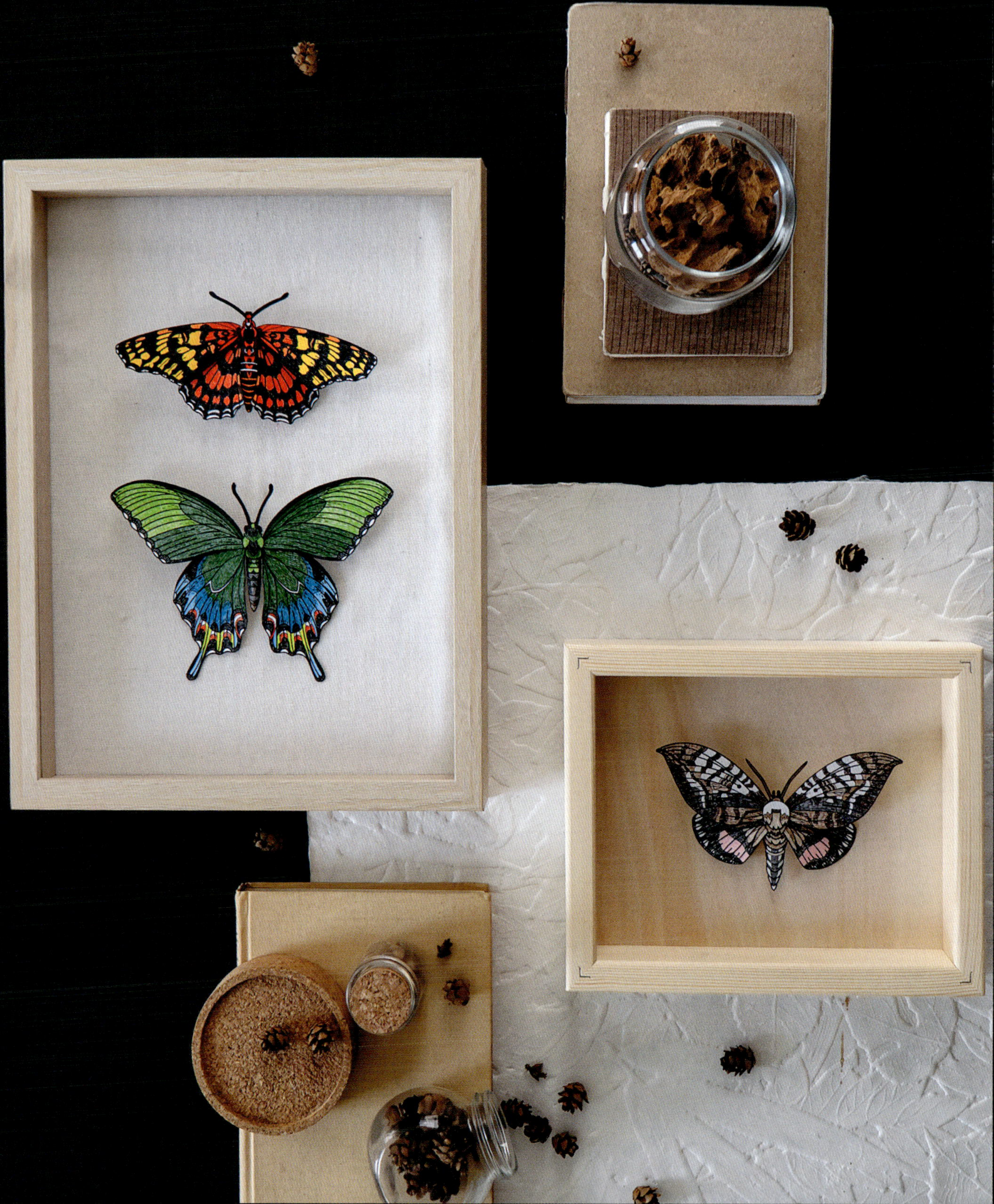

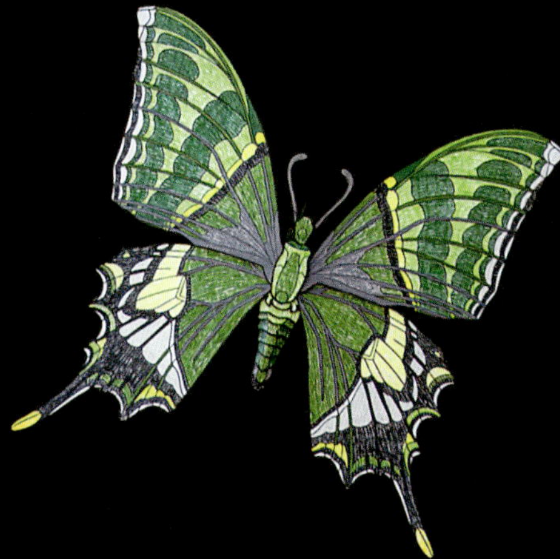

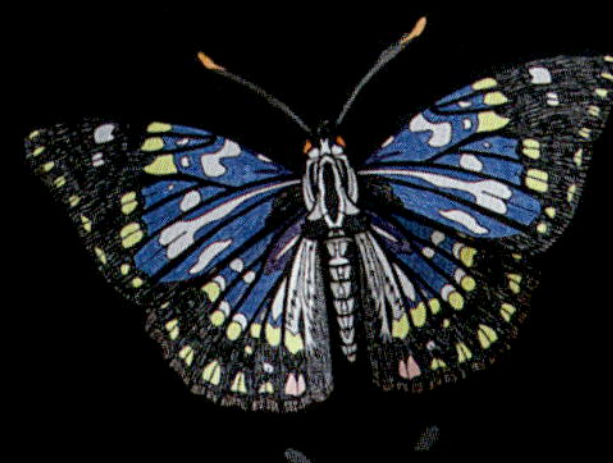

PAPERCRAFT TIPS AND TRICKS

If you are new to papercraft, you'll be happy to hear that great results come from working slowly, testing your tools and materials before you jump into the full project, and having a few simple techniques up your sleeve.

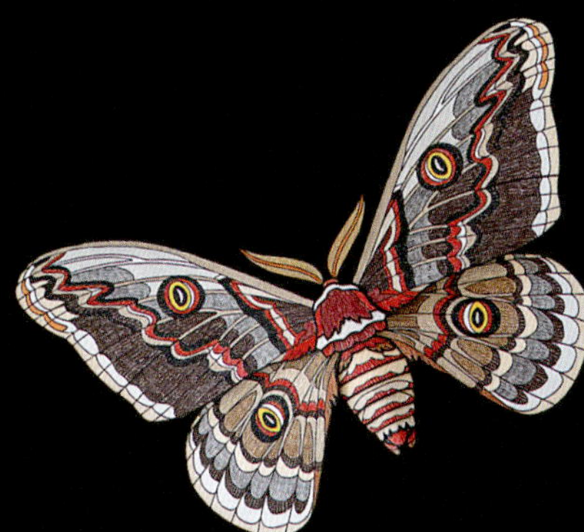

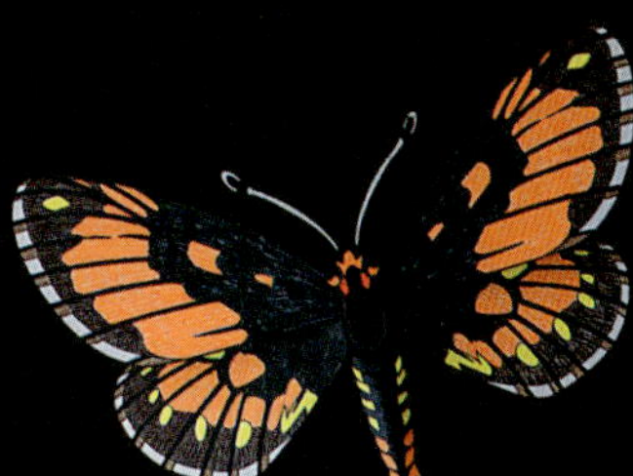

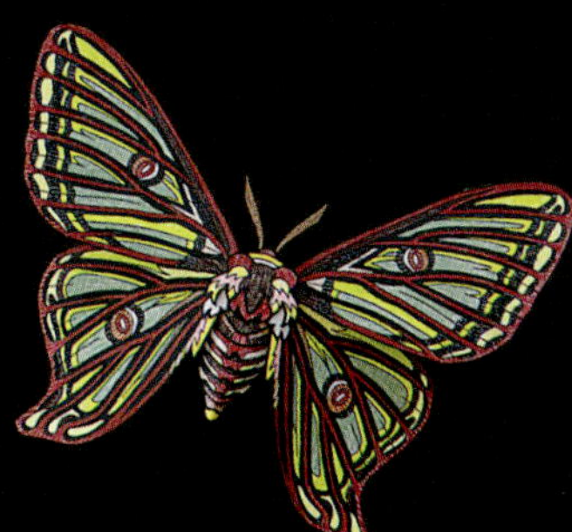

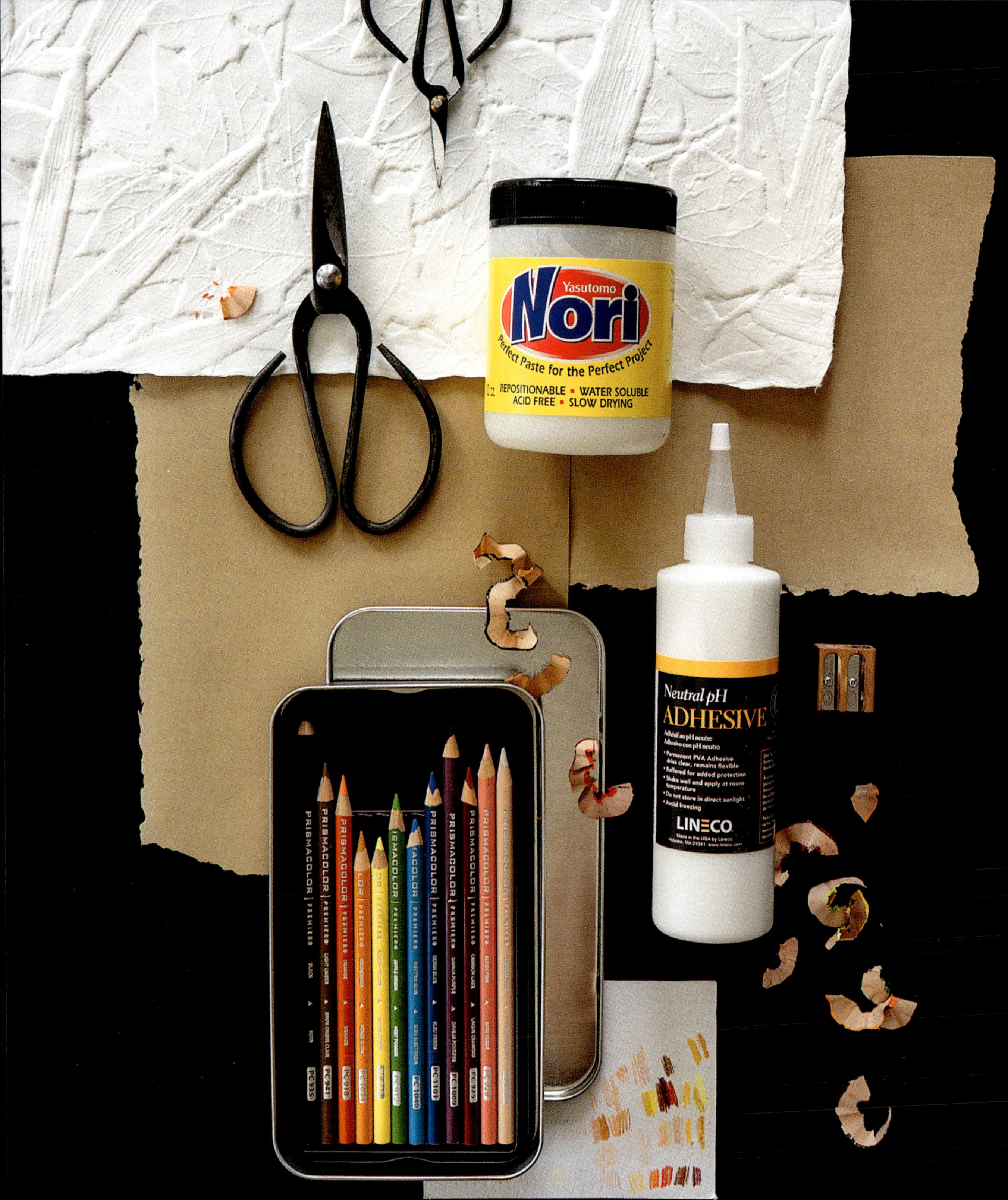
Yasutomo
Nori
Perfect Paste for the Perfect Project
REPOSITIONABLE ▪ WATER SOLUBLE
ACID FREE ▪ SLOW DRYING
Neutral pH
ADHESIVE
LINECO
PRISMACOLOR

TOOLS AND MATERIALS

Colored Pencils: The smoothest and richest color is applied with *artist-quality* colored pencils. These are softer than colored pencils intended for children and have more pigment in them. Personally, I like the brand Prismacolor® because of their wide range of available colors and their accessibility. Not only are they a more affordable artist-quality pencil brand, but they are carried by almost all arts and crafts stores. The colors needed for each individual project will be listed in its instructions. If you can't source pencils the exact same colors as the ones listed in the projects, simply use the color guides for each project to visually match to the closest pencil colors you like. While each species has specific coloration, there is a natural range of variation between individuals in a species, so you'll still be re-creating realistic coloring!

You can also use watercolors, markers, ink, or acrylic paint if you prefer those mediums. (I like gouache, myself, when creating my papercraft original works.). But avoid getting your templates too damp while you work, to prevent the cardstock from warping.

Thick Black Marker: While any black marker with a thick nib will do, I recommend using one filled with waterproof India ink. India ink is a beautiful, rich black that doesn't fade, and being waterproof will prevent the ink from bleeding across your specimen template pieces when you glue them together. Both Prismacolor and Faber-Castell® brands have nice markers that fit these suggestions.

Scissors: I have found brand does not matter as much as how you handle the scissors while working, but smaller pairs are easier to maneuver through details or corners while cutting.

Glue: There are two types of glue that work well for papercraft projects like the ones in this book.

1. PVA (polyvinyl acetate) glue is very common, though you may know it better as tacky glue or Elmer's® glue. **PH neutral PVA glue** is the higher-quality version of this glue and can be found in bookbinding sections of art stores. It is pretty runny, but thick, and dries quickly. It works well if you have a small brush to apply it with, and if you are comfortable working quickly.

2. Nori paste is my personal favorite glue to work with for papercraft, particularly with delicate elements. It is an archival glue (meaning it won't discolor, crumble, or damage what it is used on for a *very long* time) and is made of rice starch. It is thick and dries completely clear, though it does take longer to dry. This makes it great to work with if you're worried about dripping glue or would like to have time to adjust the pieces you're gluing together before they dry.

Additional helpful items for creating your papercraft insect specimens include a **pencil sharpener, scrap paper** to practice color and cutting techniques, and a **small paintbrush or toothpick** to apply glue with.

TECHNIQUES

COLORING

If you'd like a **solid, bold color approach** for your papercraft moths and butterflies, a smoother finish can be achieved by building up the color through going over each section two to three times with a lighter touch, rather than by pressing down hard. Pressing too hard can scratch or indent the cardstock the project templates are printed on, make your pencil lead prone to breaking, or even tire your hands faster.

If you'd like a **softer finish that mimics real lepidopteran wing scales**, make many small, repeating marks with your pencils, following the curves of the wing sections of the project templates. This coloring technique is called *linear hatching*.

To add **extra detail and customization** to your papercraft specimens, sprinkle small marks of darker colors through lighter areas of your templates, and vice versa, particularly along edges of wings, or along the edges where two different colors meet. This technique is called *stippling*.

To achieve **a polished finish** for your template pieces, color the edges with a black marker. To do this, hold the template piece up in one hand, and run the side of the marker nib, not the tip, along the edge of the template piece. This step is optional but does result in a cleaner look for your completed paper specimen.

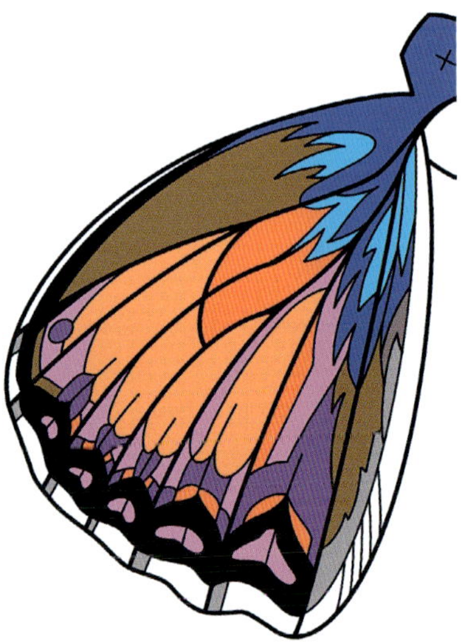

Solid color

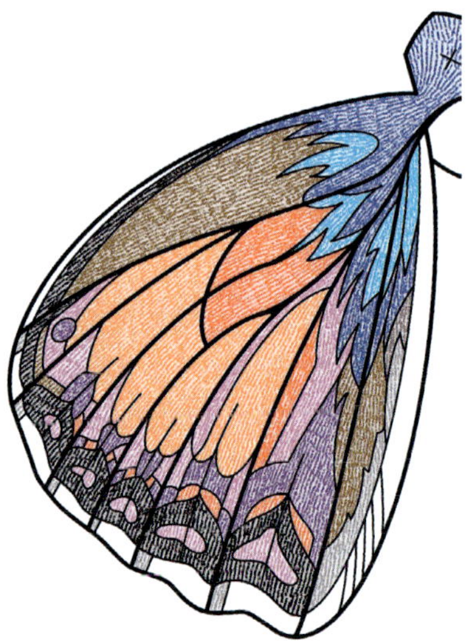

Linear hatching

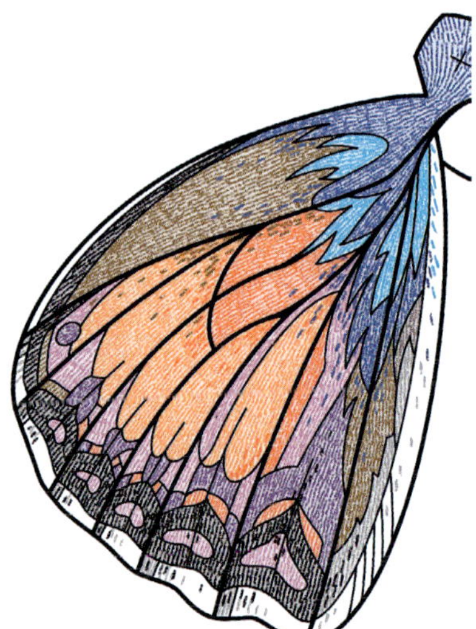

Linear hatching with stippling detail

CUTTING

Before cutting out the pieces of your project templates, first cut the template into sections, separating each template piece from the rest as indicated in the image below. This reduces the amount of paper you have to handle when doing the more detailed cutting and eliminates you accidentally cutting into or smudging another template piece.

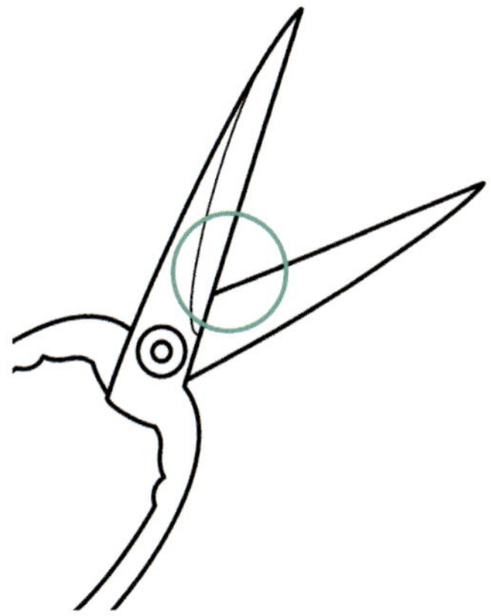

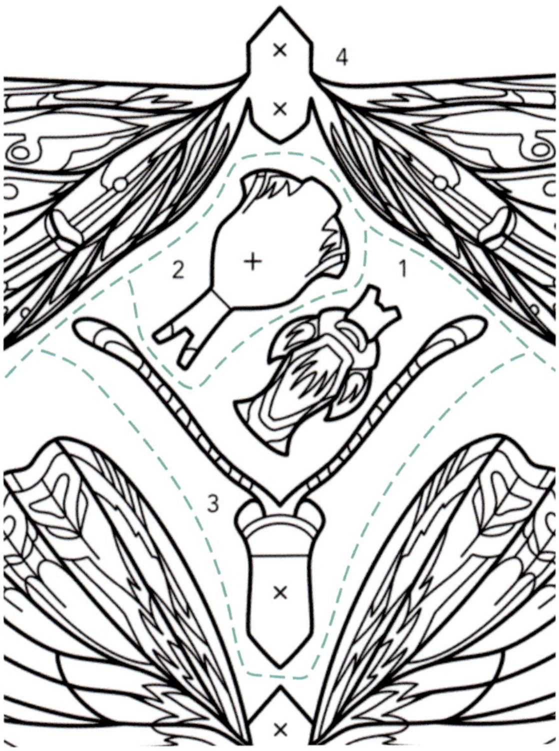

Use the inner corner of your scissors to cut. This area of your scissors, circled in the image above, is nearest the fulcrum (the point where the two blades and the handles join) and therefore the easiest to control, being more sensitive to pressure and tiny changes of direction.

Cut two-snip Vs. This means when cutting out a corner or detail area, cut down into the corner from one direction, remove your scissors, turn the paper, and cut down into the corner from the other direction. Cutting this way results in a cleaner look, and prevents your template pieces getting crumpled from twisting the scissors around trying to turn a sharp corner while you cut.

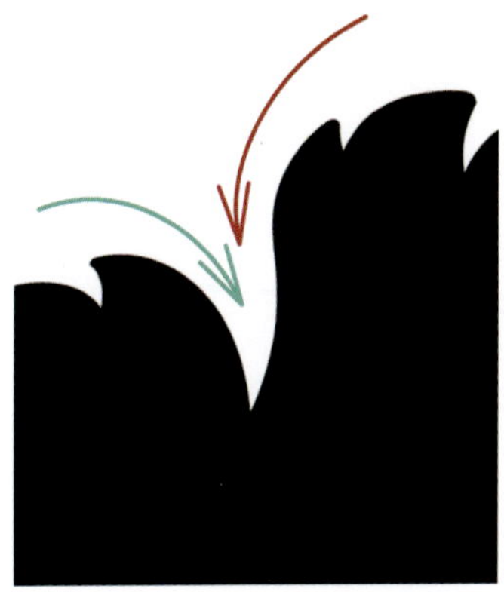

Don't go for long cuts. Utilizing many tiny repeating snips may be more work for your hand, but it will result in smoother curves and fewer chances you'll cut something off accidentally. It also works well with the previously mentioned suggestion of using the inner area of your scissors.

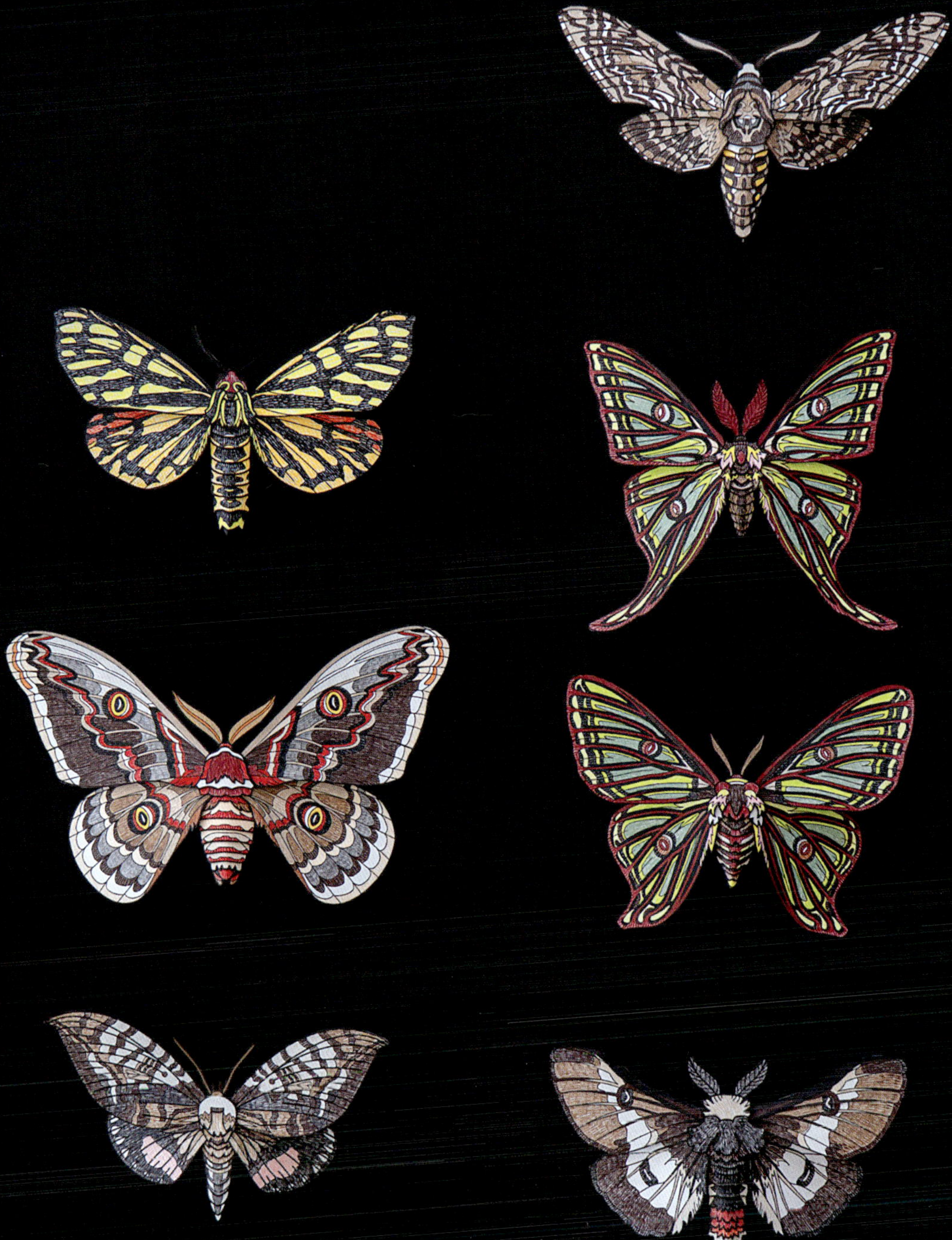

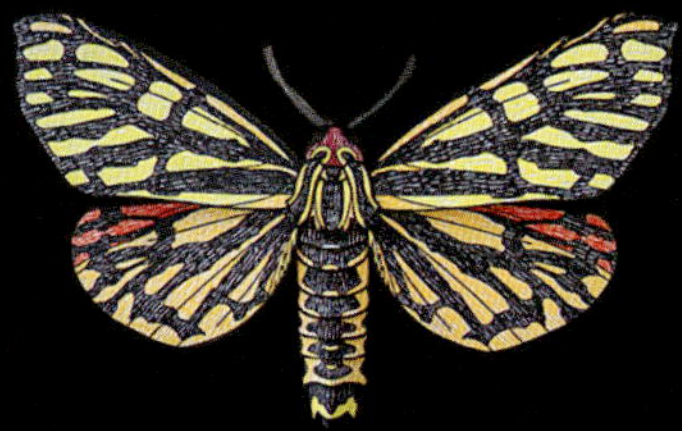

MOTHS

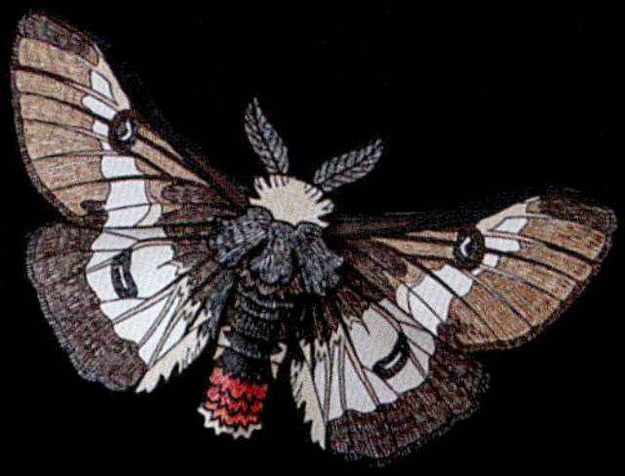

Generally nocturnal (active at night), moths are also usually fluffy and more muted in coloration than butterflies. Their fluffiness—created by their long scales that look like hairs—helps keep them warm without sunlight to bask in and mutes their movements, making them harder for nocturnal predators like bats or owls to pinpoint. The soft shades of brown, black, and gray present in many moths allow them to blend into the flora of their surroundings as they rest during the day. The brighter colors that exist in moths serve specific purposes, too. They're designed to startle daytime predators, either with sudden flashes like the hindwings of the Southern Pink Underwing Moth (page 45) or the *Warning! I'm toxic!* orange on the Menetries' Tiger Moth (page 27).

Explore the subtler, twilight-loving side of Lepidoptera in the following projects featuring moths!

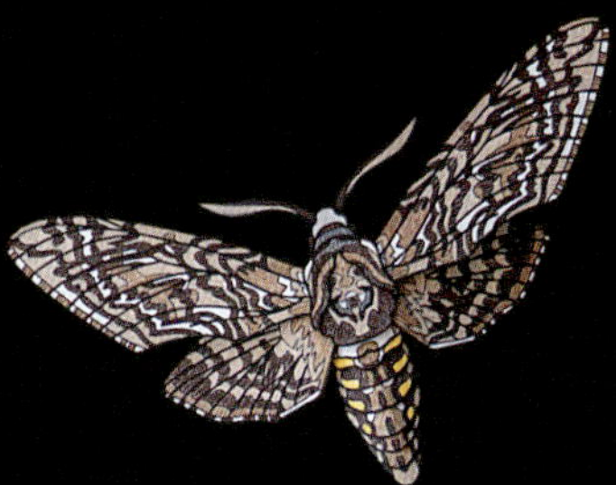

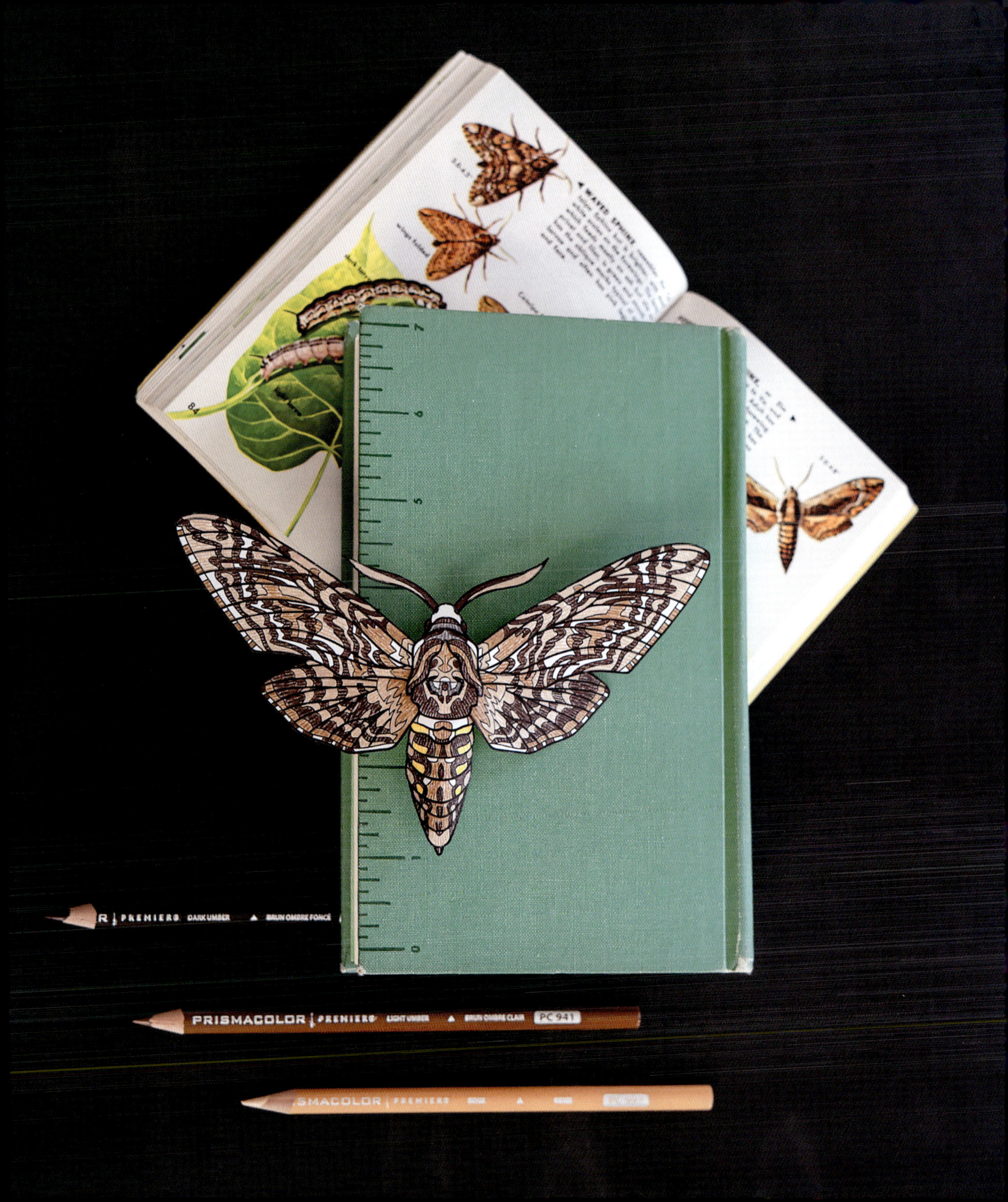
R PREMIER DARK UMBER BRUN OMBRE FONCÉ
PRISMACOLOR PREMIER LIGHT UMBER BRUN OMBRE CLAIR PC 941
SMACOLOR PREMIER

BLACKBURN'S SPHINX MOTH

The largest insect native to the islands of Hawaii, the Blackburn's sphinx moth is a noisy little powerhouse. Sphinx moths are the fastest moths in the world; some species reach over 30 miles per hour and can even hover in place like a bee or hummingbird. To fuel all this activity, sphinx moths are voracious eaters. Their proboscis, a tube-like mouthpart that works like a straw, can be almost a foot long (in the case of the Wallace's sphinx moth), and allows them to feed on cone-shaped flowers like the Hawaiian morning glory, hunakai. Such blooms produce nectar that's higher in carbohydrates, and feeding on it gives Blackburn's sphinx moths unusually high energy. As adults, they live far longer than most moths or butterflies do (up to two months) and are even capable of migration, which allows them to zoom between their homeland islands in search of mates and their next meal.

Scientific name: ***Manduca blackburni***

Habitat: ***Forests of Hawaii***

Real-life size: ***Wingspan of 5" (127 mm)***

Conservation status: ***Endangered (US Endangered Species Act)***

Template: ***Page 121***

BLACKBURN'S SPHINX MOTH COLOR GUIDE

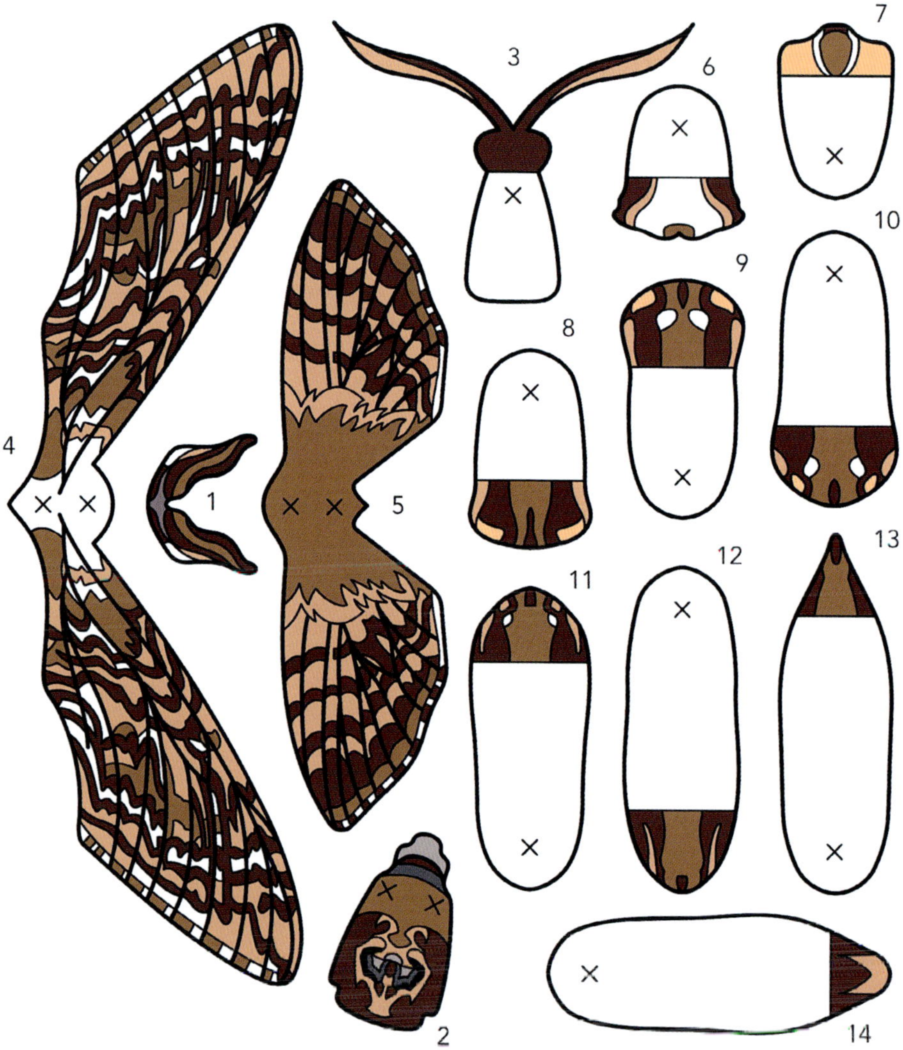

Colors Needed

- Black
- 50% warm gray
- 10% warm gray
- Dark umber
- Light umber
- Beige
- Spanish orange

BLACKBURN'S SPHINX MOTH ASSEMBLY

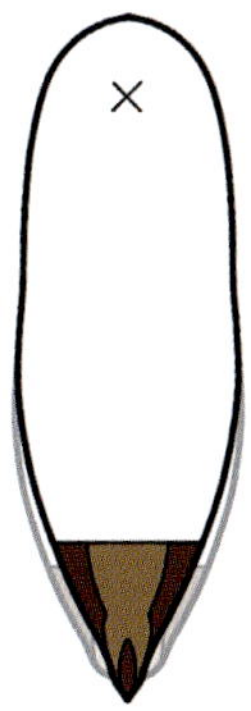

1

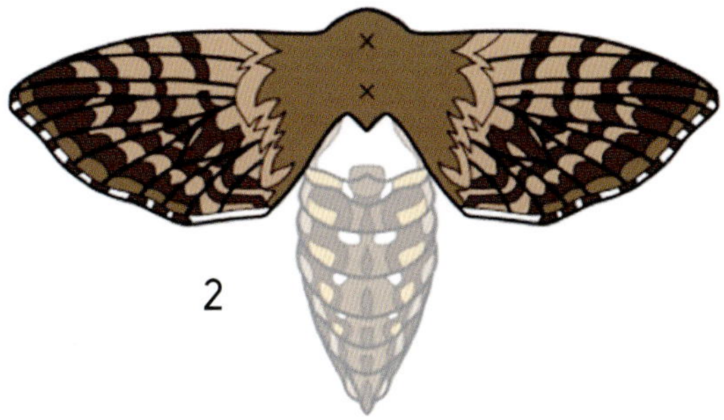

2

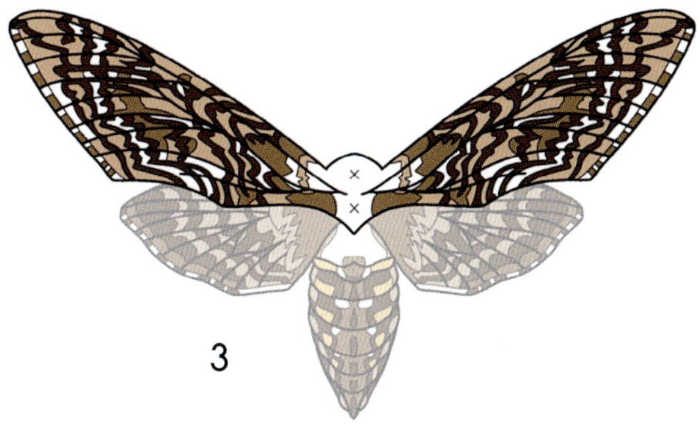

3

Remove the template for this project (page 121), and using the color guide on the left, color in the template. (You can refer to the Papercraft Tips and Tricks on page 11 for suggestions on coloring.) Once you are finished coloring, carefully cut out the template pieces along their solid black outer borders. Now it's time to assemble!

We start with the **abdomen**. Like a real lepidopteran, this paper specimen of yours has nine segments in its abdomen. Stack them in ascending order: Begin by adding glue with a toothpick or small paintbrush to the *X* mark on piece **14** and set piece **13** on top, aligning the curved top edges as shown in image 1.

Apply glue to the *X* mark on piece **13**, and set piece **12** on top. Continue this way until pieces **6** through **14** are all assembled. Set your completed abdomen aside to dry for 2 to 5 minutes. Next, mimic the curved fullness of a real moth's abdomen by pressing the abdomen over the barrel of your marker with your thumb and finger, bending the edges down.

Now for the **wings**. Apply some glue to the *X* mark on piece **6**, and set piece **5**, the **hindwings**, on top, aligning as shown in image 2.

Apply glue to the *X* marks on piece **5**, and set piece **4**, the **forewings**, on top, aligning as shown in image 3.

BLACKBURN'S SPHINX MOTH ASSEMBLY CONTINUED

4

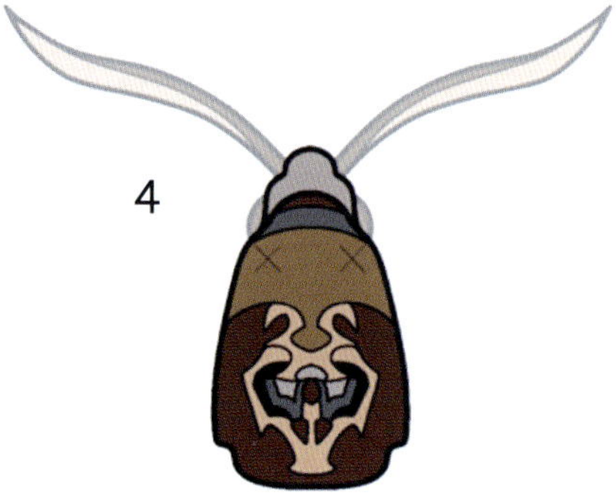

5

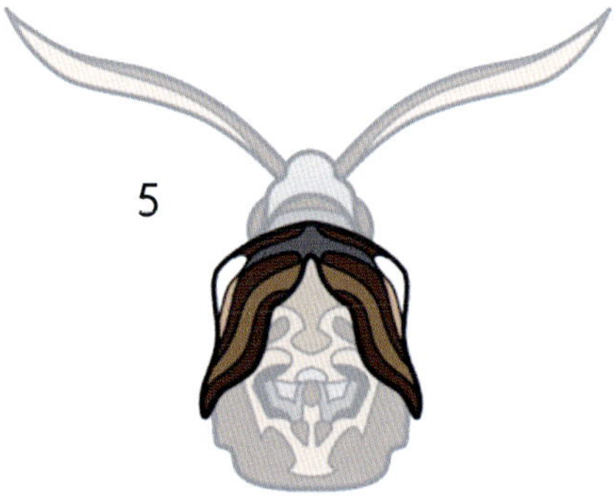

6

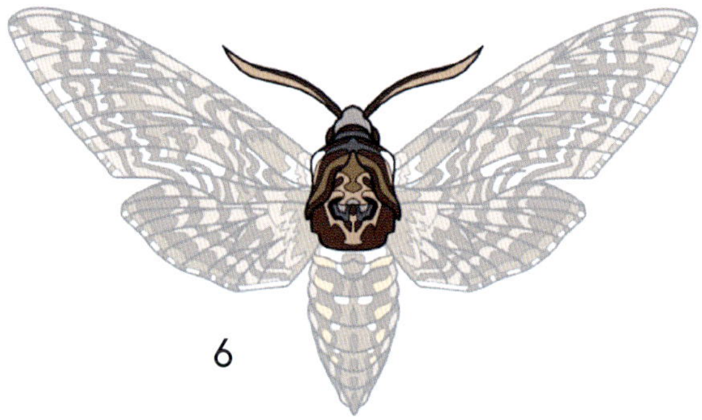

Let the wings and abdomen dry together for 2 to 5 minutes. Finally, let's assemble the **head**. Apply glue to the *X* mark on piece **3**, and set piece **2** on top, aligning as shown in image 4.

Apply glue to the two *X* marks on piece **2**, and place piece **1** on top, aligning as shown in image 5.

Set the completed head aside to dry for 2 to 5 minutes, then add glue to the *X* marks on piece **4**, and set the head on top, aligning as shown in image 6. You're done!

For a final touch of dimension, gently bend the forewings up with your fingers, and the hindwings down. If you'd like suggestions on how to display your completed moth, check out Mounting and Displaying Your Papercraft Specimens (page 109).

BOG BUCK MOTH

Scientific name: ***Hemileuca maia menyanthevora***

Habitat: ***Groundwater-fed fens in Northeastern United States and Ontario, Canada***

Real-life size: ***Wingspan of 3" (76 mm)***

Conservation status: ***Endangered (US Endangered Species Act)***

Template: ***Page 123***

While pretty, the bog buck moth is one insect I hope you don't run into unexpectedly. It's a defensive little critter native to forested wet areas that feeds on the toxic bog buckbean as a caterpillar, storing those toxins in its body to sting anything unfortunate enough to touch it. Its common name comes from the timing of the adults' emergences from their *cocoons*, which occurs in spring, the season of deer hunting. Adults only live a couple of weeks, so humans spotting them when venturing out to hunt are in the small window of time when you're less likely to get stung by a baby. But since bog buck moths remain caterpillars for up to two years and their habitat is shrinking due to deforestation, they are coming into contact with humans more often as the adults adapt to laying eggs in oak trees of developed areas like neighborhoods or parks. This has gotten the bog buck moth flagged as a pest in many areas, but they are important as *periodic defoliators* of their host plant oak trees, helping to naturally prune the branches to allow healthier growth. So, if you do run into a bog buck moth caterpillar in your backyard, recognize it'd rather be out in a thick, wet forest, left alone to do its munching work.

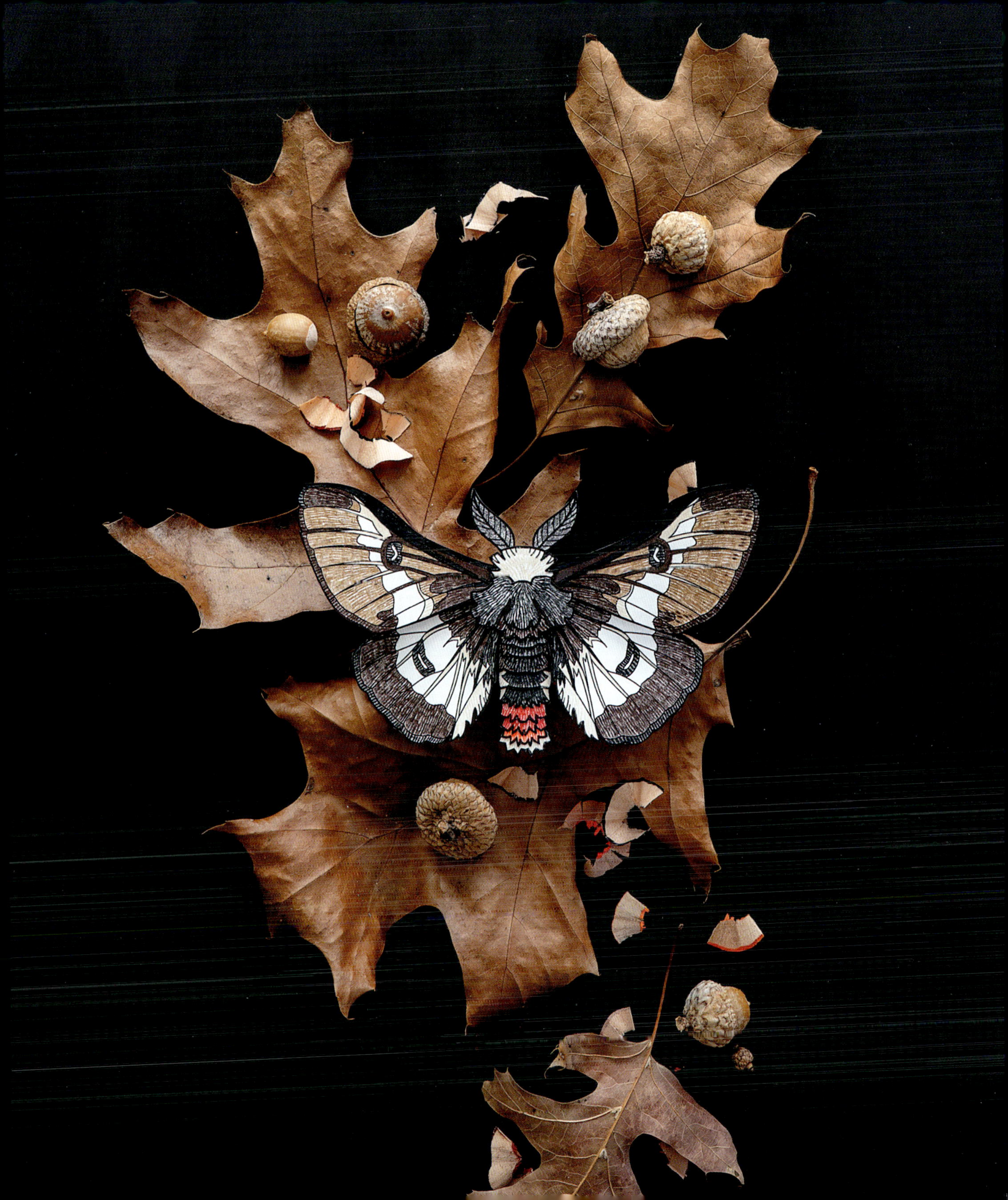

BOG BUCK MOTH COLOR GUIDE

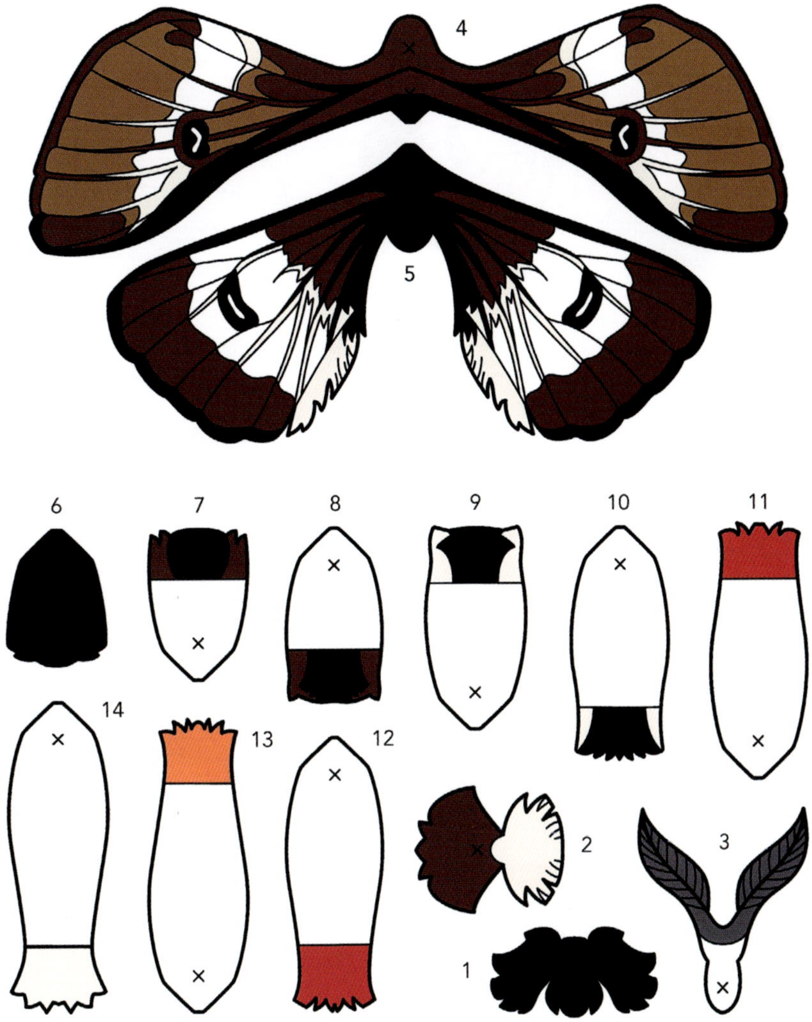

Colors Needed

- Black
- 90% warm gray
- Dark umber
- Light umber
- Crimson lake
- Poppy red
- Seashell pink

BOG BUCK MOTH ASSEMBLY

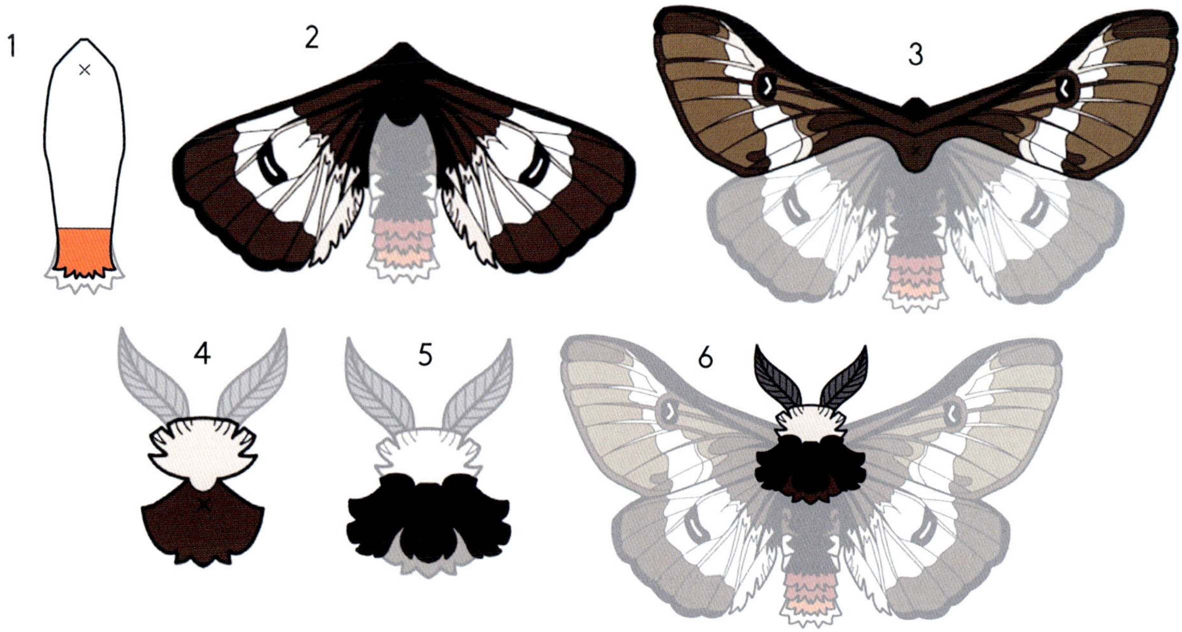

Remove the template for this project (page 123), and using the color guide on page 25, color in the template. Once you are finished coloring, carefully cut out the template pieces along their solid black outer borders. Now it's time to assemble!

We start with the **abdomen**. Like a real lepidopteran, this paper specimen of yours has nine segments in its abdomen. Stack them in ascending order: Begin by adding glue with a toothpick or small paintbrush to the *X* mark on piece **14** and set piece **13** on top, aligning the curved top edges as shown in image 1.

Apply glue to the *X* mark on piece **13** and set piece **12** on top. Continue this way until pieces **6** through **14** are all assembled. Set your completed abdomen aside to dry for 2 to 5 minutes. Next, mimic the curved fullness of a real moth's abdomen by pressing the abdomen over the barrel of your marker, bending the edges down.

Now for the **wings**. Apply some glue to the *X* mark on piece **6**, and set piece **5**, the **hindwings**, on top, aligning as shown in image 2. Apply glue to the *X* marks on piece **5**, and set piece **4**, the **forewings**, on top, aligning as shown in image 3. Let the wings and abdomen dry together for 2 to 5 minutes.

Finally, let's assemble the **head**. Apply glue to the *X* mark on piece **3**, and set piece **2** on top, aligning as shown in image 4. Apply glue to the *X* mark on piece **2**, and place piece **1** onto joined pieces **2** and **3** as shown in image 5. Set the completed head aside to dry for 2 to 5 minutes, then add glue to the *X* marks on piece **4**, and set the head on top, aligning as shown in image 6. You're done!

For a final touch of dimension, gently bend the forewings up with your fingers, and the hindwings down. Then, check out Mounting and Displaying Your Papercraft Specimens (page 109).

MENETRIES' TIGER MOTH

Like anything that lives near the Arctic Circle, the Menetries' tiger moth is hardy. And that's putting it mildly. As a *larva*, it is among one of the beloved "woolly bear" type of caterpillars, its little body surrounded by a thick coat of bristly hairs called *setae*. These setae prevent the caterpillar from freezing during the winter while it undergoes a kind of half hibernation called *quiescence*. In quiescence, the caterpillar's body produces natural antifreeze called *glycerol*, lowering its overall freezing point, while the setae keep the core of the caterpillar's body from freezing, protecting the essential organs. Not much else is known about the Menetries' tiger moth, in adult or caterpillar form, as their cold, remote habitat makes them difficult to observe. But that alone is impressive—a tiny, delicate moth fighting out a life in a space too cold and rough for most people to live comfortably.

Scientific name: ***Arctia menetriesii***

Habitat: ***Boreal forests of Northen Europe, Russia, and China***

Real-life size: ***Wingspan of 2¼" (56 mm)***

Conservation status: ***Rare; insufficient data for further ruling***

Template: ***Page 125***

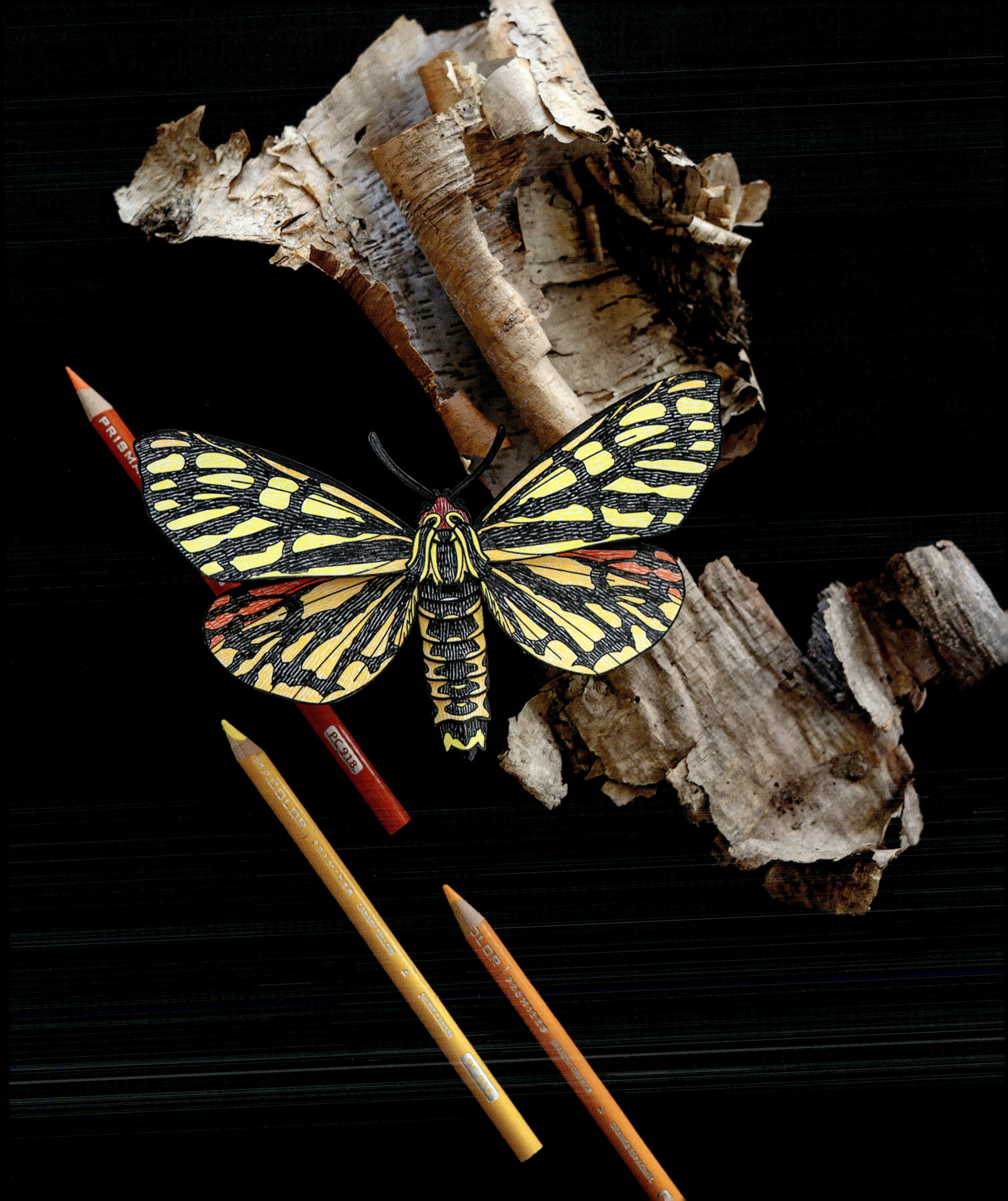
PC 918

MENETRIES' TIGER MOTH COLOR GUIDE

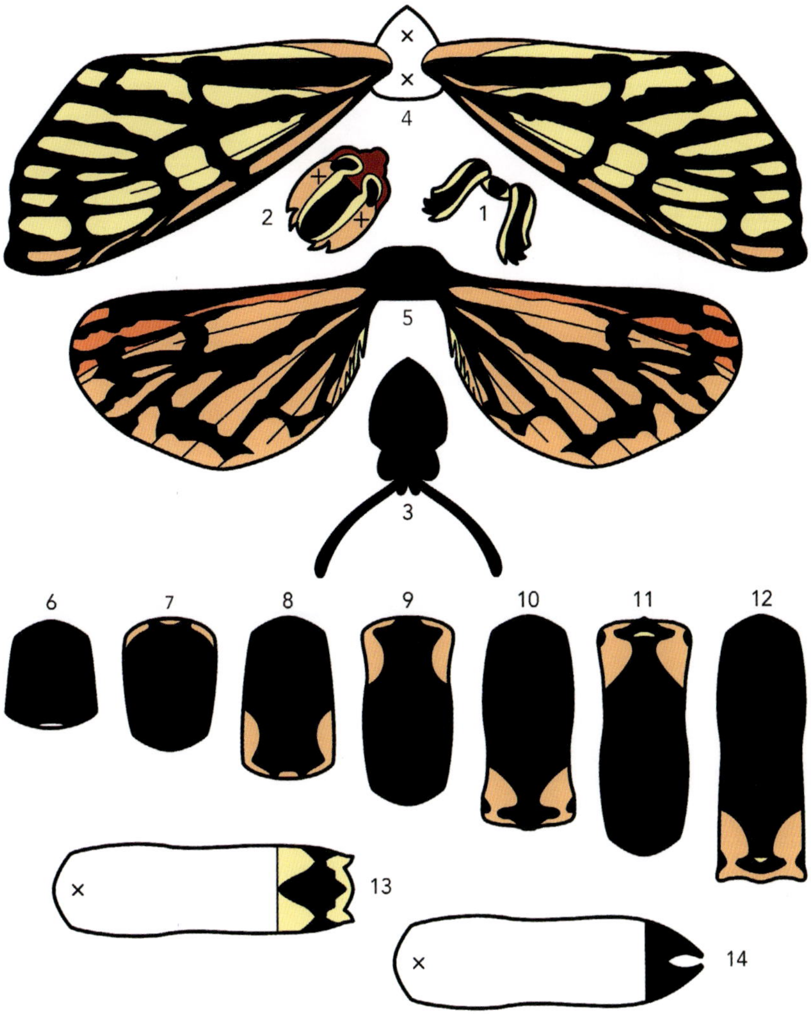

Colors Needed

- Black
- Tuscan red
- Poppy red
- Spanish orange
- Canary yellow

MENETRIES' TIGER MOTH ASSEMBLY

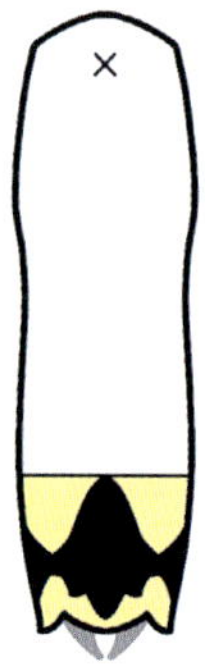

1

2

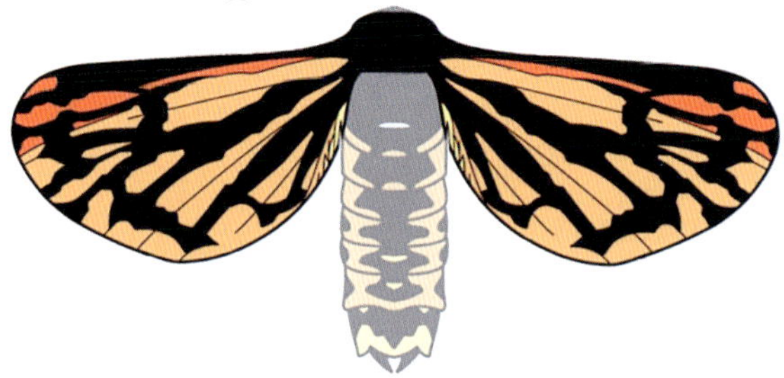

3

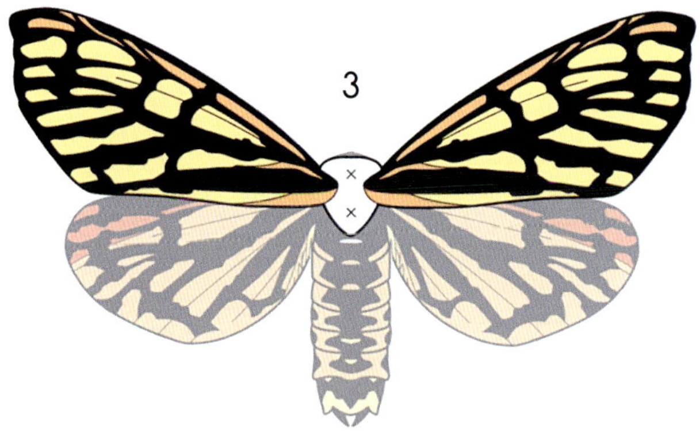

Remove the template for this project (page 125), and using the color guide on page 29, color in the template. (You can refer to the Papercraft Tips and Tricks on page 11 for suggestions on coloring.) Once you are finished coloring, carefully cut out the template pieces along their solid black outer borders. Now it's time to assemble!

We start with the **abdomen**. Like a real lepidopteran, this paper specimen of yours has nine segments in its abdomen. Stack them in ascending order: Begin by adding glue with a toothpick or small paintbrush to the *X* mark on piece **14** and set piece **13** on top, aligning the curved top edges as shown in image 1.

Apply glue to the *X* mark on piece **13** and set piece **12** on top. Continue this way until pieces **6** through **14** are all assembled. Set your completed abdomen aside to dry for 2 to 5 minutes. Next, mimic the curved fullness of a real moth's abdomen by pressing the abdomen over the barrel of your marker with your thumb and finger, bending the edges down.

Now for the **wings**. Apply some glue to the *X* mark on piece **6**, and set piece **5**, the **hindwings**, on top, aligning as shown in image 2.

Apply glue to the *X* mark on piece **5**, and set piece **4**, the **forewings**, on top, aligning as shown in image 3.

4

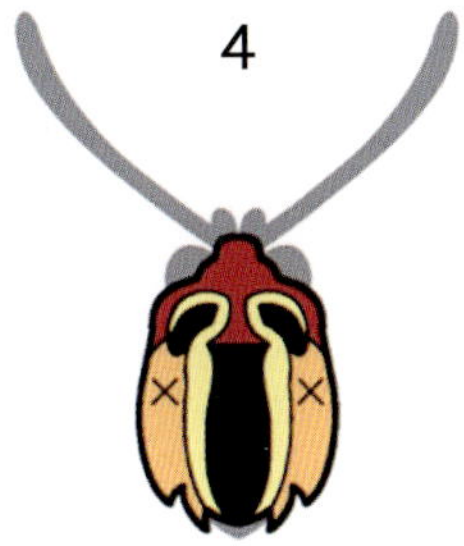

5

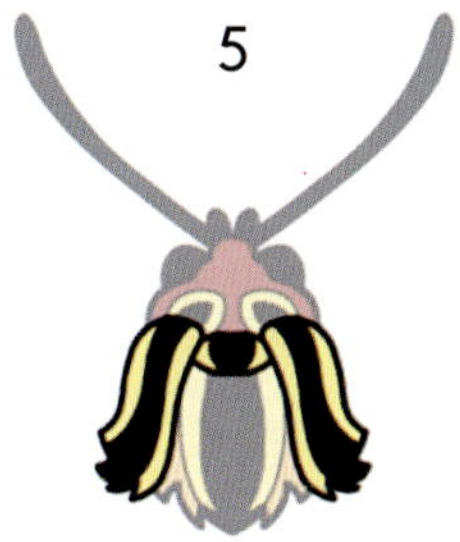

6

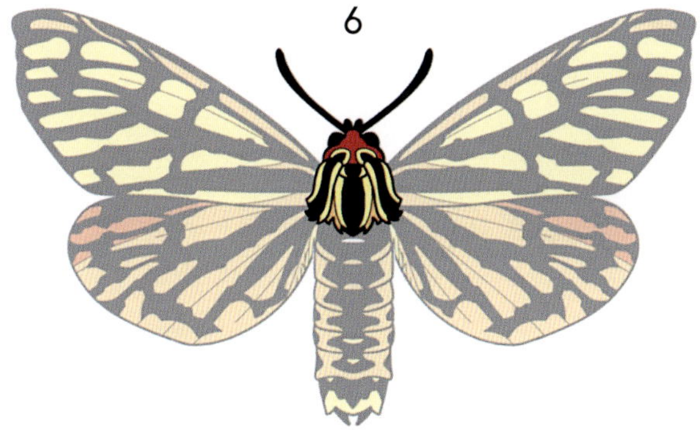

Let the wings and abdomen dry together for 2 to 5 minutes. Finally, let's assemble the **head**. Apply glue to the *X* mark on piece **3**, and set piece **2** on top, aligning as shown in image 4.

Apply glue to the *X* marks on piece **2**, and place piece **1** onto joined pieces **2** and **3** as shown in image 5.

Set the completed head aside to dry for 2 to 5 minutes, then add glue to the *X* marks on piece **4**, and set the head on top, aligning as shown in image 6. You're done!

For a final touch of dimension to your paper specimen, gently bend the forewings up with your fingers, and the hindwings down. If you'd like suggestions on how to display your completed moth, check out Mounting and Displaying Your Papercraft Specimens (page 109).

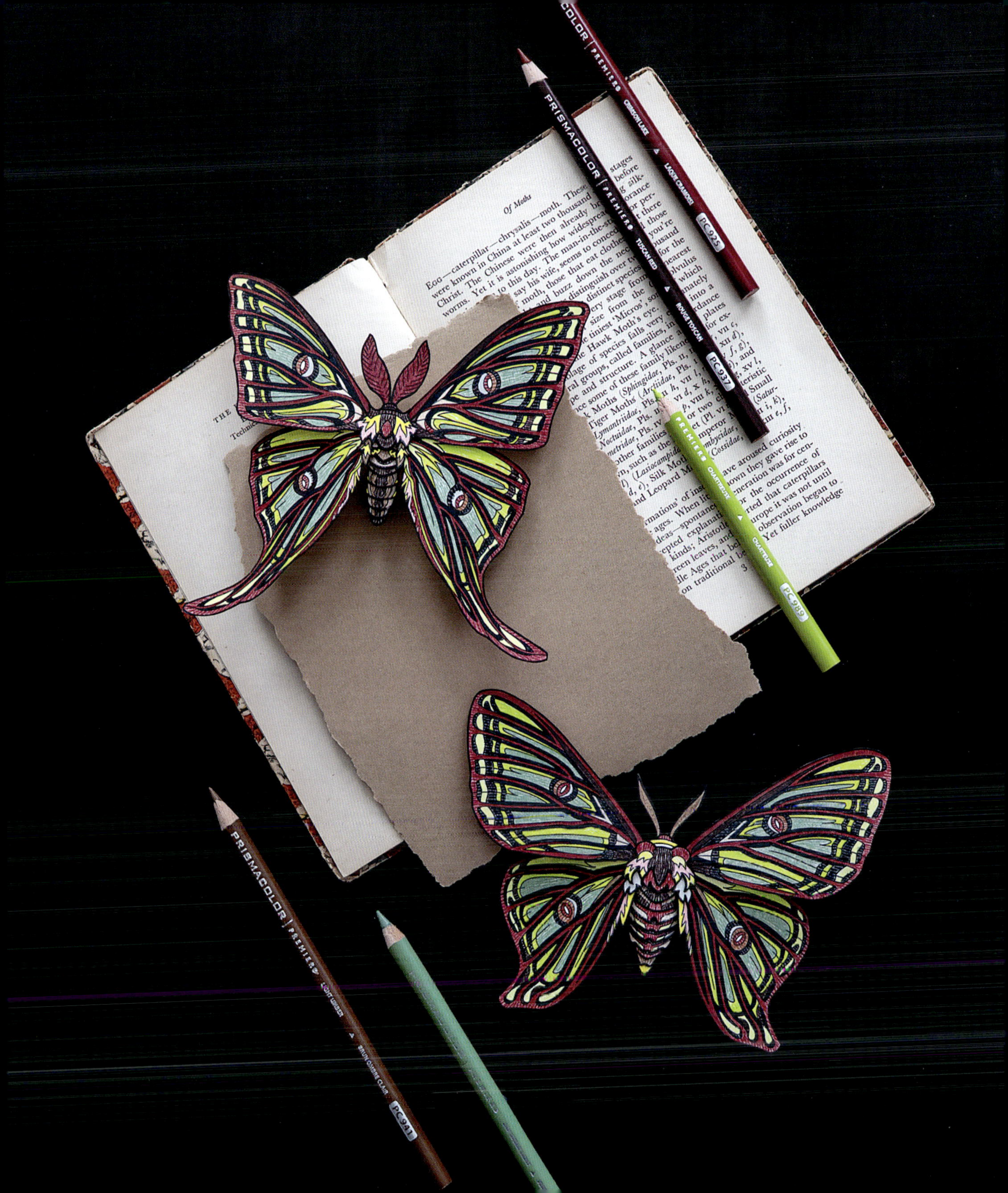
Of Moths
PRISMACOLOR | PREMIER
PC925
PC937
PC989
PRISMACOLOR | PREMIER
PC941

SPANISH MOON MOTH

Scientific name: ***Graellsia isabellae***

Habitat: ***High mountain altitudes in Spain and France***

Real-life size: ***Wingspan of 3½ to 4" (89 to 102 mm)***

Conservation status: ***Rare; Protected (Habitats Directive of the European Union and various country-specific legal measures)***

Templates: ***Pages 127 and 129***

Have you ever held a living relic in your hand? Anyone who's held a Spanish moon moth has. That's because this isolated species native to the alpine regions of the Iberian Peninsula are remnants of a prehistoric species of moth that goes all the way back to the Ice Age, as discovered by genetic testing performed in 2016! The common ancestor of these big, beautiful moths is thought to be related to moths in the Saturniidae (silk moth) subfamily of *Actias*. Over time, that common ancestor developed into different species (such as the Spanish moon moth and the Indian moon moth) due to geographic location, which is called *geographic* or *allopatric speciation*. Because of this, Spanish moon moths have been successfully hybridized with the Indian moon moth in captivity. Unfortunately, the resulting hybrid moths are born sterile, unable to reproduce young of their own. So evolution, at least in this case, is left to continue in its normal, gradual pace. A pace that suits the Spanish moon moth in its remote mountain habitat, where the primeval cold-enduring qualities it's held on to have served it well.

SPANISH MOON MOTH (MALE) COLOR GUIDE

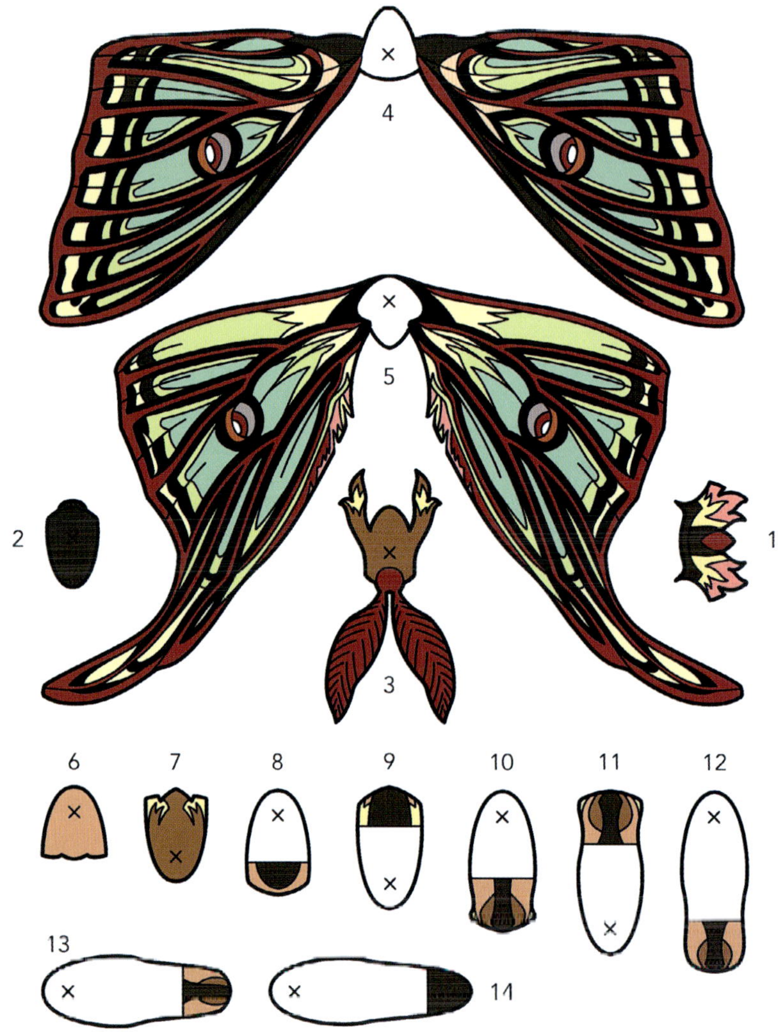

Colors Needed

- Black
- 10% warm gray
- Dark umber
- Light umber
- Sienna brown
- Beige sienna
- Beige
- Tuscan red
- Blush pink
- Seashell pink
- Lemon yellow
- Canary yellow
- Chartreuse
- Sap green light

SPANISH MOON MOTH (MALE) ASSEMBLY

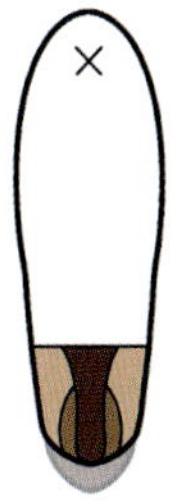

1

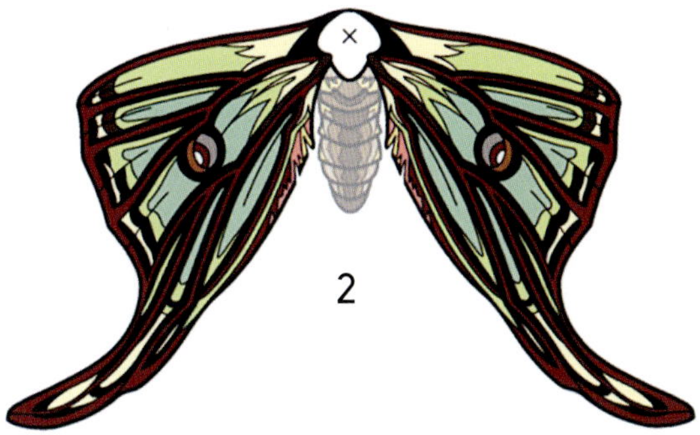

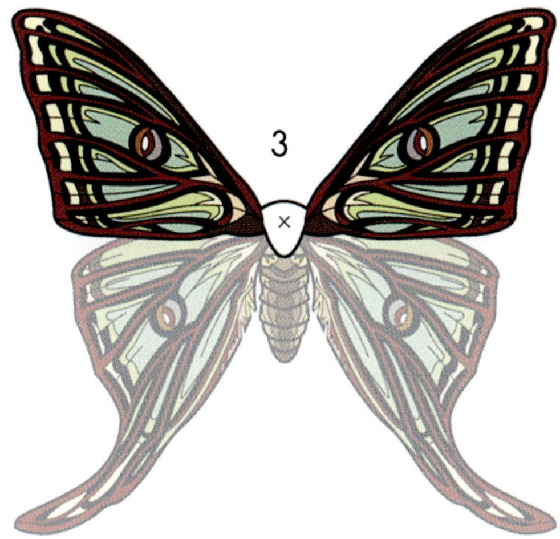

Note: There are two variants of this project available in this book. This project is for the Male, which is smaller than the Female, but has the distinctive elongated hindwing "tails" and larger comb-like antennae.

Remove the template for this project (page 127), and using the color guide on the left, color in the template. (You can refer to the Papercraft Tips and Tricks on page 11 for suggestions on coloring.) Once you are finished coloring, carefully cut out the template pieces along their solid black outer borders. Now it's time to assemble!

We start with the **abdomen**. Like a real lepidopteran, this paper specimen of yours has nine segments in its abdomen. Stack them in ascending order: Begin by adding glue with a toothpick or small paintbrush to the *X* mark on piece **14** and set piece **13** on top, aligning the curved top edges as shown in image 1.

Apply glue to the *X* mark on piece **13** and set piece **12** on top. Continue this way until pieces **6** through **14** are all assembled. Set your completed abdomen aside to dry for 2 to 5 minutes. Next, mimic the curved fullness of a real moth's abdomen by pressing the abdomen over the barrel of one of your colored pencils with your thumb and finger, bending the edges down.

Now for the **wings**. Apply some glue to the *X* mark on piece **6**, and set piece **5**, the **hindwings**, on top, aligning as shown in image 2.

Apply glue to the *X* mark on piece **5**, and set piece **4**, the **forewings**, on top, aligning as shown in image 3.

SPANISH MOON MOTH (MALE) ASSEMBLY CONTINUED

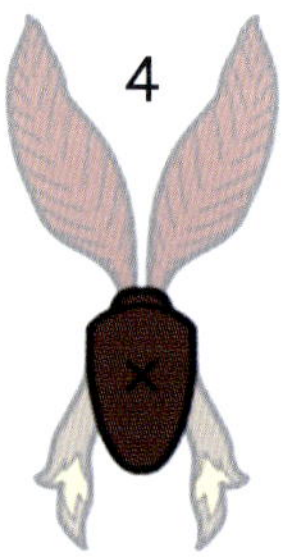

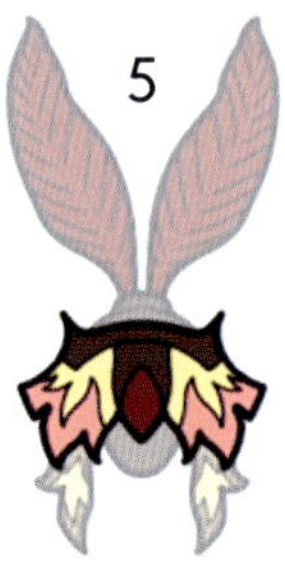

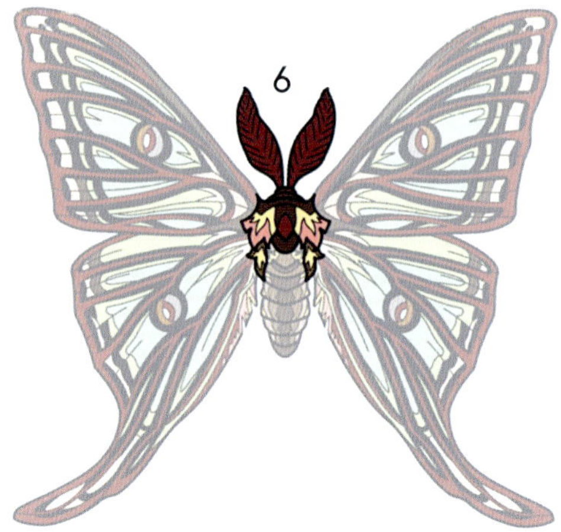

Let the wings and abdomen dry together for 2 to 5 minutes. Finally, let's assemble the **head**. Apply glue to the *X* mark on piece **3**, and set piece **2** on top, aligning as shown in image 4.

Apply glue to the *X* mark on piece **2**, and place piece **1** onto joined pieces **2** and **3** as shown in image 5.

Set the completed head aside to dry for 2 to 5 minutes, then add glue to the *X* mark on piece **4**, and set the head on top, aligning as shown in image 6. You're done!

For a final touch of dimension to your paper specimen, gently bend the forewings up with your fingers, and the hindwings down. If you'd like suggestions on how to display your completed moth, check out Mounting and Displaying Your Papercraft Specimens (page 109).

SPANISH MOON MOTH (FEMALE) COLOR GUIDE

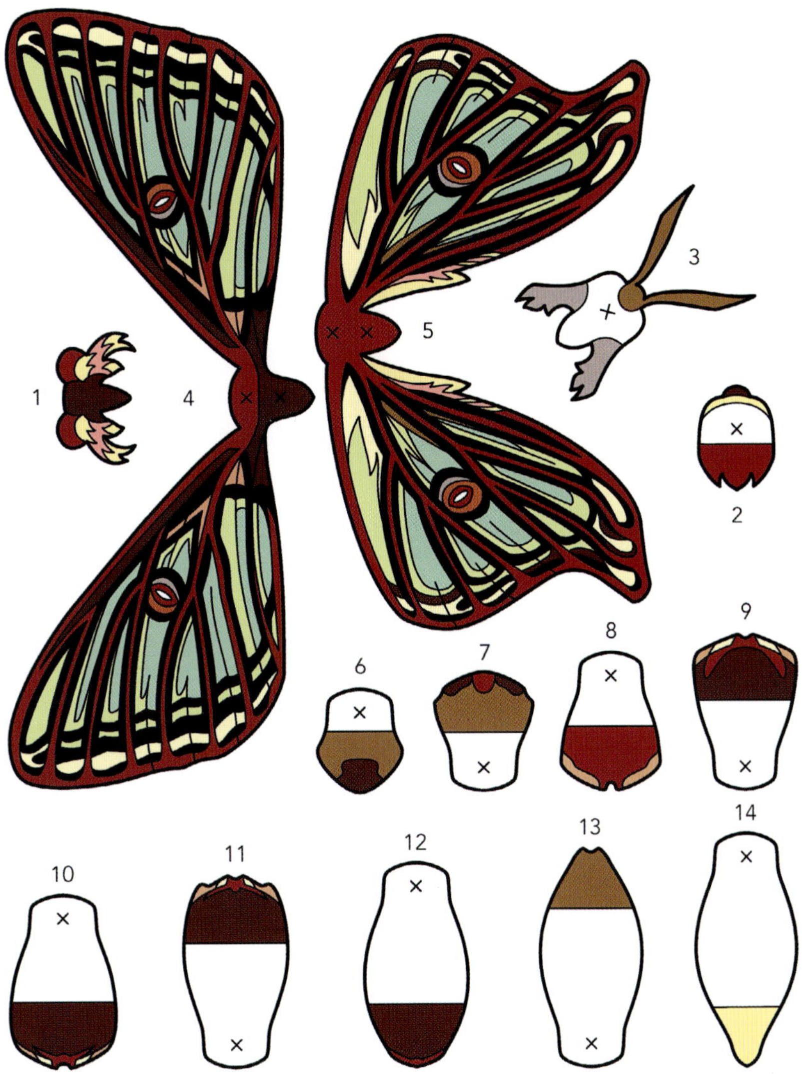

Colors Needed

- Black
- 10% warm gray
- Dark umber
- Light umber
- Sienna brown
- Beige sienna
- Beige
- Tuscan red
- Blush pink
- Seashell pink
- Lemon yellow
- Canary yellow
- Chartreuse
- Sap green light

SPANISH MOON MOTH (FEMALE) ASSEMBLY

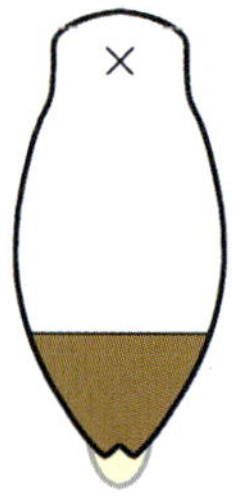

1

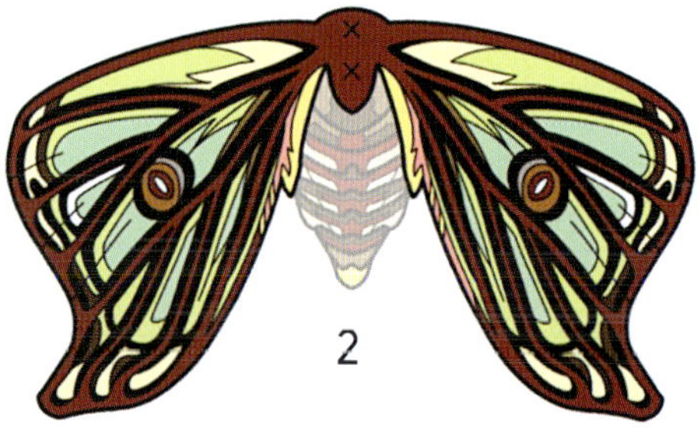

2

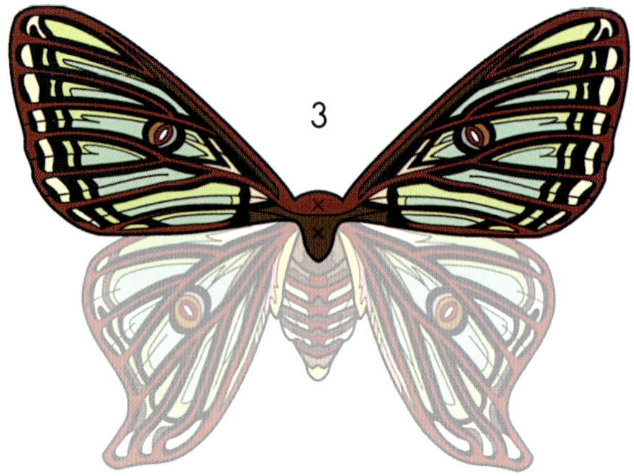

3

> **Note:** There are two variants of this project available in this book. This project is for the Female, which is larger than the Male, with broader wings and a fatter abdomen.

Remove the template for this project (page 129), and using the color guide on page 37, color in the template. (You can refer to the Papercraft Tips and Tricks on page 11 for suggestions on coloring.) Once you are finished coloring, carefully cut out the template pieces along their solid black outer borders. Now it's time to assemble!

We start with the **abdomen**. Like a real lepidopteran, this paper specimen of yours has nine segments in its abdomen. Stack them in ascending order: Begin by adding glue with a toothpick or small paintbrush to the *X* mark on piece **14** and set piece **13** on top, aligning the curved top edges as shown in image 1.

Apply glue to the *X* mark on piece **13** and set piece **12** on top. Continue this way until pieces **6** through **14** are all assembled. Set your completed abdomen aside to dry for 2 to 5 minutes. Next, mimic the curved fullness of a real moth's abdomen by pressing the abdomen over the barrel of your marker with your thumb and finger, bending the edges down.

Now for the **wings**. Apply some glue to the *X* mark on piece **6**, and set piece **5**, the **hindwings**, on top, aligning as shown in image 2.

Apply glue to the *X* marks on piece **5**, and set piece **4**, the **forewings**, on top, aligning as shown in image 3.

4

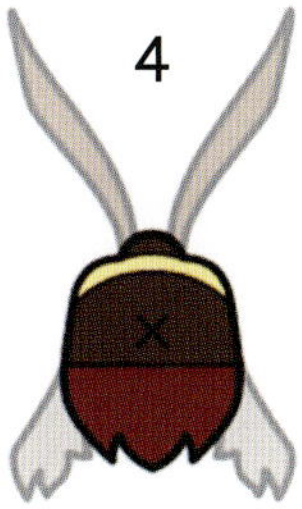

5

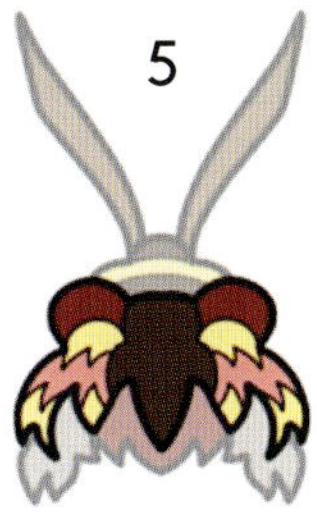

6

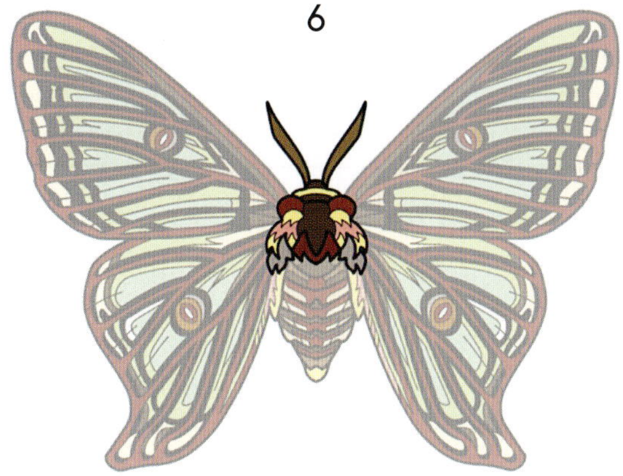

Let the wings and abdomen dry together for 2 to 5 minutes. Finally, let's assemble the **head**. Apply glue to the *X* mark on piece **3**, and set piece **2** on top, aligning as shown in image 4.

Apply glue to the *X* mark on piece **2**, and place piece **1** onto joined pieces **2** and **3** as shown in image 5.

Set the completed head aside to dry for 2 to 5 minutes, then add glue to the *X* marks on piece **4**, and set the head on top, aligning as shown in image 6. You're done!

For a final touch of dimension to your paper specimen, gently bend the forewings up with your fingers, and the hindwings down. If you'd like suggestions on how to display your completed moth, check out Mounting and Displaying Your Papercraft Specimens (page 109).

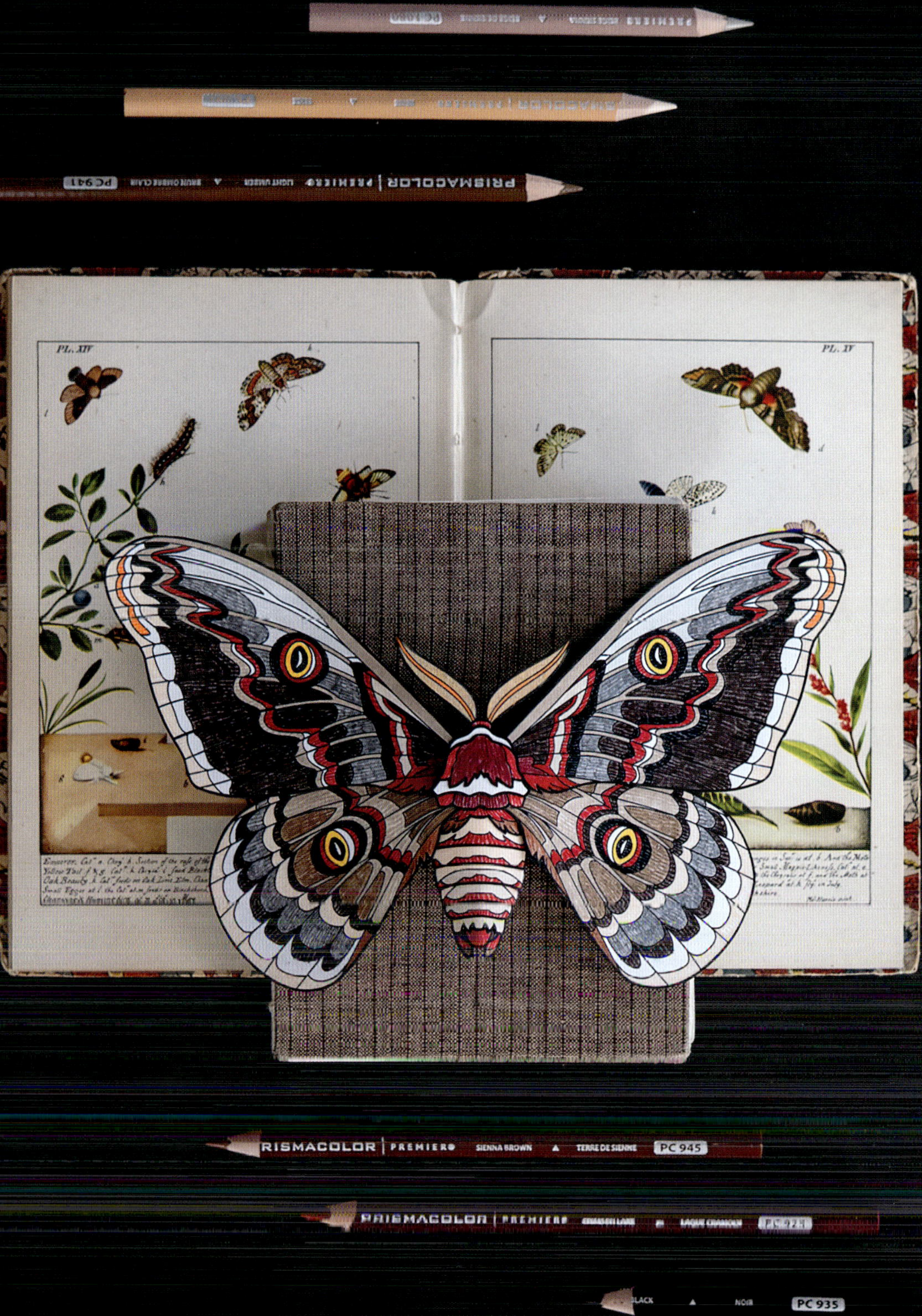
RISMACOLOR | PREMIER SIENNA BROWN ▲ TERRE DE SIENNE PC 945
PRISMACOLOR | PREMIER
BLACK ▲ NOIR PC 935

GIANT PEACOCK MOTH

Containing some of the largest moths in the world, the Saturniidae family of moths is so named because the ringed defensive *eyespots* on their wings are shaped similarly to the planet Saturn. The giant peacock moth is no exception, being the largest moth in mainland Europe, and its *ocelli* (the scientific term for eyespots) are translucent to add to the illusion of light glinting off real eyes. This is a very useful tactical detail for the giant peacock moth. With their small heads, reduced mouthparts, and fat bodies, built from a caterpillar youth spent stuffing themselves with food, giant peacock moths aren't great fliers. They're built to last just long enough to find a mate—usually, only about a week. So, instead of fleeing when a predator appears, they reserve their energy for finding love, and instead pop open their wings, revealing a flash of giant eyes glinting fiercely in the moonlight.

Scientific name: ***Saturnia pyri***

Habitat: ***Woodlands and shrublands of Southern and Mediterranean Europe and West Asia***

Real-life size: ***Wingspan of 6 to 8" (152 to 203 mm)***

Conservation status: ***Rare; not officially protected***

Template: ***Pages 131 and 133***

GIANT PEACOCK MOTH COLOR GUIDE

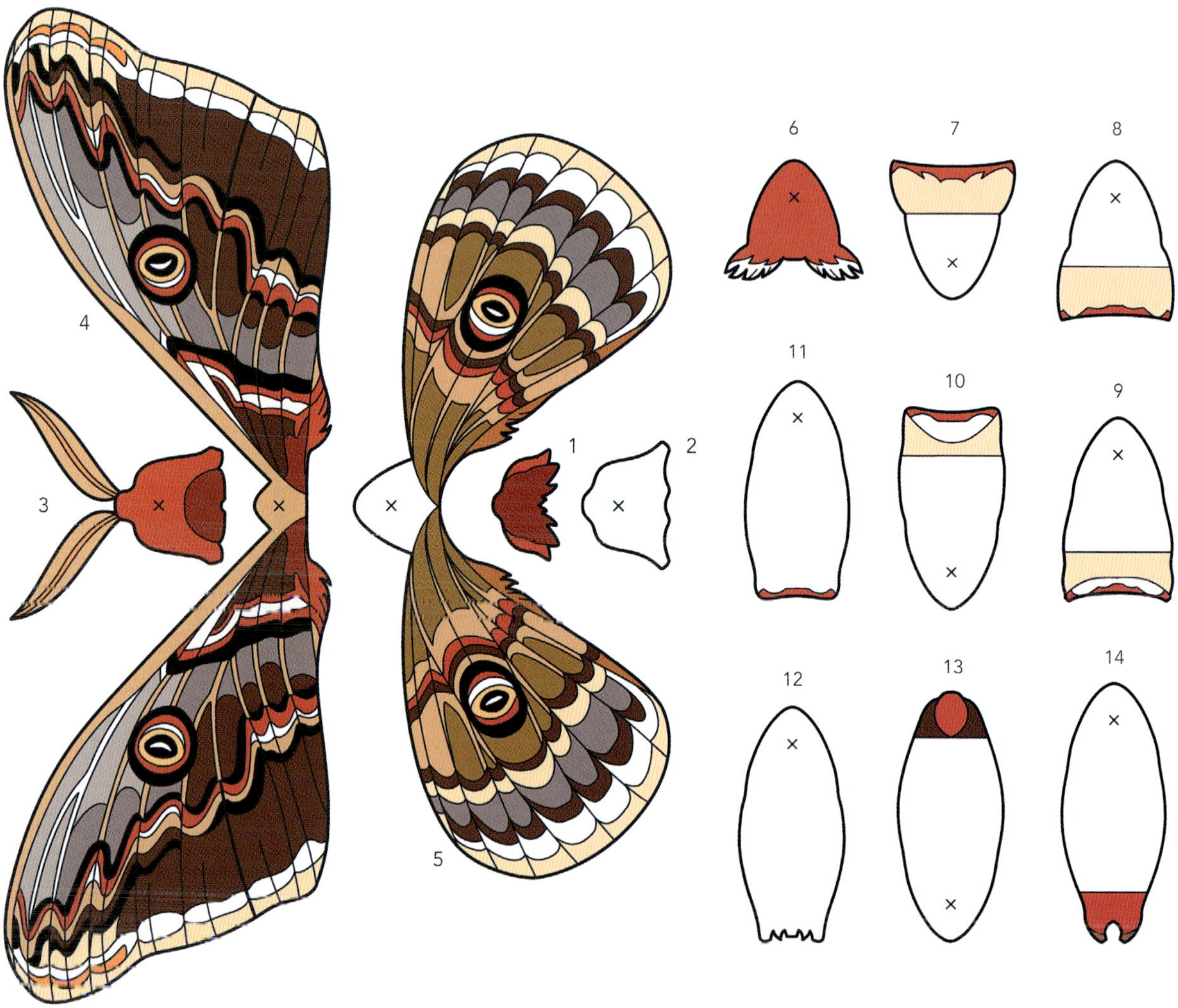

Colors Needed

- Black
- 50% warm gray
- 10% warm gray
- Dark umber
- Light umber
- Sienna brown
- Beige sienna
- Beige
- Spanish orange
- Orange
- Crimson lake
- Tuscan red
- Seashell pink

GIANT PEACOCK MOTH ASSEMBLY

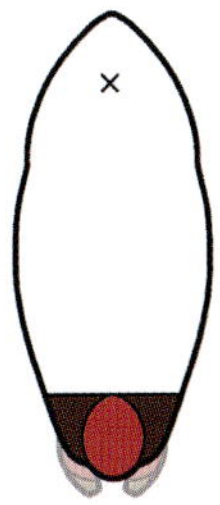

1

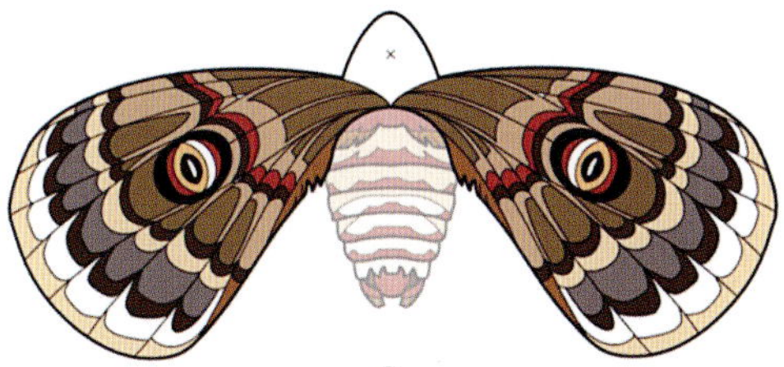

2

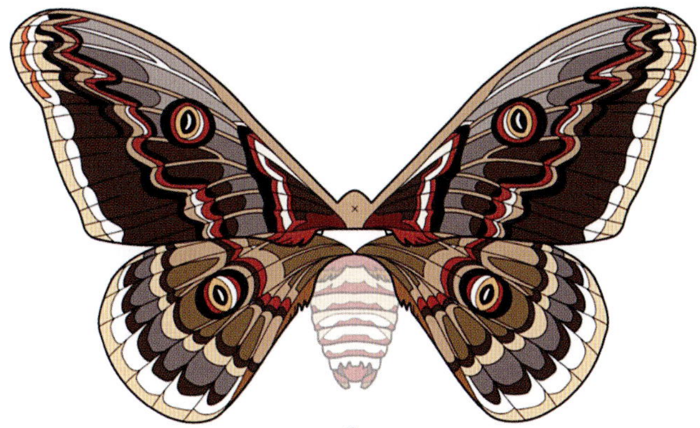

3

Remove the template for this project (page 131 and 133), and using the color guide on the left, color in the template. (You can refer to the Papercraft Tips and Tricks on page 11 for suggestions on coloring.) Once you are finished coloring, carefully cut out the template pieces along their solid black outer borders. Now it's time to assemble!

We start with the **abdomen**. Like a real lepidopteran, this paper specimen of yours has nine segments in its abdomen. Stack them in ascending order: Begin by adding glue with a toothpick or small paintbrush to the *X* mark on piece **14** and set piece **13** on top, aligning the curved top edges as shown in image 1.

Apply glue to the *X* mark on piece **13** and set piece **12** on top. Continue this way until pieces **6** through **14** are all assembled. Set your completed abdomen aside to dry for 2 to 5 minutes. Next, mimic the curved fullness of a real moth's abdomen by pressing the abdomen over the barrel of your marker with your thumb and finger, bending the edges down.

Now for the **wings**. Apply some glue to the *X* mark on piece **6**, and set piece **5**, the **hindwings**, on top, aligning as shown in image 2.

Apply glue to the *X* mark on piece 5, and set piece **4**, the **forewings**, on top, aligning as shown in image 3.

GIANT PEACOCK MOTH ASSEMBLY CONTINUED

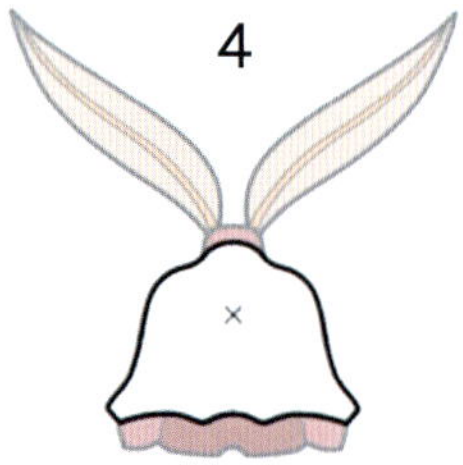

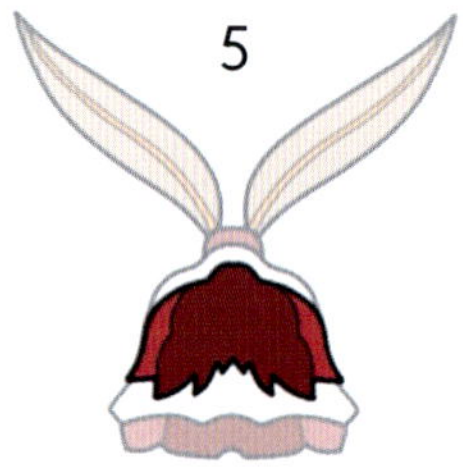

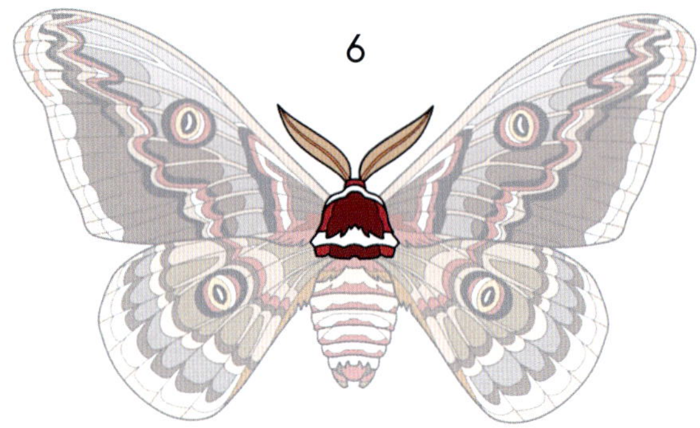

Let the wings and abdomen dry together for 2 to 5 minutes. Finally, let's assemble the **head**. Apply glue to the *X* mark on piece **3**, and set piece **2** on top, aligning as shown in image 4.

Apply glue to the *X* mark on piece **2**, and place piece **1** onto joined pieces **2** and **3** as shown in image 5.

Set the completed head aside to dry for 2 to 5 minutes, then add glue to the *X* mark on piece **4**, and set the head on top, aligning as shown in image 6. You're done!

For a final touch of dimension to your paper specimen, gently bend the forewings up with your fingers, and the hindwings down. If you'd like suggestions on how to display your completed moth, check out Mounting and Displaying Your Papercraft Specimens (page 109).

SOUTHERN PINK UNDERWING MOTH

The pink underwing moth is an actor both in its *larval* (caterpillar) stage and its *imago* (adult) stage. The caterpillars start as either green or brown, and mature to a dark brown and red coloration, up to 4½ inches (11 cm) in length, with a striking "skull" marking on the back of their head. This "skull" is made up of two large, yellow-circled black "eyes" on either side with two rows of fake teeth. When startled, the caterpillar tucks its head down to reveal this marking to full effect in an example of *aggressive mimicry*. Aggressive mimicry develops to keep predators away by tricking them into thinking a smaller creature, like a caterpillar, is actually a larger and fiercer beast. The adult pink underwing moth still has its teeth, so to speak, in the white markings along its namesake pink underwings, which it flashes if threatened. But the wilder theatrics of its youth are over, and the pink underwing moth adult sticks to staying safe mostly through folding its wings in a steepled position that looks like eucalyptus leaves, a trick it pulls off thanks to *cryptic* (camouflage) *coloring*.

Scientific name: ***Phyllodes imperialis***

Habitat: ***Subtropical rainforest in Southeastern Australia***

Real-life size: ***Wingspan of 5½ to 6¾" (140 to 172 mm)***

Conservation status: ***Endangered (Australian Environment Protection and Biodiversity Conservation Act, 1999)***

Template: ***Page 135***

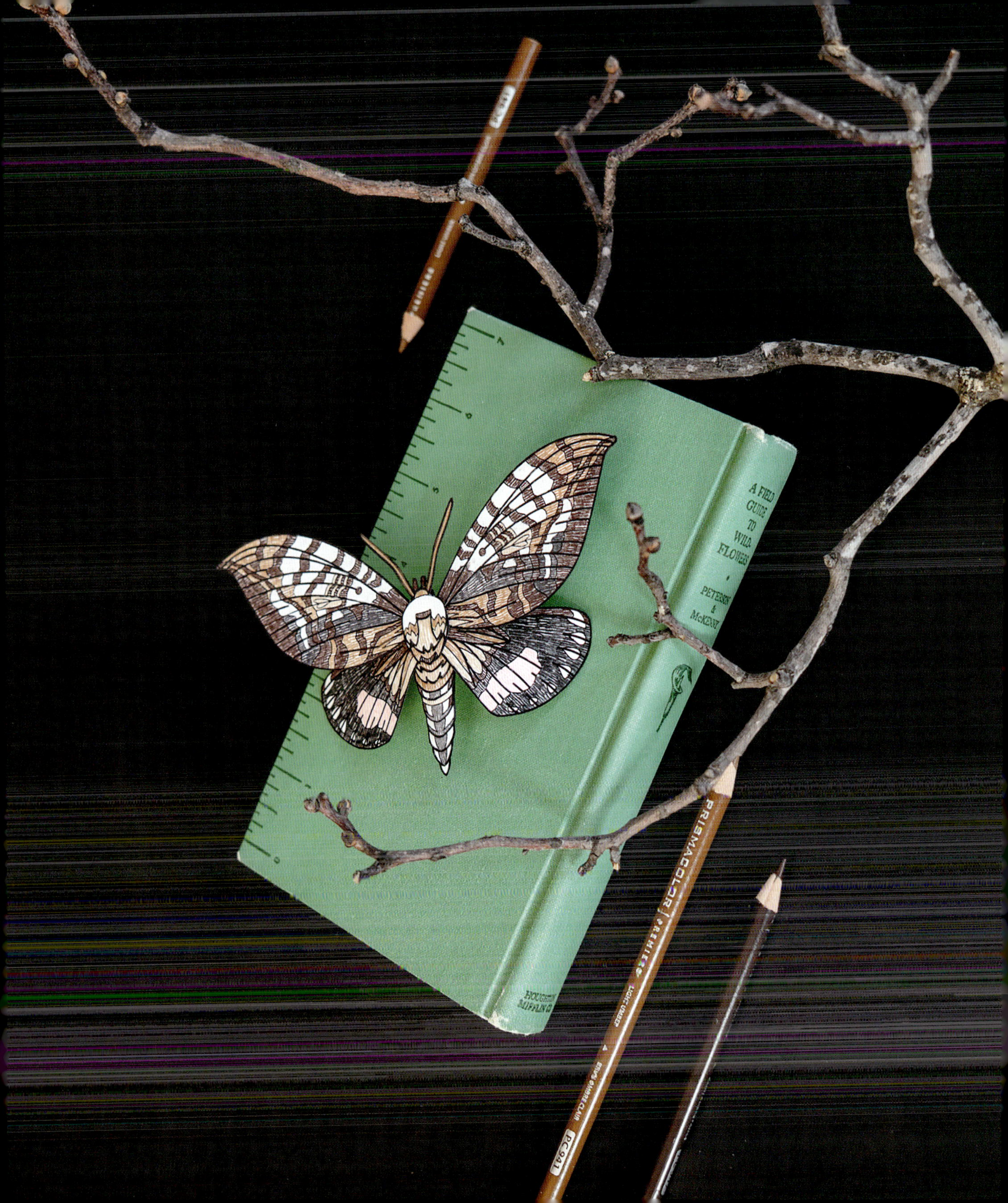
A FIELD GUIDE TO WILDFLOWERS
PRISMACOLOR | PREMIER
PC941

SOUTHERN PINK UNDERWING MOTH COLOR GUIDE

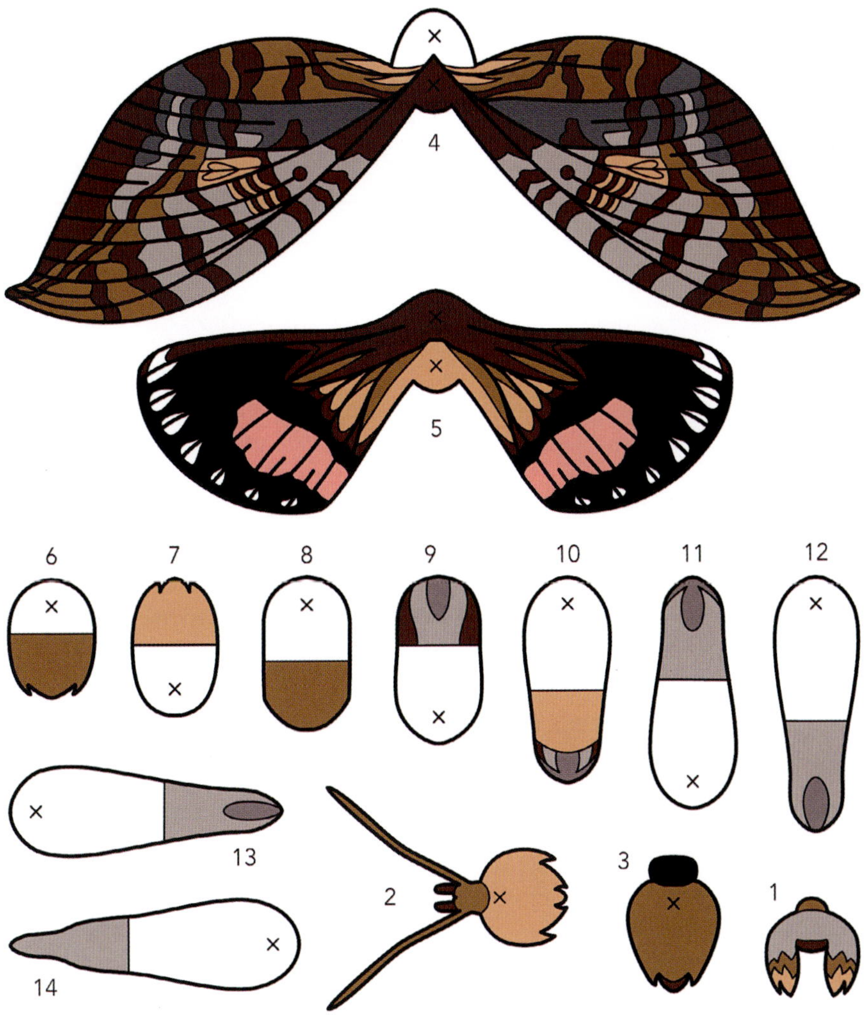

Colors Needed

- Black
- 90% warm gray
- 50% warm gray
- 10% warm gray
- Dark umber
- Light umber
- Beige sienna
- Blush pink

SOUTHERN PINK UNDERWING MOTH ASSEMBLY

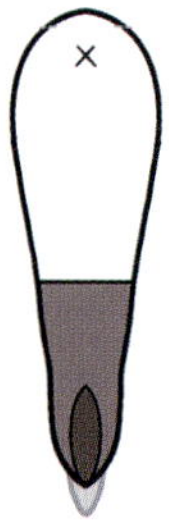

1

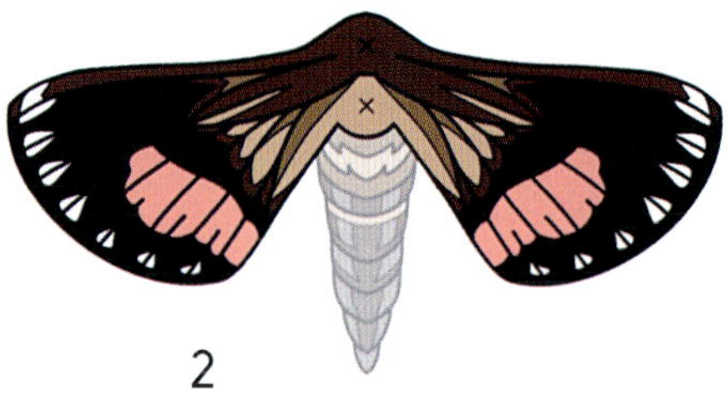

2

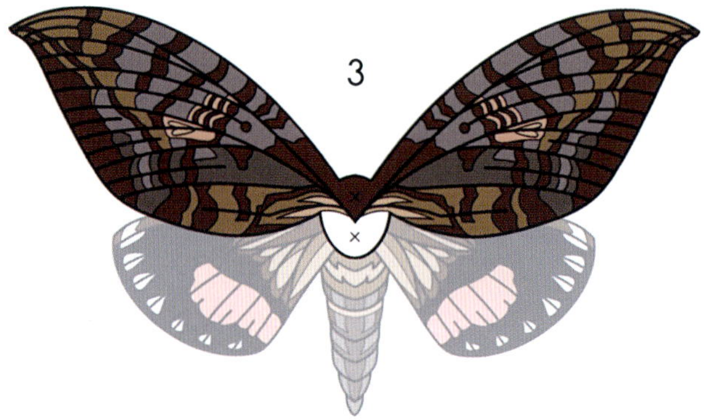

3

Remove the template for this project (page 135), and using the color guide on page 47, color in the template. (You can refer to the Papercraft Tips and Tricks on page 11 for suggestions on coloring.) Once you are finished coloring, carefully cut out the template pieces along their solid black outer borders. Now it's time to assemble!

We start with the **abdomen**. Like a real lepidopteran, this paper specimen of yours has nine segments in its abdomen. Stack them in ascending order: Begin by adding glue with a toothpick or small paintbrush to the *X* mark on piece **14** and set piece **13** on top, aligning the curved top edges as shown in image 1.

Apply glue to the *X* mark on piece **13** and set piece **12** on top. Continue this way until pieces **6** through **14** are all assembled. Set your completed abdomen aside to dry for 2 to 5 minutes. Next, mimic the curved fullness of a real moth's abdomen by pressing the abdomen over the barrel of one of your colored pencils with your thumb and finger, bending the edges down.

Now for the **wings**. Apply some glue to the *X* mark on piece **6**, and set piece **5**, the **hindwings**, on top, aligning as shown in image 2.

Apply glue to the *X* marks on piece **5**, and set piece **4**, the **forewings**, on top, aligning as shown in image 3.

4

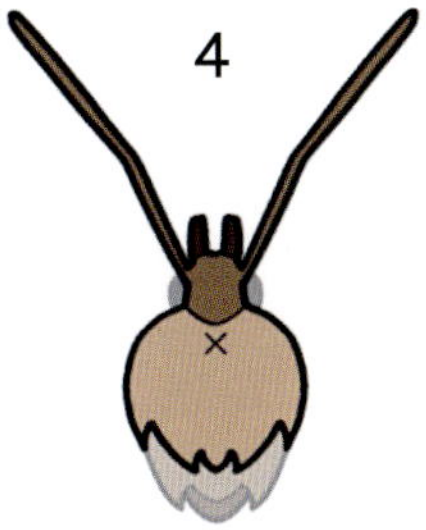

5

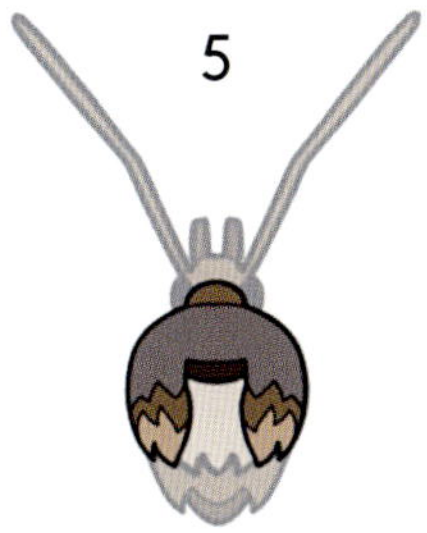

6

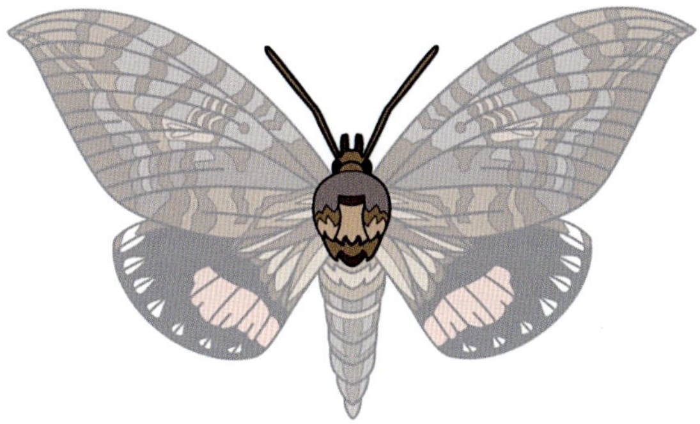

Let the wings and abdomen dry together for 2 to 5 minutes. Finally, let's assemble the **head**. Apply glue to the *X* mark on piece **3**, and set piece **2** on top, aligning as shown in image 4.

Apply glue to the *X* mark on piece **2**, and place piece **1** onto joined pieces **2** and **3** as shown in image 5.

Set the completed head aside to dry for 2 to 5 minutes, then add glue to the *X* marks on piece **4**, and set the head on top, aligning as shown in image 6. You're done!

For a final touch of dimension to your paper specimen, gently bend the forewings up with your fingers, and the hindwings down. If you'd like suggestions on how to display your completed moth, check out Mounting and Displaying Your Papercraft Specimens (page 109).

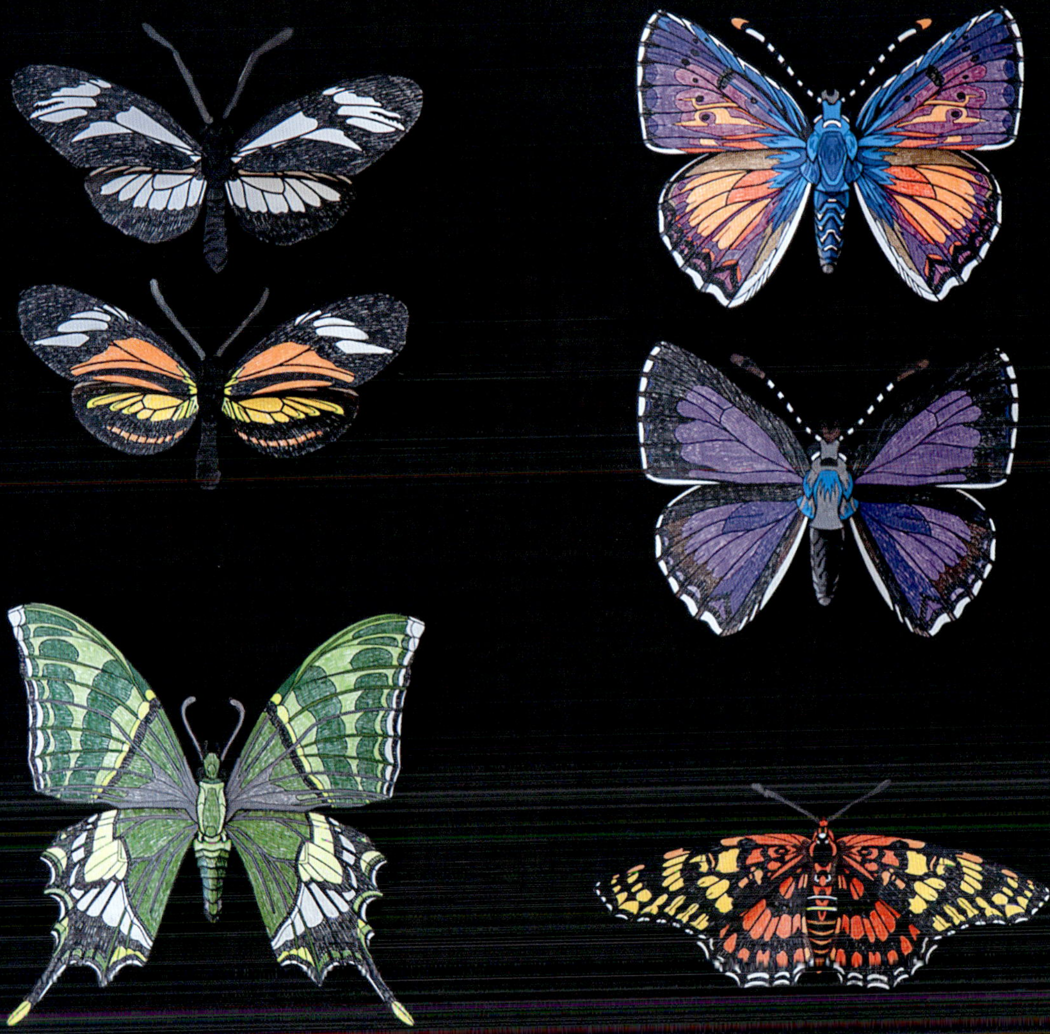

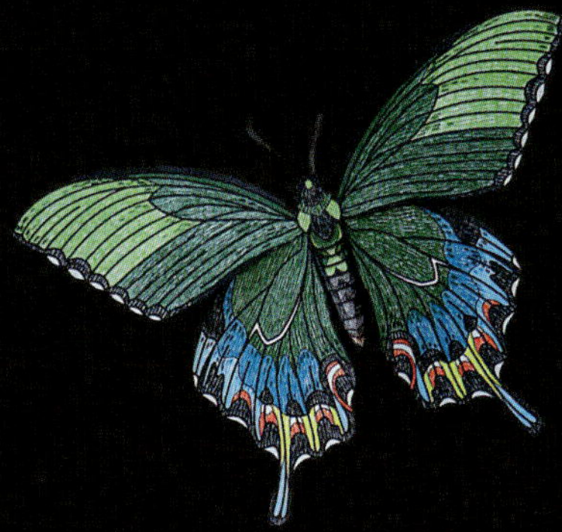

BUTTERFLIES

While far fewer species of butterflies exist than moths (about 17,000 butterfly species to roughly 160,000 moth species worldwide), butterflies have stolen prominence and common association with the scientific order of Lepidoptera both because they're diurnal (active in daytime) and far flashier in coloration than moths in general. We see far more butterflies than we do moths, generally being awake during the day ourselves, and who can resist watching a butterfly's flight when its bright colors catch the eye?

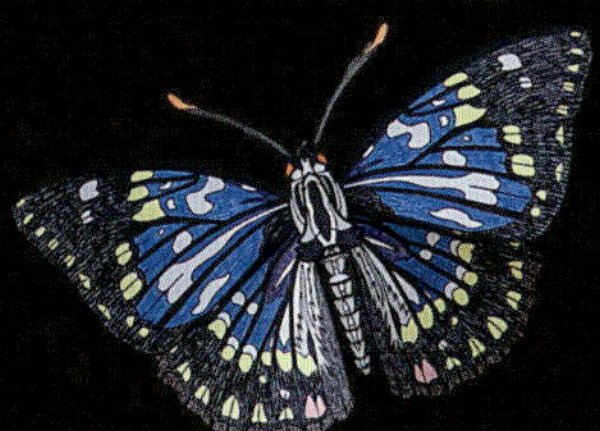

However, those colors are for nonhuman eyes first and foremost. Far more dependent on visuals than moths are, butterflies use their colors to communicate: identifying potential mates, confusing predators (see the Luzon Peacock Swallowtail Butterfly, page 57), and even disguising themselves as similar species that would be dangerous to eat (see Wallace's Golden Birdwing Butterfly [female], page 75).

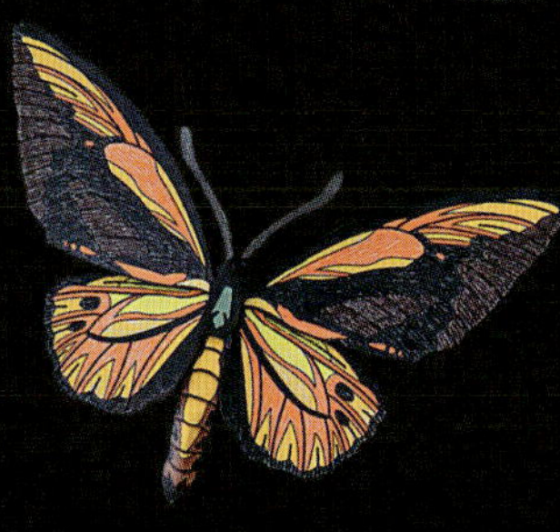

Discover the hidden meanings behind butterflies' many hues and more in the following projects!

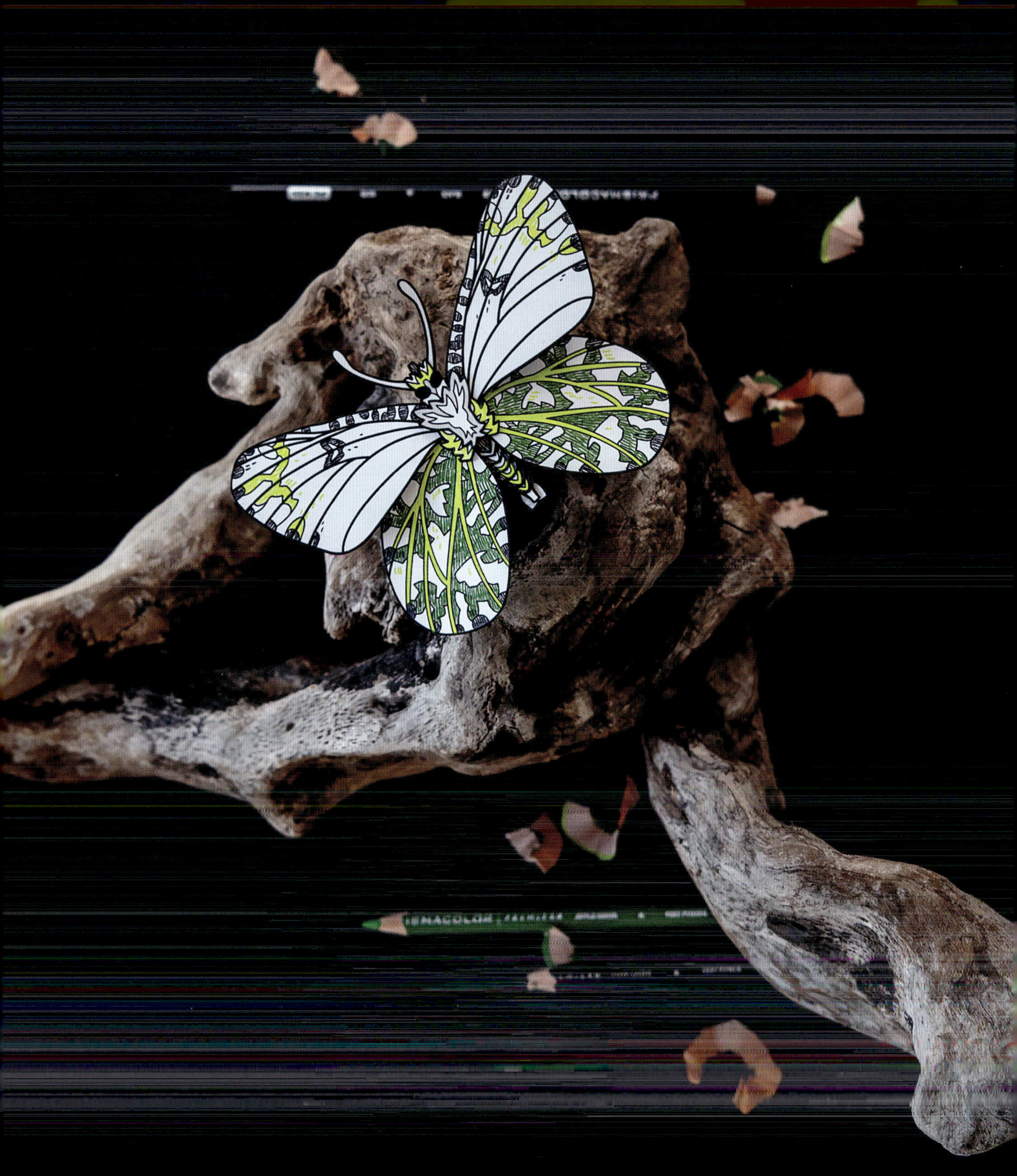

ISLAND MARBLE BUTTERFLY

Scientific name: ***Euchloe ausonides insulanus***

Habitat: ***Island prairie of the Pacific Northwestern United States***

Real-life size: ***Wingspan of 1¾" (44 mm)***

Conservation status: ***Endangered (US Endangered Species Act)***

Template: ***Page 137***

A tiny butterfly on a tiny island, the island marble butterfly lives up to its name with a vibrant, green-yellow and white coloring speckled with black. Coloring is a famous aspect of the Pieridae family, and these species produce their signature yellowy tints by processing nitrogen waste in their bodies into pigments. Yellow is so closely associated with these species, in fact, that they are the reason the word *butterfly* even exists. One early English naturalist famously described the Pieridae species *Gonepteryx rhamni* as "butter-colored," and the descriptor stuck.

Not so famous, however, is the island marble. Up through the 1900s, this little species was thought to be extinct, but was spotted during a butterfly survey on San Juan Island in 1998. It's been located many times since, but pretty much only on San Juan Island, and the season to spot them is short. The majority of the island marble butterfly's life is spent as a caterpillar, or in a *chrysalis*, where it metamorphosizes for 10 to 12 months. Finally, it emerges during the peak of wildflower blooming season, fluttering about pollinating and mating for just a couple of weeks among its equally brightly colored host plant of choice, the white and yellow-blooming Virginia pepperweed.

ISLAND MARBLE BUTTERFLY COLOR GUIDE

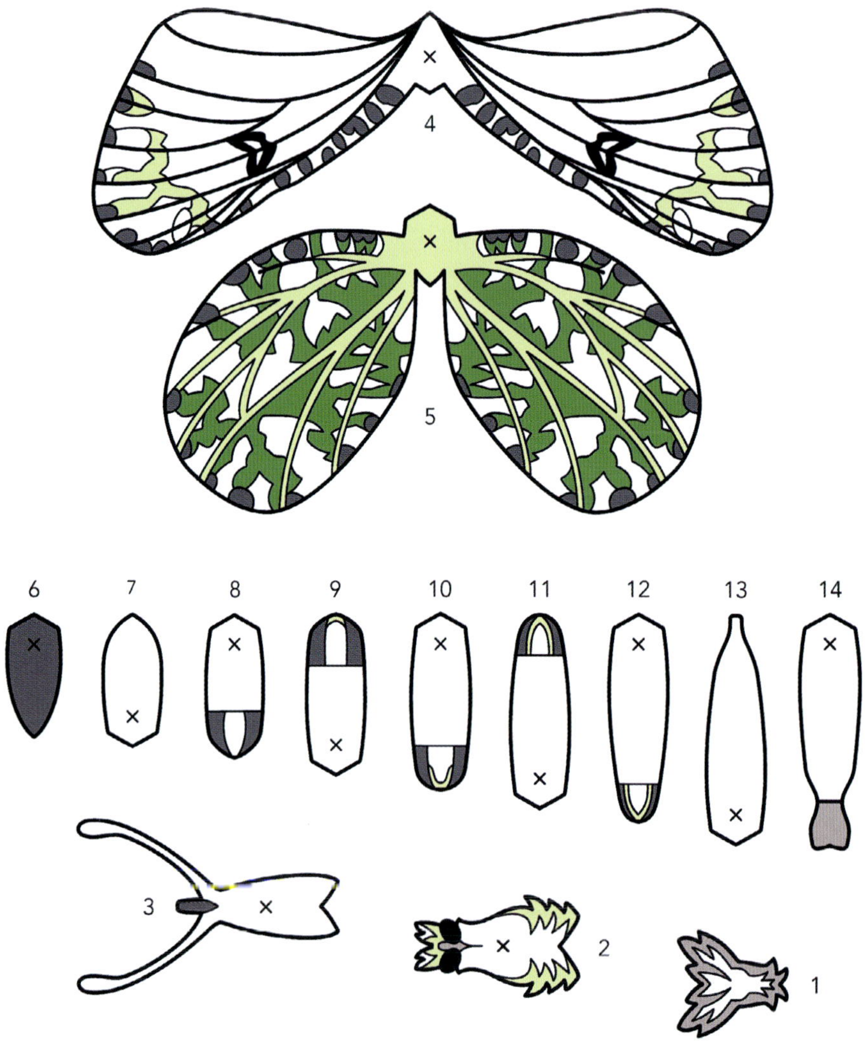

Colors Needed

- Black
- 90% warm gray
- 10% warm gray
- Chartreuse
- Olive green

ISLAND MARBLE BUTTERFLY ASSEMBLY

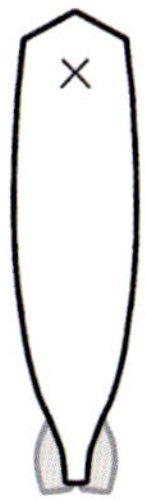

1

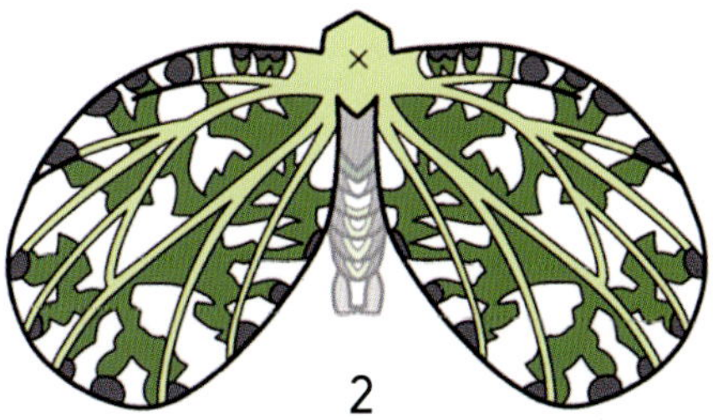

2

Remove the template for this project (page 137), and using the color guide on the left, color in the template. (You can refer to the Papercraft Tips and Tricks on page 11 for suggestions on coloring.) Once you are finished coloring, carefully cut out the template pieces along their solid black outer borders. Now it's time to assemble!

We start with the **abdomen**. Like a real lepidopteran, this paper specimen of yours has nine segments in its abdomen. Stack them in ascending order: Begin by adding glue with a toothpick or small paintbrush to the *X* mark on piece **14** and set piece **13** on top, aligning the curved top edges as shown in image 1.

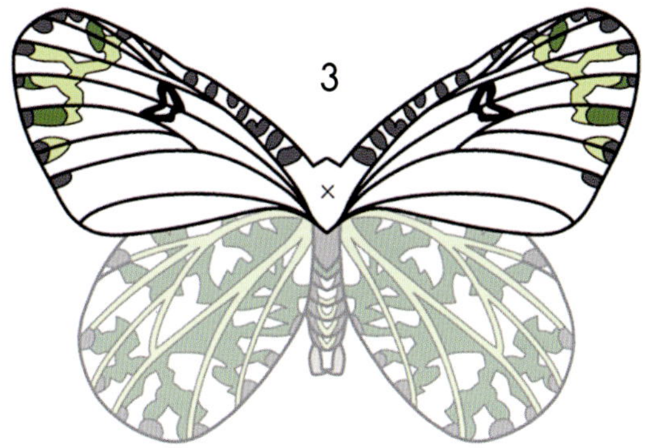

3

Apply glue to the *X* mark on piece **13** and set piece **12** on top. Continue this way until pieces **6** through **14** are all assembled. Set your completed abdomen aside to dry for 2 to 5 minutes.

Now for the **wings**. Apply some glue to the *X* mark on piece **6**, and set piece **5**, the **hindwings**, on top, aligning as shown in image 2.

Apply glue to the *X* mark on piece **5**, and set piece **4**, the **forewings**, on top, aligning as shown in image 3.

ISLAND MARBLE BUTTERFLY ASSEMBLY CONTINUED

4

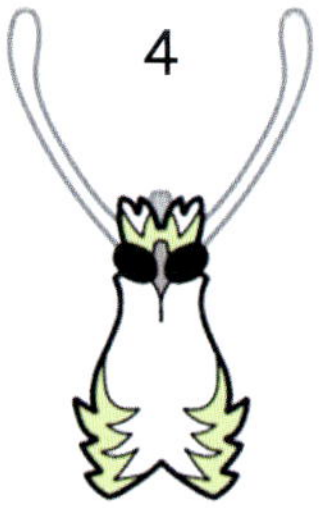

5

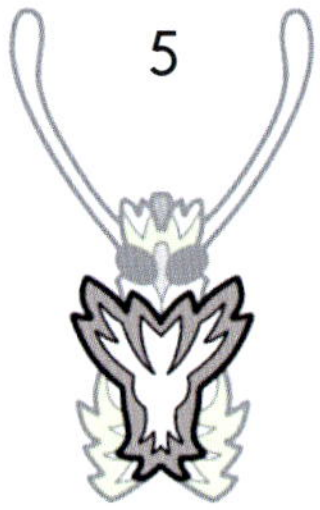

6

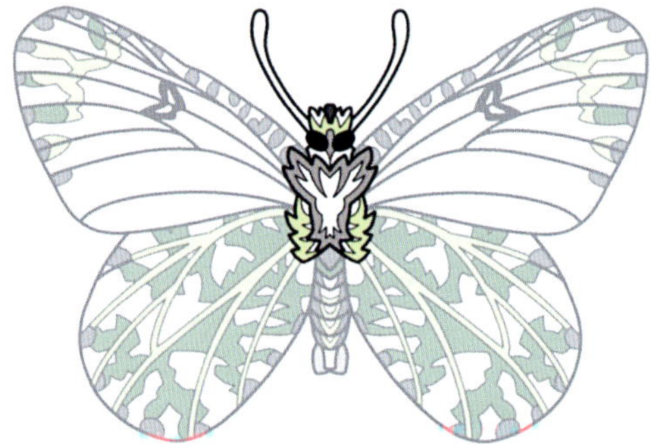

Let the wings and abdomen dry together for 2 to 5 minutes. Finally, let's assemble the **head**. Apply glue to the *X* mark on piece **3**, and set piece **2** on top, aligning as shown in image 4.

Apply glue to the *X* mark on piece **2**, and place piece **1** onto joined pieces **2** and **3** as shown in image 5.

Set the completed head aside to dry for 2 to 5 minutes, then add glue to the *X* mark on piece **4**, and set the head on top, aligning as shown in image 6. You're done!

For a final touch of dimension to your paper specimen, gently bend the forewings up with your fingers, and the hindwings down. If you'd like suggestions on how to display your completed butterfly, check out Mounting and Displaying Your Papercraft Specimens (page 109).

LUZON PEACOCK SWALLOWTAIL BUTTERFLY

The Luzon peacock is a stunning example of the well-known family of swallowtail butterflies and their tricky hind ends. So named for the long, decorative tails on the adults' hindwings, swallowtails also feature a strange, forked appendage in their youth: the *osmeterium*. This appendage is hidden in the caterpillar's body until it feels threatened, at which point it shoots out the osmeterium like shaking a pitchfork, and secretes a stinky, bitter liquid that lets predators know: *I eat toxic plants, and that makes me taste bad*. The osmeterium is unique to swallowtails, just like their wing tails, but while it provides defense through *aposematic warning* (bright colors that warn of toxic or poisonous traits), the tails defend through *automimicry*. The length and shape of the swallowtails' tails serve as *false heads*. False heads confuse predators into biting the butterfly's tail rather than their real head, and the swallowtail flutters on to live another day.

Scientific name: ***Papilio chikae***

Habitat: ***Mountainous areas of the Philippines***

Real-life size: ***Wingspan of 4¾" (120 mm)***

Conservation status: ***Endangered (International Union for Conservation of Nature)***

Template: ***Page 139***

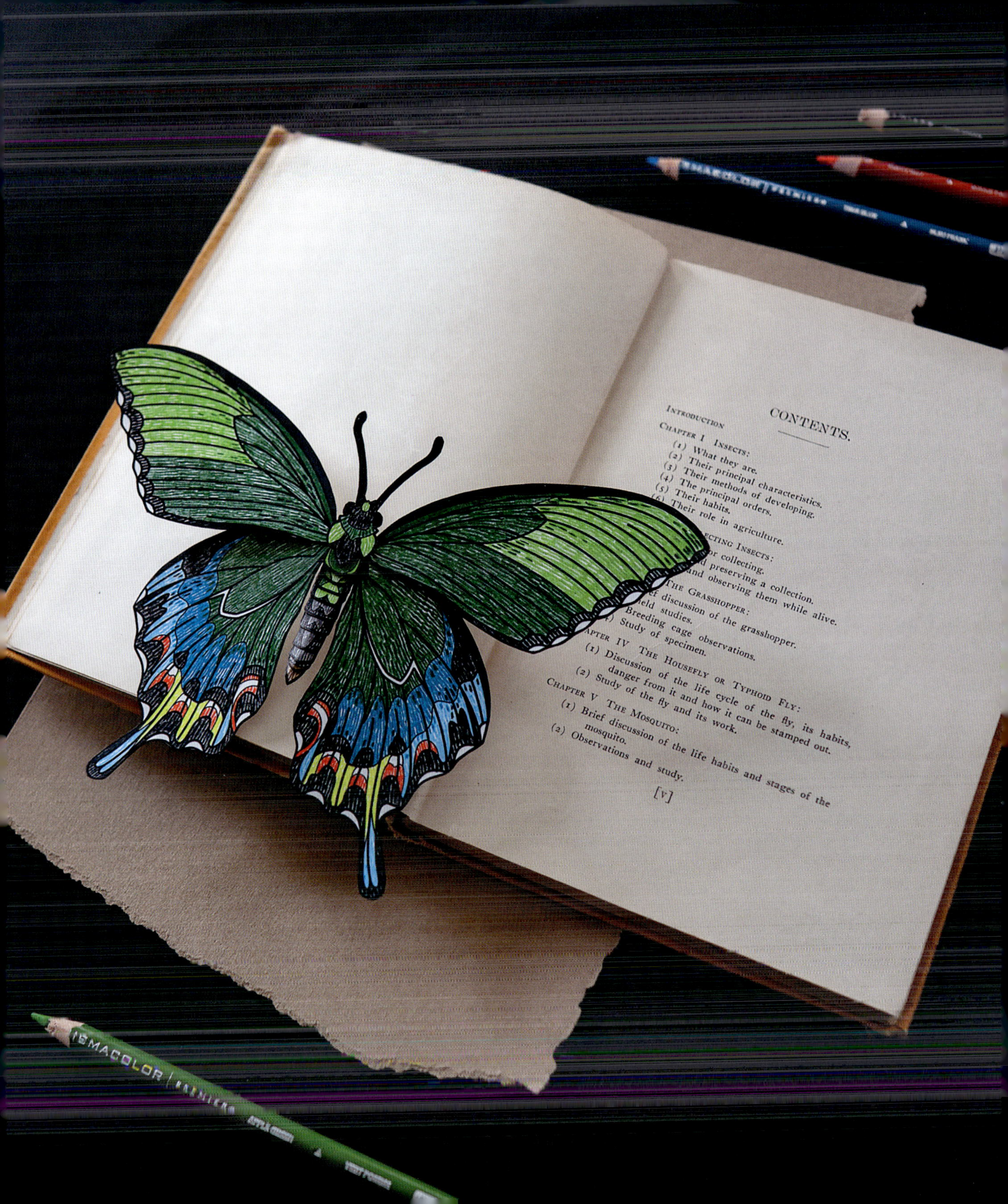
Introduction
CONTENTS.
Chapter I Insects:
(1) What they are.
(2) Their principal characteristics.
(3) Their methods of developing.
(4) The principal orders.
(5) Their habits.
Breeding cage observations.
Study of specimen.
(1) Discussion of the life cycle of the fly, its habits,
danger from it and how it can be stamped out.
(2) Study of the fly and its work.
Chapter V The Mosquito:
(1) Brief discussion of the life habits and stages of the
mosquito.
(2) Observations and study.
[v]

LUZON PEACOCK SWALLOWTAIL BUTTERFLY COLOR GUIDE

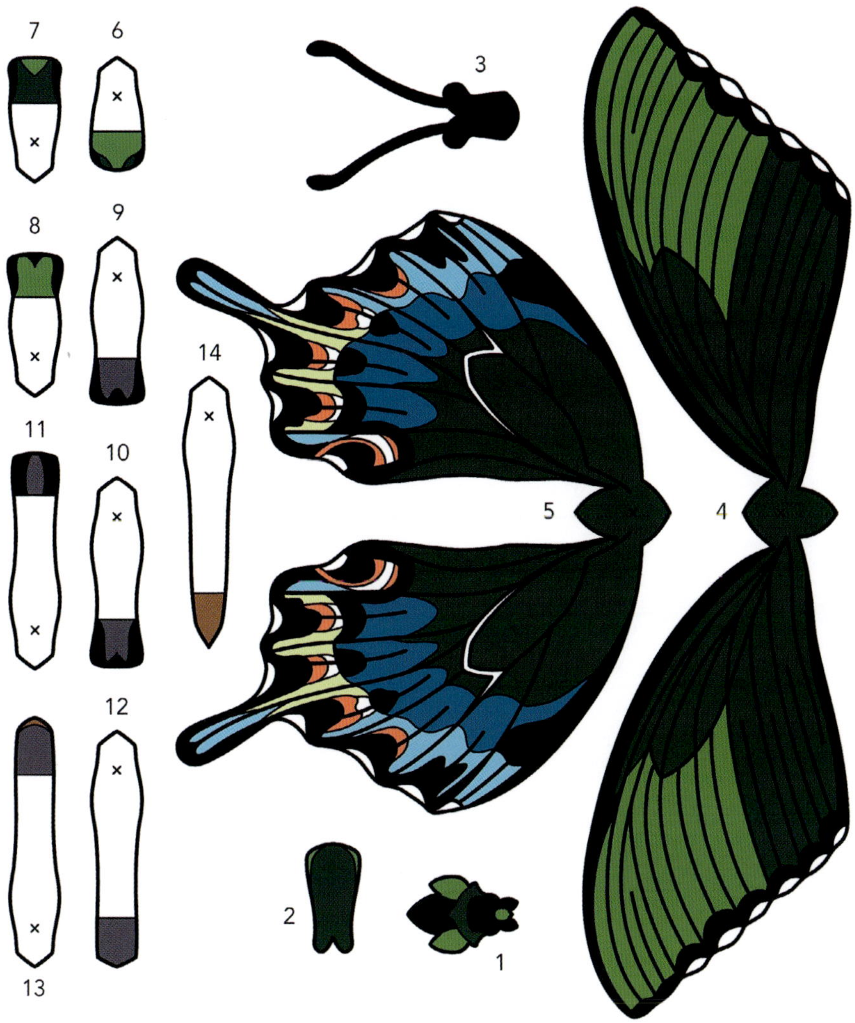

Colors Needed

- Black
- 50% warm gray
- Light umber
- Poppy red
- Chartreuse
- Apple green
- Olive green
- Dark green
- Peacock blue
- Electric blue

LUZON PEACOCK SWALLOWTAIL BUTTERFLY ASSEMBLY

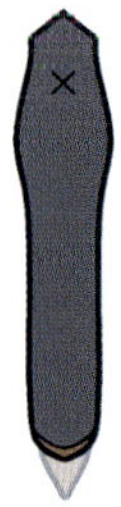

1

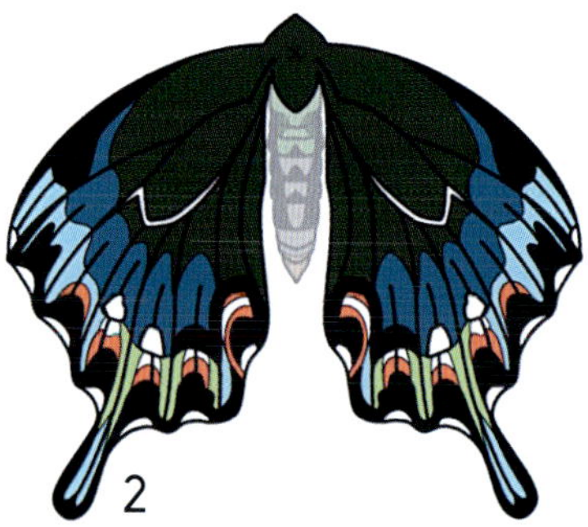

2

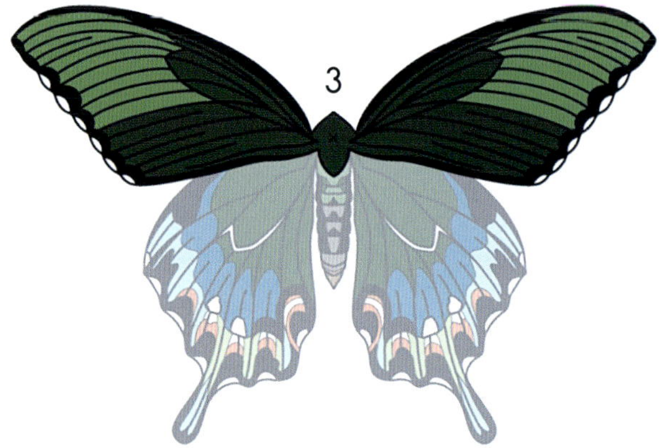

3

Remove the template for this project (page 139), and using the color guide on page 59, color in the template. (You can refer to the Papercraft Tips and Tricks on page 11 for suggestions on coloring.) Once you are finished coloring, carefully cut out the template pieces along their solid black outer borders. Now it's time to assemble!

We start with the **abdomen**. Like a real lepidopteran, this paper specimen of yours has nine segments in its abdomen. Stack them in ascending order: Begin by adding glue with a toothpick or small paintbrush to the *X* mark on piece **14** and set piece **13** on top, aligning the curved top edges as shown in image 1.

Apply glue to the *X* mark on piece **13** and set piece **12** on top. Continue this way until pieces **6** through **14** are all assembled. Set your completed abdomen aside to dry for 2 to 5 minutes. Next, mimic the curved fullness of a real butterfly's abdomen by pressing the abdomen over the barrel of one of your colored pencils with your thumb and finger, bending the edges down.

Now for the **wings**. Apply some glue to the *X* mark on piece **6**, and set piece **5**, the **hindwings**, on top, aligning as shown in image 2.

Apply glue to the *X* mark on piece **5**, and set piece **4**, the **forewings**, on top, aligning as shown in image 3.

4

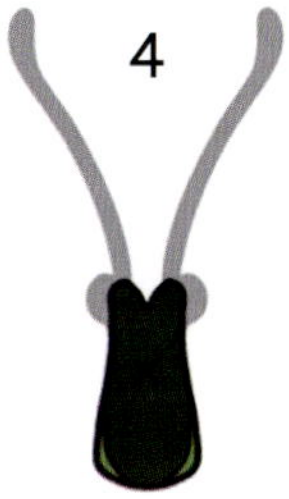

5

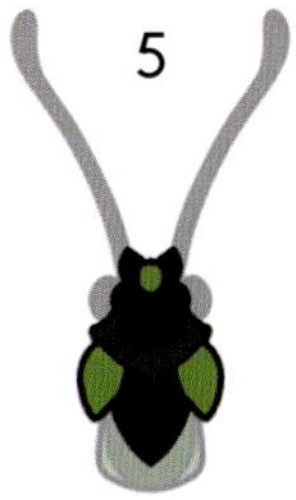

6

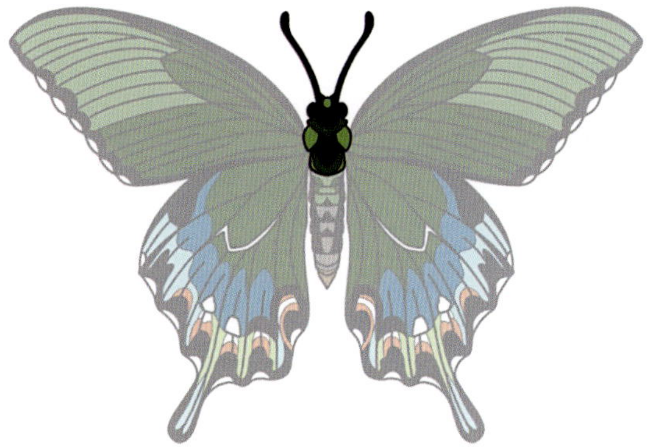

Let the wings and abdomen dry together for 2 to 5 minutes. Finally, let's assemble the **head**. Apply glue to the *X* mark on piece **3**, and set piece **2** on top, aligning as shown in image 4.

Apply glue to the back of piece **1**, and place it onto joined pieces **2** and **3** as shown in image 5.

Set the completed head aside to dry for 2 to 5 minutes, then add glue to the *X* mark on piece **4**, and set the head on top, aligning as shown in image 6. You're done!

For a final touch of dimension to your paper specimen, gently bend the forewings up with your fingers, and the hindwings down. If you'd like suggestions on how to display your completed butterfly, check out Mounting and Displaying Your Papercraft Specimens (page 109).

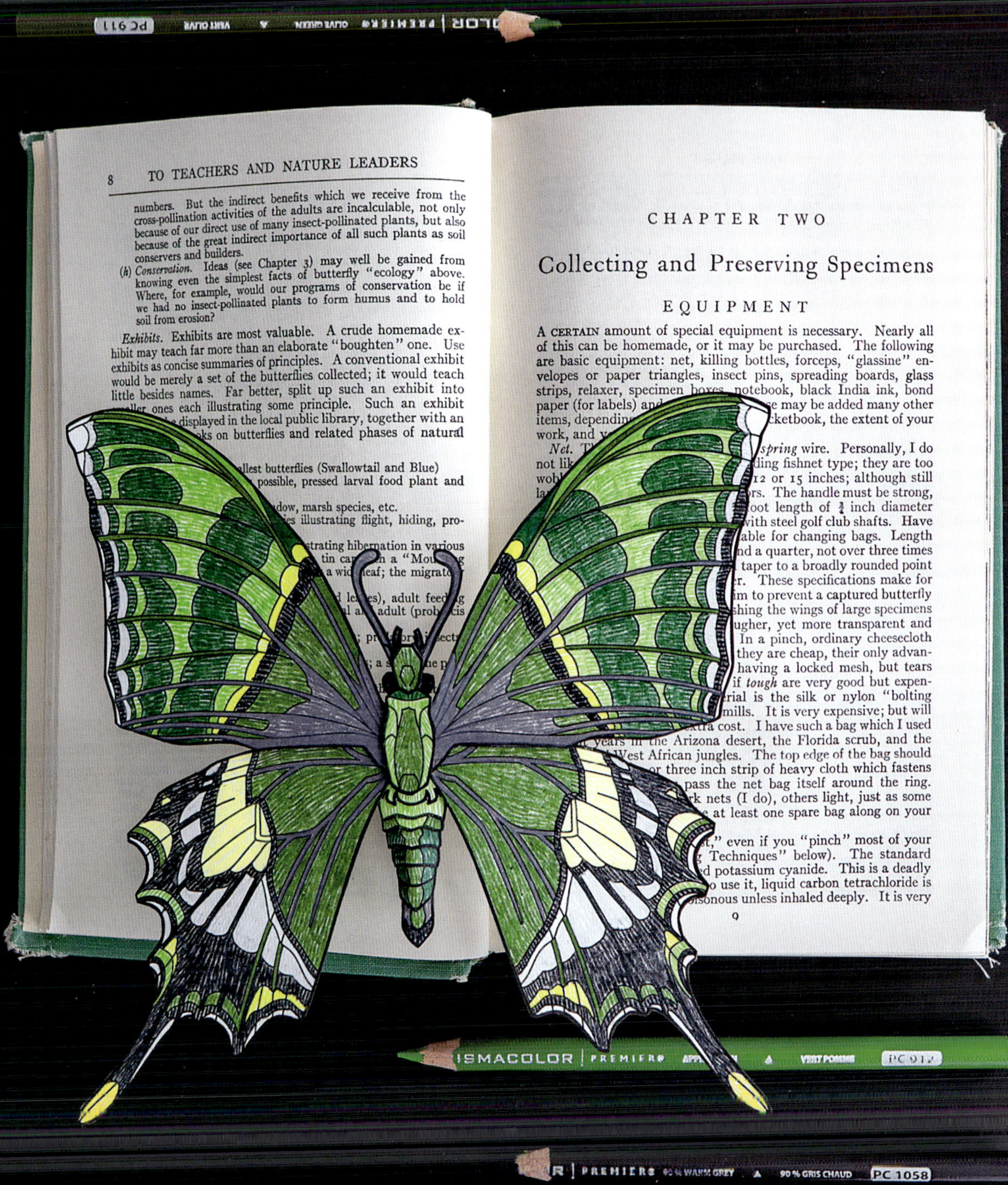
PC 911
OLIVE GREEN
8 TO TEACHERS AND NATURE LEADERS
numbers. But the indirect benefits which we receive from the cross-pollination activities of the adults are incalculable, not only because of our direct use of many insect-pollinated plants, but also because of the great indirect importance of all such plants as soil conservers and builders.
(h) Conservation. Ideas (see Chapter 3) may well be gained from knowing even the simplest facts of butterfly "ecology" above. Where, for example, would our programs of conservation be if we had no insect-pollinated plants to form humus and to hold soil from erosion?
Exhibits. Exhibits are most valuable. A crude homemade exhibit may teach far more than an elaborate "boughten" one. Use exhibits as concise summaries of principles. A conventional exhibit would be merely a set of the butterflies collected; it would teach little besides names. Far better, split up such an exhibit into
ones each illustrating some principle. Such an exhibit
displayed in the local public library, together with an
on butterflies and related phases of natural
CHAPTER TWO
Collecting and Preserving Specimens
EQUIPMENT
A CERTAIN amount of special equipment is necessary. Nearly all of this can be homemade, or it may be purchased. The following are basic equipment: net, killing bottles, forceps, "glassine" envelopes or paper triangles, insect pins, spreading boards, glass strips, relaxer, specimen
notebook, black India ink, bond paper (for labels)
may be added many other items, depending
ketbook, the extent of your
spring wire. Personally, I do
The handle must be strong,
inch diameter
with steel golf club shafts. Have
able for changing bags. Length
taper to a broadly rounded point
These specifications make for
to prevent a captured butterfly
In a pinch, ordinary cheesecloth
they are cheap, their only advan-
having a locked mesh, but tears
tough are very good but expen-
It is very expensive; but will
I have such a bag which I used
Arizona desert, the Florida scrub, and the
West African jungles. The top edge of the bag should
inch strip of heavy cloth which fastens
pass the net bag itself around the ring.
at least one spare bag along on your
even if you "pinch" most of your
Techniques" below). The standard
potassium cyanide. This is a deadly
use it, liquid carbon tetrachloride is
unless inhaled deeply. It is very
9
PRISMACOLOR PREMIER
VERT POMME
PC 912
PREMIER
90% WARM GREY
90% GRIS CHAUD
PC 1058

GOLDEN KAISER-I-HIND BUTTERFLY

Scientific name: **Teinopalpus aureus**

Habitat: **Mountainous forests in Southeastern Asia**

Real-life size: **Wingspan of 4¾" (120 mm)**

Conservation status: **Rare; Protected (Chinese Wildlife Protection Law of the PRC)**

Template: **Pages 141 and 143**

Not all that glitters in the Himalayas and other Southeastern Asian mountains is ice. The golden Kaiser-i-Hind butterfly sparkles in a uniquely beautiful way due to the *structural color* of its wings. Look at a golden Kaiser-i-Hind from different angles, and your eyes will pick up different colors (I particularly recommend using the stippling technique [page 14] to mimic this look for this project). This is due to the individual *scales* on this butterfly's wings containing *nanostructures* that scatter and reflect light, rather than just containing pigment.

Unfortunately, this gorgeous coloration makes the Kaiser-i-Hind particularly valuable to insect collectors. Like all butterflies, this species is *ectothermic* (cold-blooded) and needs to sunbathe in its chilly high-altitude habitat before it can move, so it doesn't even try to fly on cloudy days, making it an easy catch for harvesters. Thankfully, the Convention on International Trade in Endangered Species of Wild Fauna and Flora (CITES) has recognized this threat and has declared the selling or purchasing of this species illegal internationally. There is hope yet that this treasure will not be lost.

GOLDEN KAISER-I-HIND BUTTERFLY COLOR GUIDE

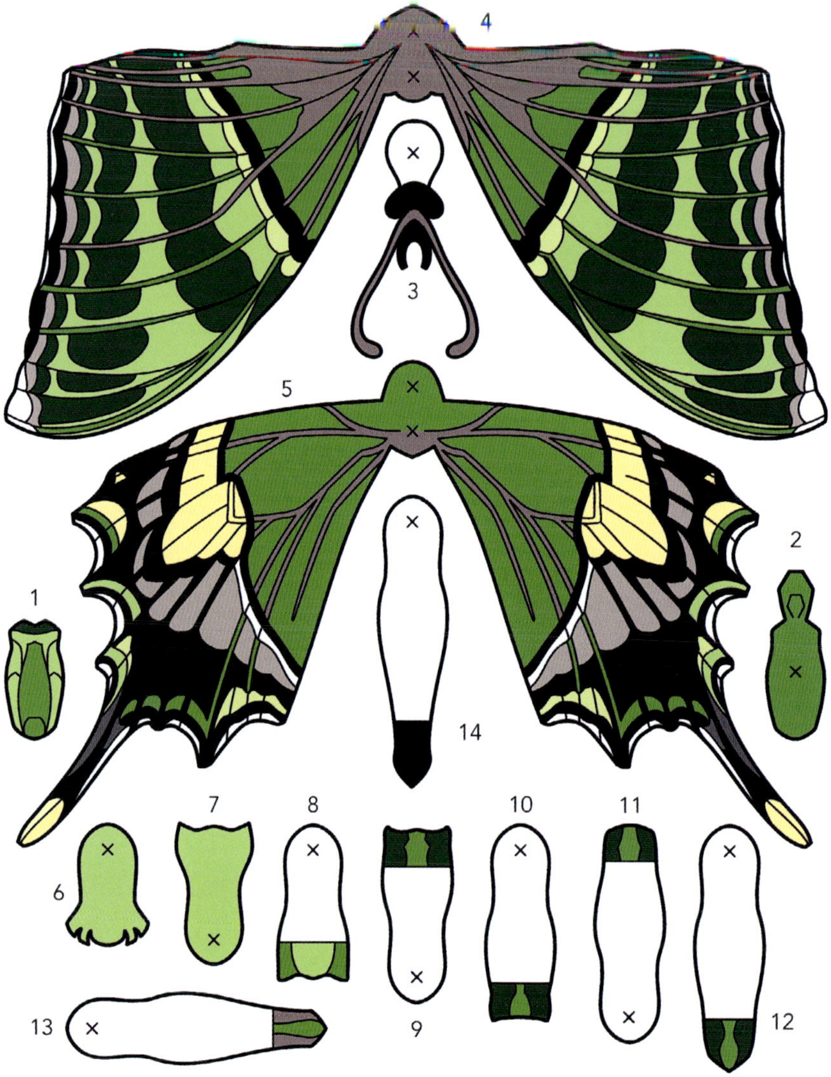

Colors Needed

- Black
- 90% warm gray
- 50% warm gray
- 10% warm gray
- Lemon yellow
- Canary yellow
- Chartreuse
- Apple green
- Olive green
- Dark green

GOLDEN KAISER-I-HIND BUTTERFLY ASSEMBLY

1

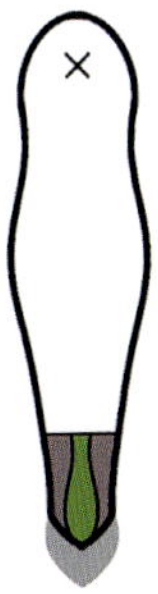

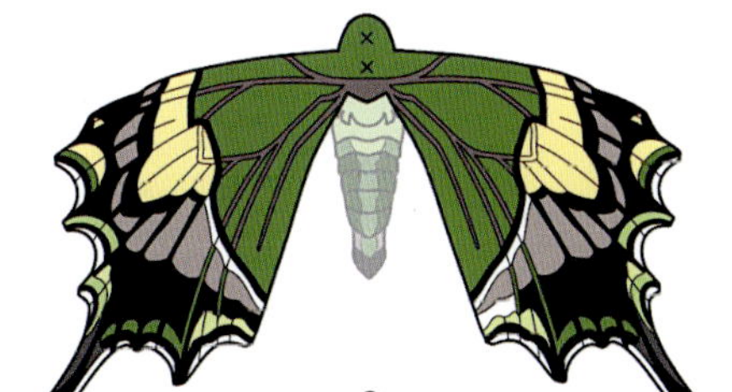

2

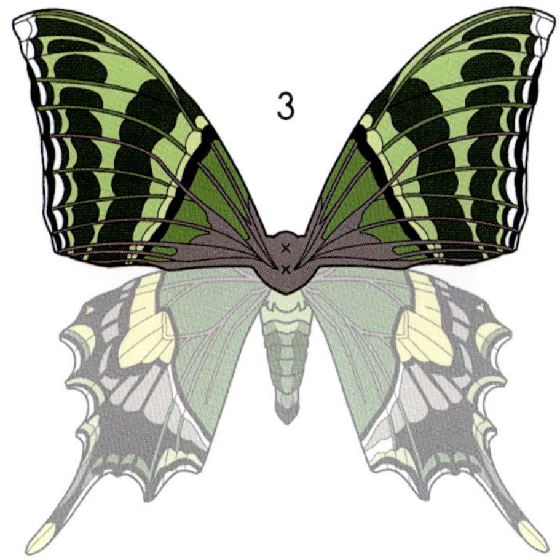

3

Remove the template for this project (page 141 and 143), and using the color guide on the left, color in the template. (You can refer to the Papercraft Tips and Tricks on page 11 for suggestions on coloring.) Once you are finished coloring, carefully cut out the template pieces along their solid black outer borders. Now it's time to assemble!

We start with the **abdomen**. Like a real lepidopteran, this paper specimen of yours has nine segments in its abdomen. Stack them in ascending order: Begin by adding glue with a toothpick or small paintbrush to the *X* mark on piece **14** and set piece **13** on top, aligning the curved top edges as shown in image 1.

Apply glue to the *X* mark on piece **13** and set piece **12** on top. Continue this way until pieces **6** through **14** are all assembled. Set your completed abdomen aside to dry for 2 to 5 minutes. Next, mimic the curved fullness of a real butterfly's abdomen by pressing the abdomen over the barrel of one of your colored pencils with your thumb and finger, bending the edges down.

Now for the **wings**. Apply some glue to the *X* mark on piece **6**, and set piece **5**, the **hindwings**, on top, aligning as shown in image 2.

Apply glue to the *X* marks on piece **5**, and set piece **4**, the **forewings**, on top, aligning as shown in image 3.

GOLDEN KAISER-I-HIND BUTTERFLY ASSEMBLY CONTINUED

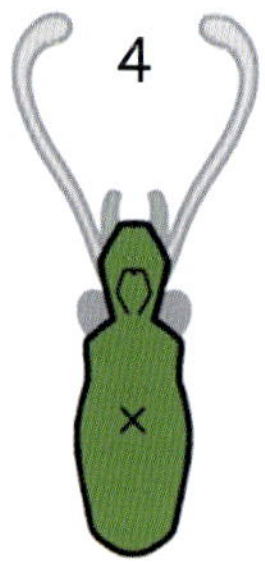

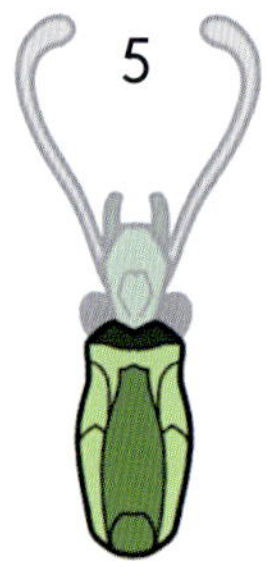

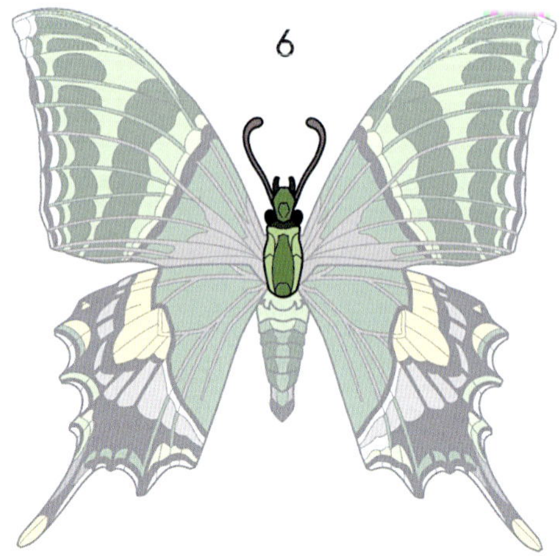

Let the wings and abdomen dry together for 2 to 5 minutes. Finally, let's assemble the **head**. Apply glue to the *X* mark on piece **3**, and set piece **2** on top, aligning as shown in image 4.

Apply glue to the *X* mark on piece **2**, and place piece **1** onto joined pieces **2** and **3** as shown in image 5.

Set the completed head aside to dry for 2 to 5 minutes, then add glue to the *X* marks on piece **4**, and set the head on top, aligning as shown in image 6. You're done!

For a final touch of dimension to your paper specimen, gently bend the forewings up with your fingers, and the hindwings down. If you'd like suggestions on how to display your completed butterfly, check out Mounting and Displaying Your Papercraft Specimens (page 109).

GREAT PURPLE EMPEROR BUTTERFLY

Scientific name: **Sasakia charonda**

Habitat: **Forests of China, Japan, the Korean Peninsula, and Vietnam**

Real-life size: **Wingspan of 2 to 2¾" (50 to 70 mm)**

Conservation status: **Rare; Near Threatened (Japanese Ministry of the Environment)**

Templates: **Pages 145 and 147**

As a youngster, the great purple emperor lives up to its name as the official butterfly species of Japan, with an adorably *kawaii* green body topped with a deer-like head that features tiny brown "antler" spikes and a black "nose." And while the male *imago* (adult) butterflies are indeed gorgeous, with namesake rich purple coloring and many yellow, white, and even pink spots, they are surprisingly scrappy and gross.

Male great purple emperors are famously territorial, seeking out high vantage points on boulders or trees where they keep an eye out over their territory and launch attacks on other encroaching males. To keep up their strength, they eat a varied diet, sucking up liquids from sap, rotting fruit, and decaying animals, and even tolerate other males during *puddling behavior*, gathering at dung or rain puddles to source minerals and salts. They sometimes resort to landing on humans to snack on sweat. While the males pick fights and hunt for wide-ranging food sources, the females remain solitary, fluttering near their preferred host plant, Chinese or Japanese hackberry, and sipping primarily on sap in a much more regal manner.

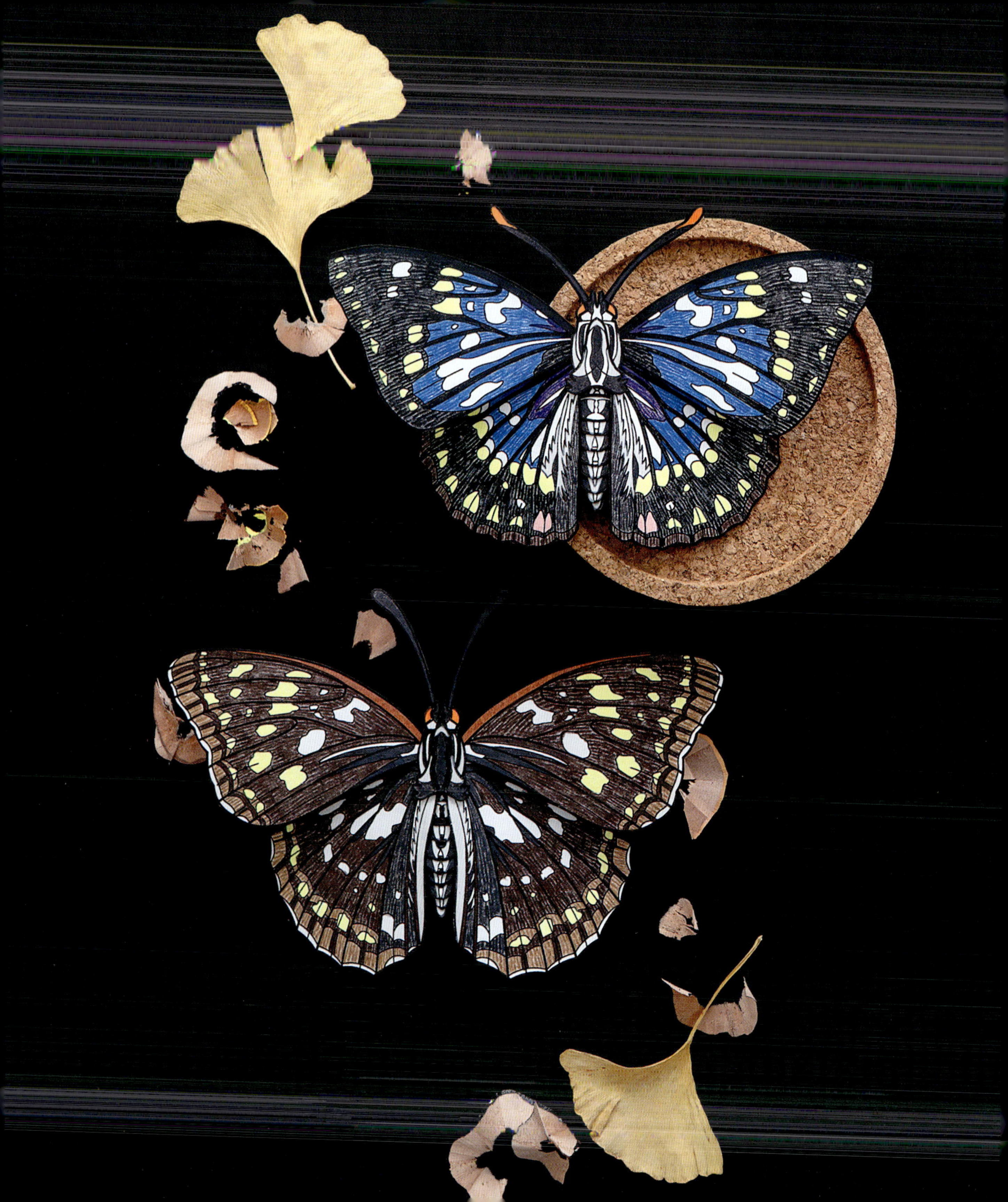

GREAT PURPLE EMPEROR BUTTERFLY (MALE) COLOR GUIDE

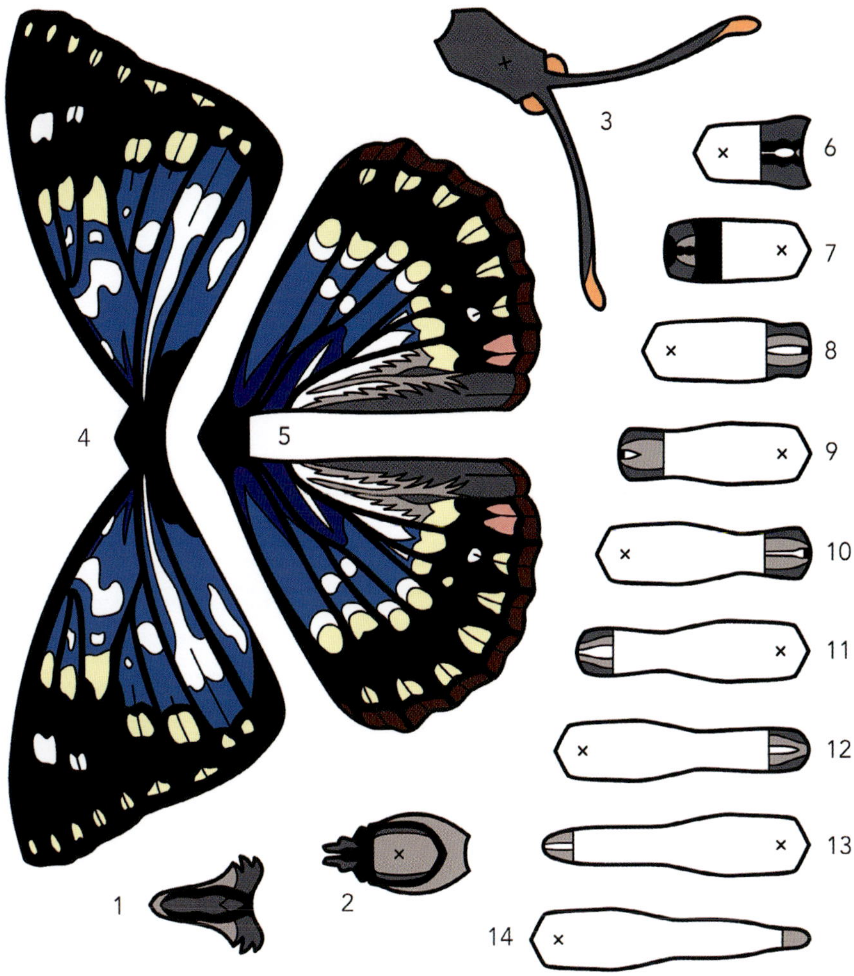

Colors Needed

- Black
- 90% warm gray
- 10% warm gray
- Dark umber
- Orange
- Blush pink
- Lemon yellow
- Denim blue
- Dioxazine purple hue

GREAT PURPLE EMPEROR BUTTERFLY (MALE) ASSEMBLY

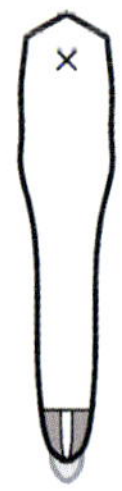

1

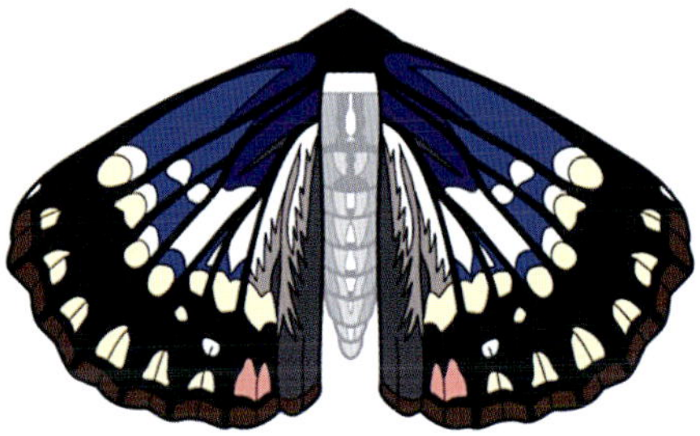

2

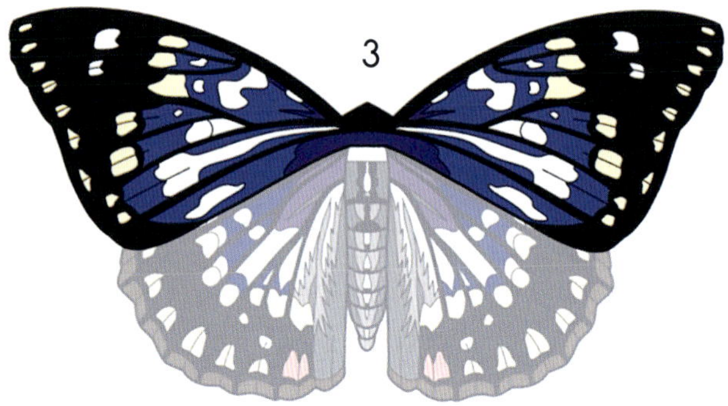

3

Note: There are two variants of this project available in this book. This project is for the Male, which has the deep purplish coloring the species is named for.

Remove the template for this project (page 145), and using the color guide on page 69, color in the template. (You can refer to the Papercraft Tips and Tricks on page 11 for suggestions on coloring.) Once you are finished coloring, carefully cut out the template pieces along their solid black outer borders. Now it's time to assemble!

We start with the **abdomen**. Like a real lepidopteran, this paper specimen of yours has nine segments in its abdomen. Stack them in ascending order: Begin by adding glue with a toothpick or small paintbrush to the *X* mark on piece **14** and set piece **13** on top, aligning the curved top edges as shown in image 1.

Apply glue to the *X* mark on piece **13** and set piece **12** on top. Continue this way until pieces **6** through **14** are all assembled. Set your completed abdomen aside to dry for 2 to 5 minutes. Next, mimic the curved fullness of a real butterfly's abdomen by pressing the abdomen over the barrel of one of your colored pencils with your thumb and finger, bending the edges down.

Now for the **wings**. Apply some glue to the *X* mark on piece **6**, and set piece **5**, the **hindwings**, on top, aligning as shown in image 2.

Apply glue to the *X* mark on piece **5**, and set piece **4**, the **forewings**, on top, aligning as shown in image 3.

4

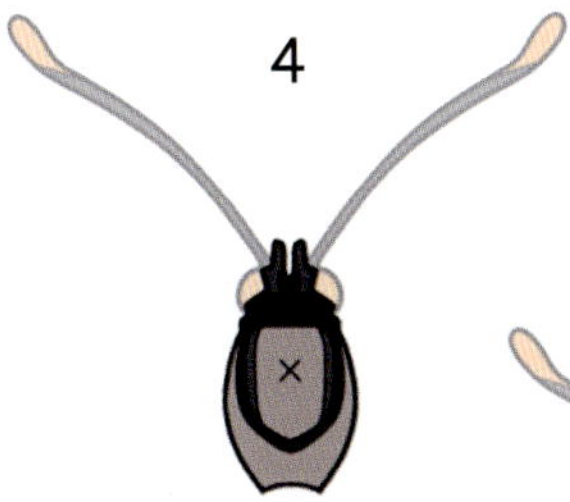

5

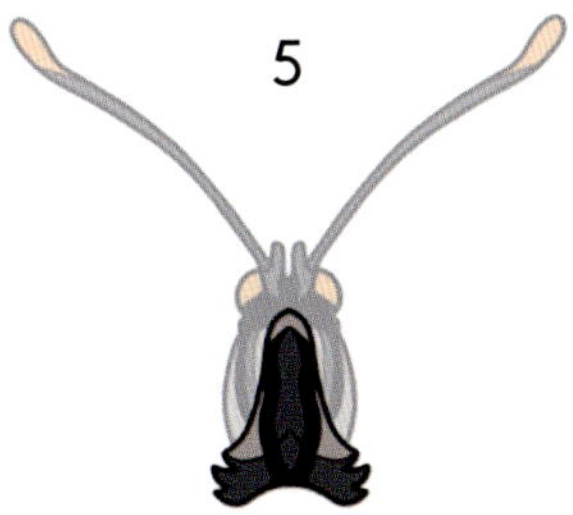

6

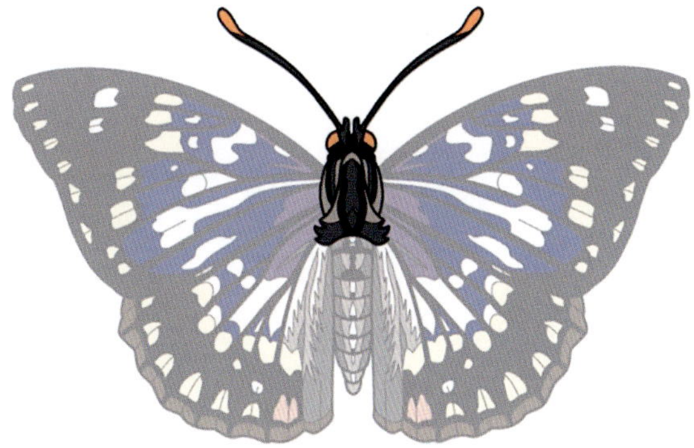

Let the wings and abdomen dry together for 2 to 5 minutes. Finally, let's assemble the **head**. Apply glue to the *X* mark on piece **3**, and set piece **2** on top, aligning as shown in image 4.

Apply glue to the *X* mark on piece **2**, and place piece **1** onto joined pieces **2** and **3** as shown in image 5.

Set the completed head aside to dry for 2 to 5 minutes, then add glue to the *X* mark on piece **4**, and set the head on top, aligning as shown in image 6. You're done!

For a final touch of dimension to your paper specimen, gently bend the forewings up with your fingers, and the hindwings down. If you'd like suggestions on how to display your completed butterfly, check out Mounting and Displaying Your Papercraft Specimens (page 109).

GREAT PURPLE EMPEROR BUTTERFLY (FEMALE) COLOR GUIDE

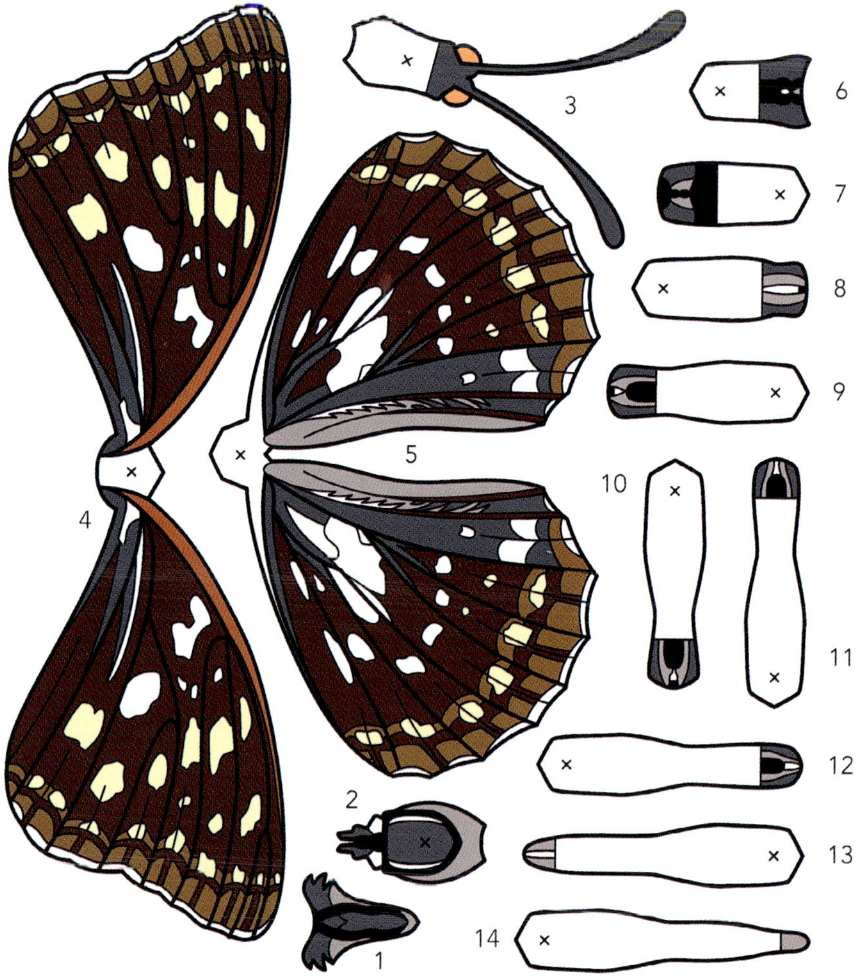

Colors Needed

- Black
- 90% warm gray
- 10% warm gray
- Dark umber
- Light umber
- Sienna orange
- Orange
- Lemon yellow

GREAT PURPLE EMPEROR BUTTERFLY (FEMALE) ASSEMBLY

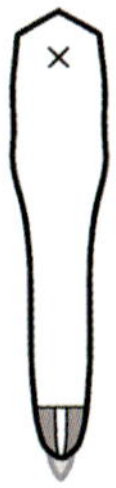

1

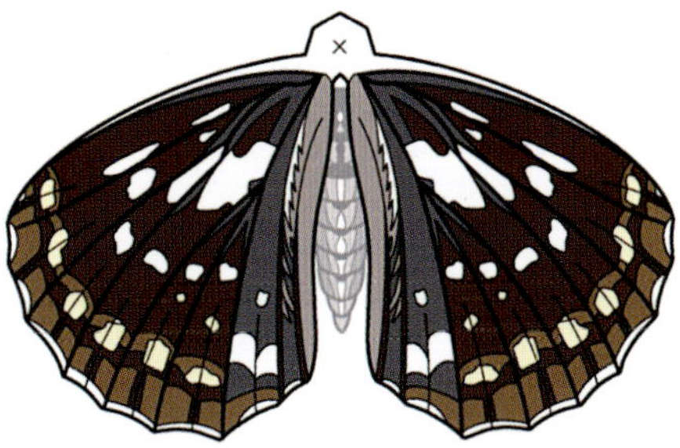

2

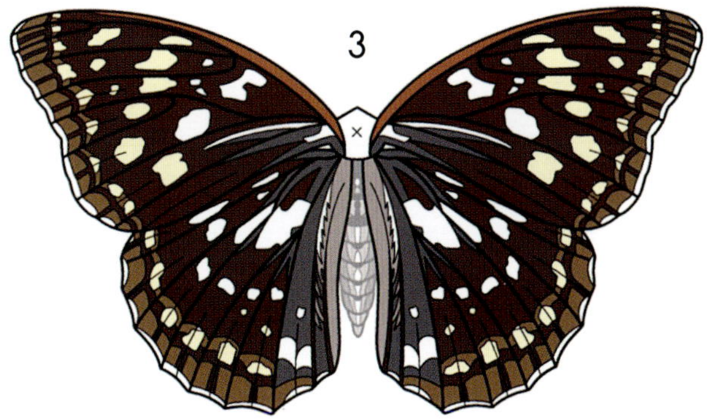

3

Note: There are two variants of this project available in this book. This project is for the Female. Her subtler coloring of browns and grays blends in with the bark and leaves of her tree canopy home in cryptic coloring camouflage, making her a rarer sight for butterfly watchers than the males.

Remove the template for this project (page 147), and using the color guide on the left, color in the template. (You can refer to the Papercraft Tips and Tricks on page 11 for suggestions on coloring.) Once you are finished coloring, carefully cut out the template pieces along their solid black outer borders. Now it's time to assemble!

We start with the **abdomen**. Like a real lepidopteran, this paper specimen of yours has nine segments in its abdomen. Stack them in ascending order: Begin by adding glue with a toothpick or small paintbrush to the *X* mark on piece **14** and set piece **13** on top, aligning the curved top edges as shown in image 1.

Apply glue to the *X* mark on piece **13** and set piece **12** on top. Continue this way until pieces **6** through **14** are all assembled. Set your completed abdomen aside to dry for 2 to 5 minutes. Next, mimic the curved fullness of a real butterfly's abdomen by pressing the abdomen over the barrel of one of your colored pencils with your thumb and finger, bending the edges down.

Now for the **wings**. Apply some glue to the *X* mark on piece **6**, and set piece **5**, the **hindwings**, on top, aligning as shown in image 2.

Apply glue to the *X* mark on piece **5**, and set piece **4**, the **forewings**, on top, aligning as shown in image 3.

4

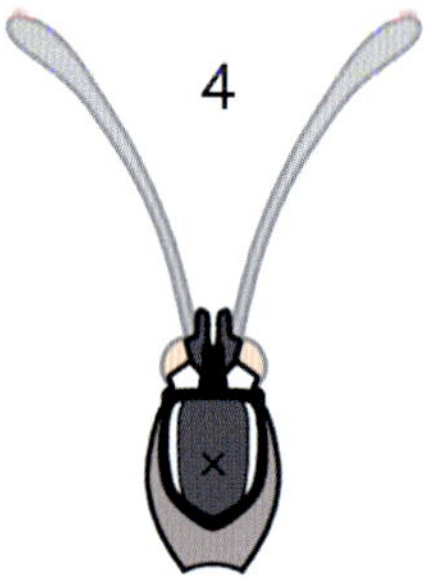

5

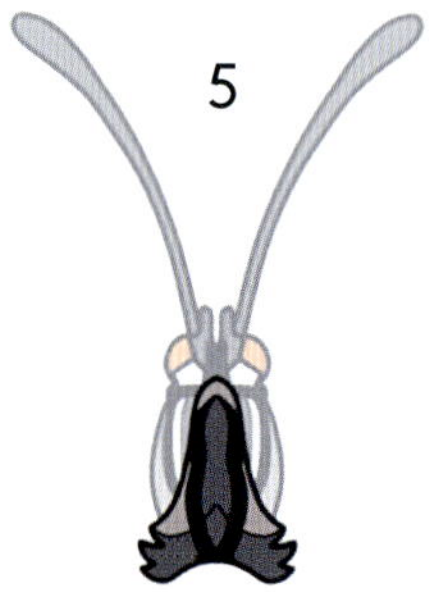

6

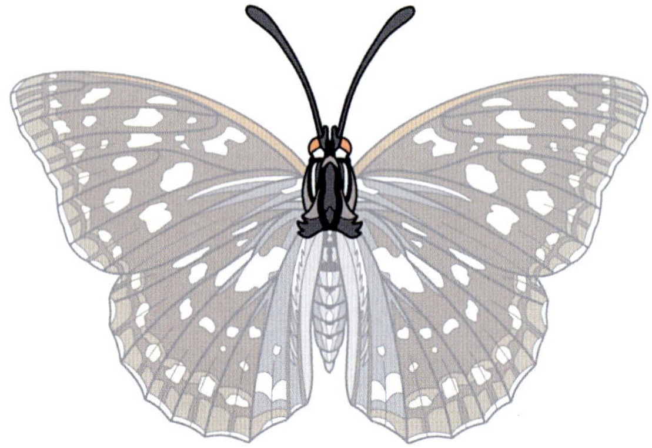

Let the wings and abdomen dry together for 2 to 5 minutes. Finally, let's assemble the **head**. Apply glue to the *X* mark on piece **3**, and set piece **2** on top, aligning as shown in image 4.

Apply glue to the *X* mark on piece **2**, and place piece **1** onto joined pieces **2** and **3** as shown in image 5.

Set the completed head aside to dry for 2 to 5 minutes, then add glue to the *X* mark on piece **4**, and set the head on top, aligning as shown in image 6. You're done!

For a final touch of dimension to your paper specimen, gently bend the forewings up with your fingers, and the hindwings down. If you'd like suggestions on how to display your completed butterfly, check out Mounting and Displaying Your Papercraft Specimens (page 109).

WALLACE'S GOLDEN BIRDWING BUTTERFLY

Scientific name: ***Ornithoptera croesus***

Habitat: ***Lowland forests of Indonesia***

Real-life size: ***Wingspan of 7½" (191 mm)***

Conservation status: ***Rare; Threatened (International Union for Conservation of Nature)***

Templates: ***Pages 149, 151, and 153***

Named *birdwing* for the size of their wings and swooping flight, the *Ornithoptera* butterflies include the largest butterflies of the world and feature flashy males and more muted, but clever, females. Unsurprisingly, Wallace's golden birdwing butterflies are strong fliers. The male performs special searching flights called *aerial pursuits*. First, they fly after any moving thing that catches their attention, and once close enough, they inspect it and sense the air with their antennae to test for *sex pheromones* (chemicals that indicate a female is ready to mate). If he has successfully chased down a female, the male then performs a fluttering mating dance over her. Doing this scatters his own pheromones and is his attempt to impress the female with his flying ability. The females are not nearly so active, remaining close to their preferred host plant, Aristolochia or the Dutchman's pipe vine. Unlike the males, the females don't depend on agility or color-based *aposematic warning* of their toxicity to avoid predators, but instead, they use a different, sneaky type of warning called *batesian mimicry*. In developing coloration similar to the poisonous butterfly species of Danainae, they fend off any attacks simply sunbathing on the Dutchman's pipe, letting the bright males veer and soar alone in the treetops.

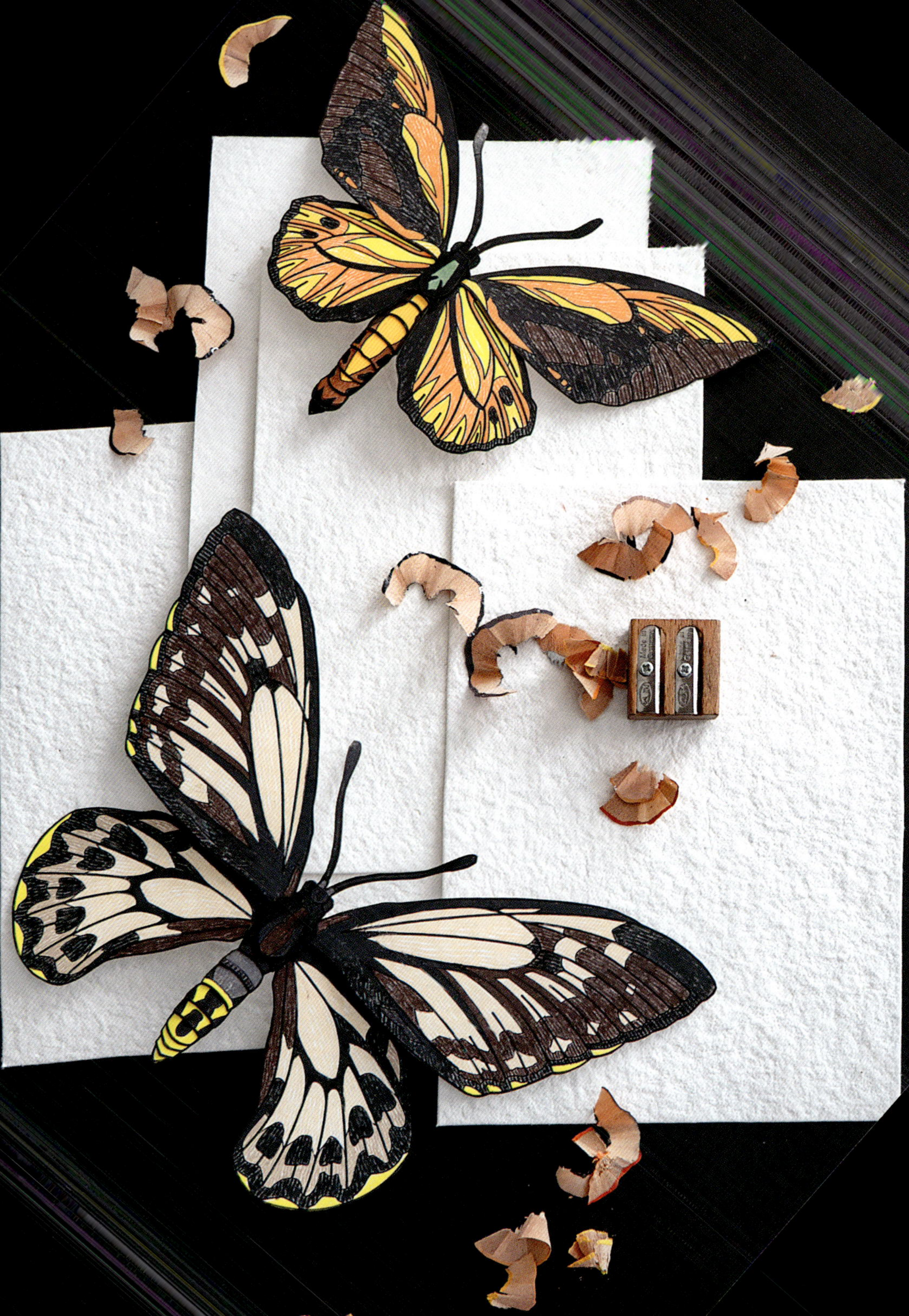

WALLACE'S GOLDEN BIRDWING BUTTERFLY (MALE) COLOR GUIDE

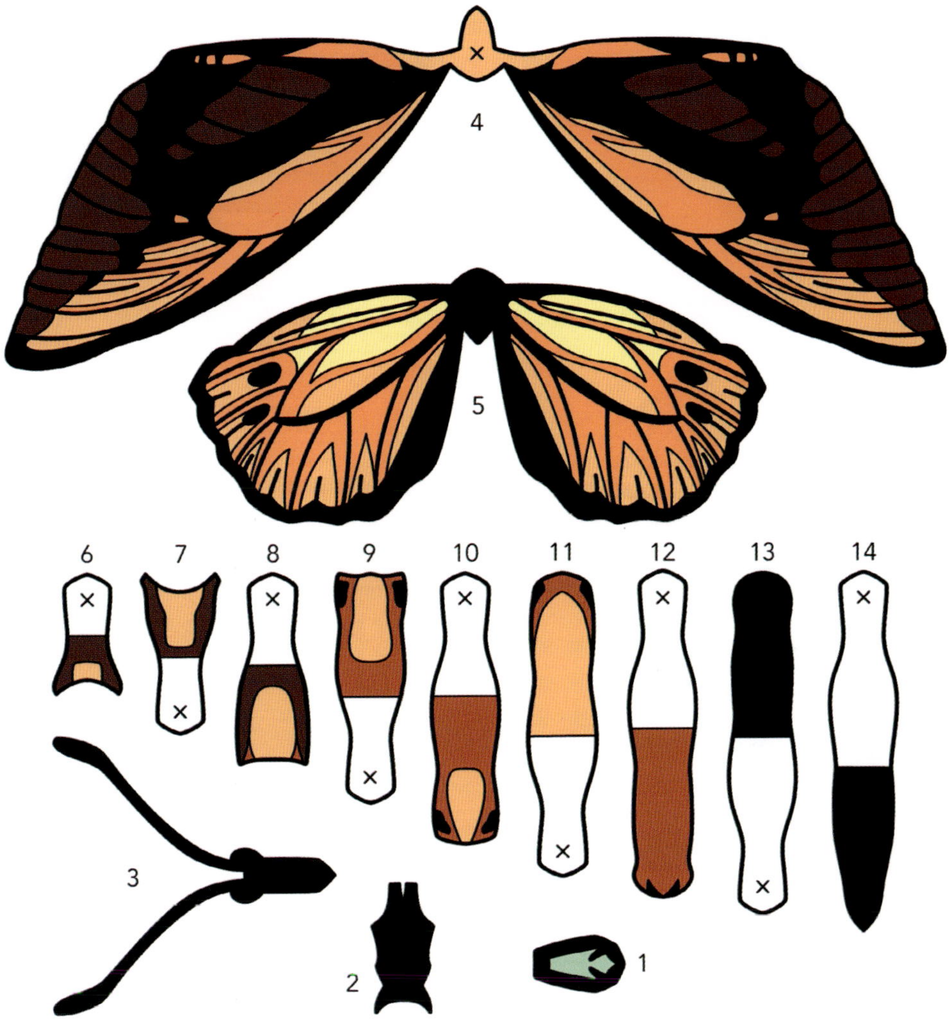

Colors Needed

- Black
- Dark umber
- Sienna brown
- Spanish orange
- Orange
- Canary yellow
- Sap green light

WALLACE'S GOLDEN BIRDWING BUTTERFLY (MALE) ASSEMBLY

1

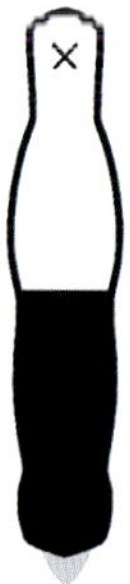

2

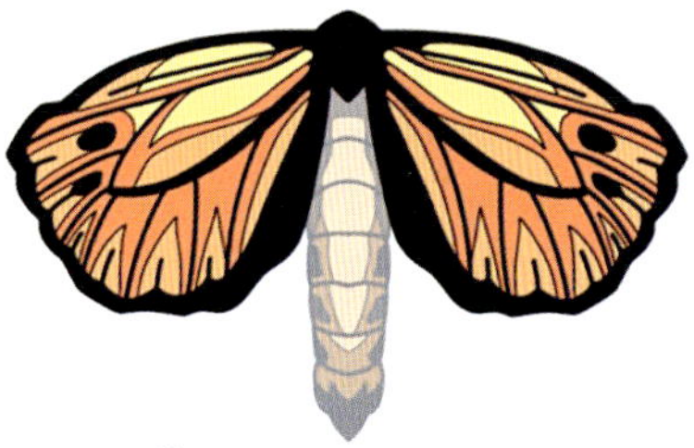

3

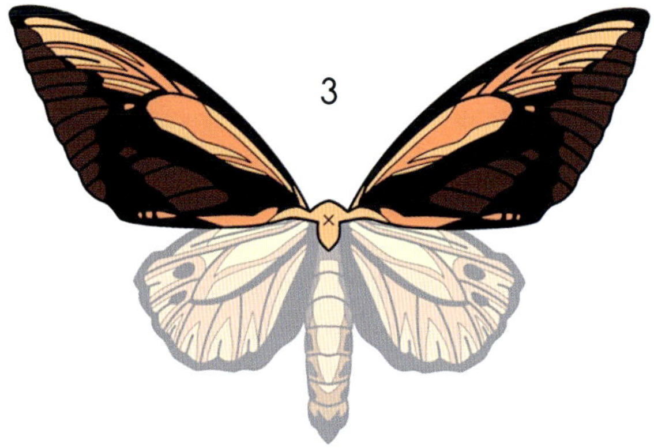

> **Note:** There are two variants of this project available in this book. This project is for the Male, which has the glistening golden wings this species is named for.

Remove the template for this project (page 149), and using the color guide on page 77, color in the template. (You can refer to the Papercraft Tips and Tricks on page 11 for suggestions on coloring.) Once you are finished coloring, carefully cut out the template pieces along their solid black outer borders. Now it's time to assemble!

We start with the **abdomen**. Like a real lepidopteran, this paper specimen of yours has nine segments in its abdomen. Stack them in ascending order: Begin by adding glue with a toothpick or small paintbrush to the *X* mark on piece **14** and set piece **13** on top, aligning the curved top edges as shown in image 1.

Apply glue to the *X* mark on piece **13** and set piece **12** on top. Continue this way until pieces **6** through **14** are all assembled. Set your completed abdomen aside to dry for 2 to 5 minutes. Next, mimic the curved fullness of a real butterfly's abdomen by pressing the abdomen over the barrel of one of your colored pencils with your thumb and finger, bending the edges down.

Now for the **wings**. Apply some glue to the *X* mark on piece **6**, and set piece **5**, the **hindwings**, on top, aligning as shown in image 2.

Apply glue to the *X* mark on piece **5**, and set piece **4**, the **forewings**, on top, aligning as shown in image 3.

4

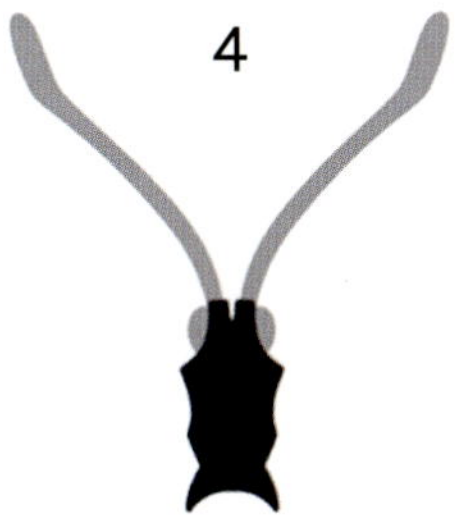

5

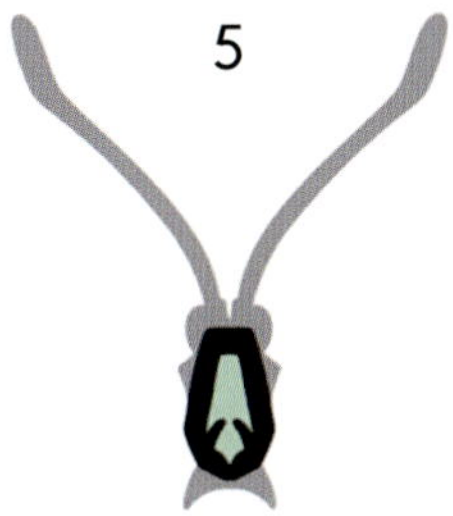

Let the wings and abdomen dry together for 2 to 5 minutes. Finally, let's assemble the **head**. Apply glue to the *X* mark on piece **3**, and set piece **2** on top, aligning as shown in image 4.

Apply glue to the *X* mark on piece **2**, and place piece **1** onto joined pieces **2** and **3** as shown in image 5.

6

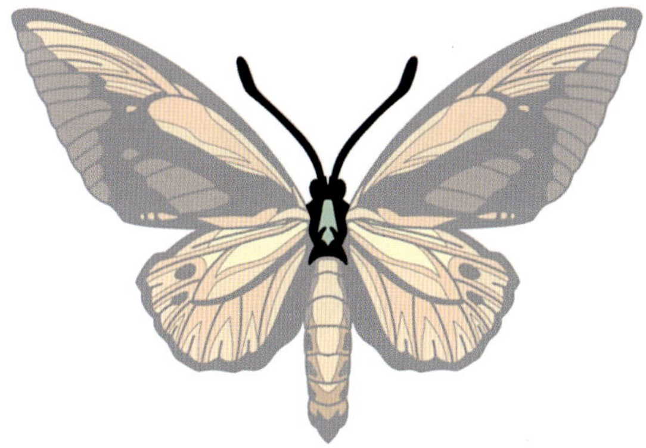

Set the completed head aside to dry for 2 to 5 minutes, then add glue to the *X* mark on piece **4**, and set the head on top, aligning as shown in image 6. You're done!

For a final touch of dimension to your paper specimen, gently bend the forewings up with your fingers, and the hindwings down. If you'd like suggestions on how to display your completed butterfly, check out Mounting and Displaying Your Papercraft Specimens (page 109).

WALLACE'S GOLDEN BIRDWING BUTTERFLY (FEMALE) COLOR GUIDE

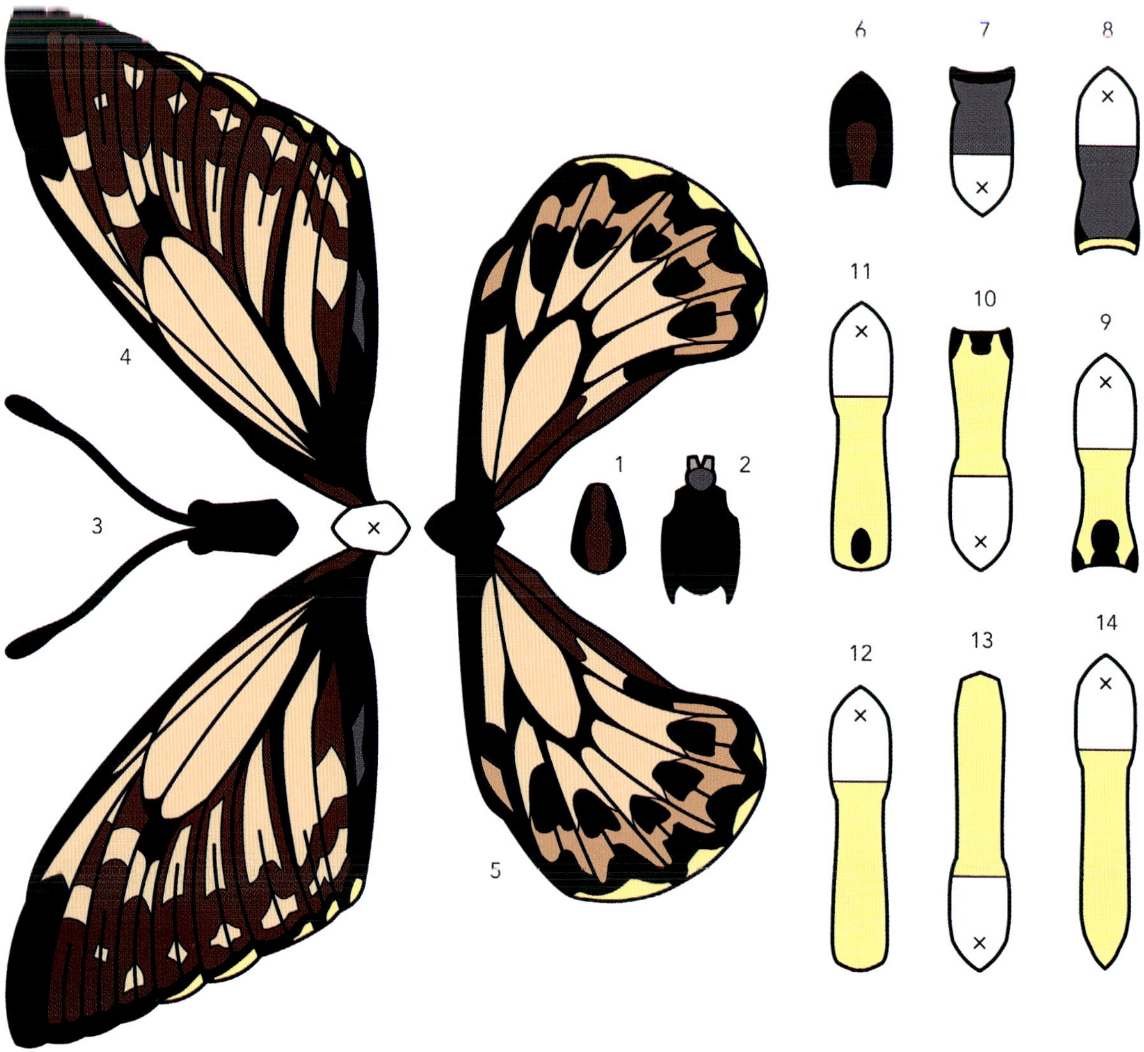

Colors Needed

- Black
- 90% warm gray
- 50% warm gray
- Dark umber
- Beige sienna
- Beige
- Canary yellow

WALLACE'S GOLDEN BIRDWING BUTTERFLY (FEMALE) ASSEMBLY

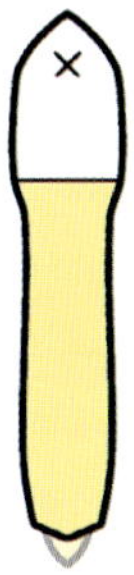

1

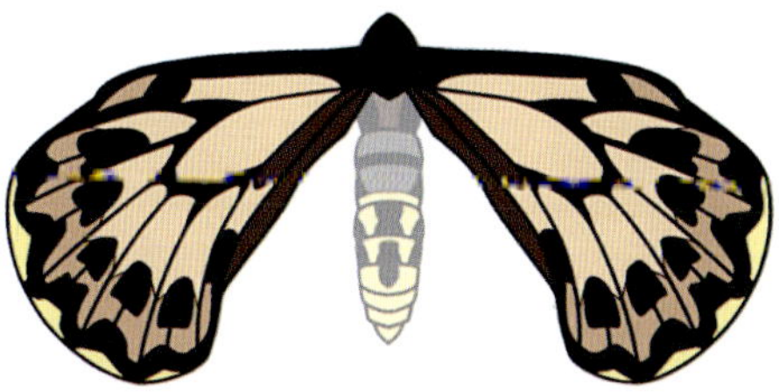

2

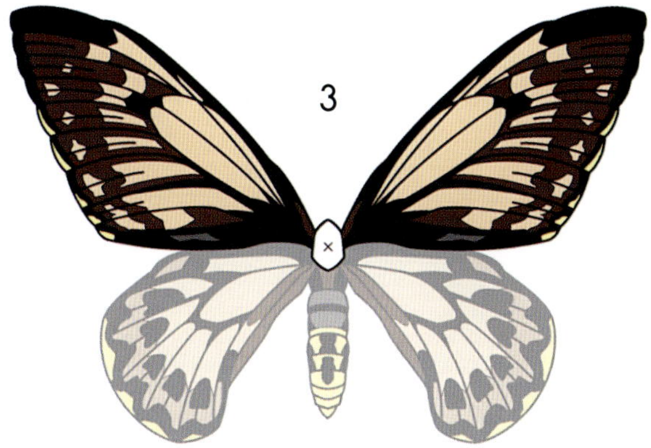

3

Note: There are two variants of this project available in this book. This project is for the Female, which is bigger than the Male and not as flashy.

Remove the template for this project (page 151 and 153), and using the color guide on the left, color in the template. (You can refer to the Papercraft Tips and Tricks on page 11 for suggestions on coloring.) Once you are finished coloring, carefully cut out the template pieces along their solid black outer borders. Now it's time to assemble!

We start with the **abdomen**. Like a real lepidopteran, this paper specimen of yours has nine segments in its abdomen. Stack them in ascending order: Begin by adding glue with a toothpick or small paintbrush to the *X* mark on piece **14** and set piece **13** on top, aligning the curved top edges as shown in image 1.

Apply glue to the *X* mark on piece **13** and set piece **12** on top. Continue this way until pieces **6** through **14** are all assembled. Set your completed abdomen aside to dry for 2 to 5 minutes. Next, mimic the curved fullness of a real butterfly's abdomen by pressing the abdomen over the barrel of one of your colored pencils with your thumb and finger, bending the edges down.

Now for the **wings**. Apply some glue to the *X* mark on piece **6**, and set piece **5**, the **hindwings**, on top, aligning as shown in image 2.

Apply glue to the *X* mark on piece **5**, and set piece **4**, the **forewings**, on top, aligning as shown in image 3.

WALLACE'S GOLDEN BIRDWING BUTTERFLY (FEMALE) ASSEMBLY CONTINUED

4

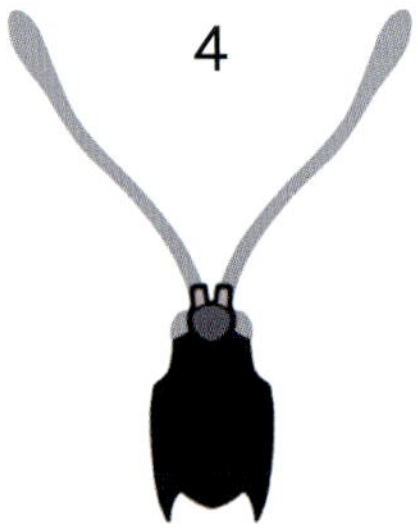

5

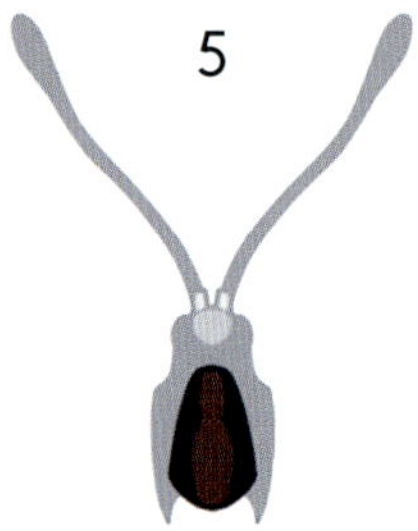

6

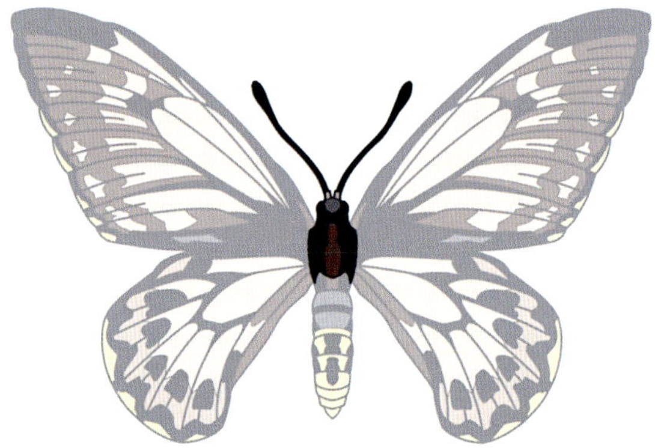

Let the wings and abdomen dry together for 2 to 5 minutes. Finally, let's assemble the **head**. Apply glue to the *X* mark on piece **3**, and set piece **2** on top, aligning as shown in image 4.

Apply glue to the *X* mark on piece **2**, and place piece **1** onto joined pieces **2** and **3** as shown in image 5.

Set the completed head aside to dry for 2 to 5 minutes, then add glue to the *X* mark on piece **4**, and set the head on top, aligning as shown in image 6. You're done!

For a final touch of dimension to your paper specimen, gently bend the forewings up with your fingers, and the hindwings down. If you'd like suggestions on how to display your completed butterfly, check out Mounting and Displaying Your Papercraft Specimens (page 109).

NATTERER'S LONGWING BUTTERFLY

Scientific name: ***Heliconius nattereri***

Habitat: ***Lowland forests of Indonesia***

Real-life size: ***Wingspan between 2¾ to 4" (70 to 100 cm)***

Conservation status: ***Rare; Threatened (International Union for Conservation of Nature)***

Templates: ***Pages 155 and 157***

Uniquely among butterflies, species that belong to the *Heliconius* group—such as the Natterer's longwing butterfly—eat pollen as well as sip on nectar. This additional food source is higher in protein and amino acids, helping the Natterer's longwing bulk up for an unusually long lifetime (for a butterfly) that is filled with strategic interactions with the host plant that they likely co-evolved with: native Indonesian passion flowers.

Like all *Heliconius* butterflies, Natterer's longwing butterflies will eat a large portion of their host plant, but the passion flowers have tried their best to stop this by developing defenses. They grow a variety of leaf shapes to keep the females from identifying them as a host plant and produce fake "egg" nodules on their leaves to convince the females there's no room for more eggs to be laid. But the females learned to take their time inspecting plants to find the correct one, poking at decoy eggs to identify them, and laying eggs that hatch into larvae so hairy, the spikes don't affect them. So as a final defense, the passion flowers recruited allies: ants. While some butterflies and ants have symbiotic relationships, that's not the case here. The passion flower plants secrete a sugary liquid from various points in their stems and leaves, attracting ants that defend this food source from anything that moves too close—including baby caterpillars. These recruited ants work well in protecting the passion flower plant, leaving the female with only one last resort in the battle for the next generation: laying her eggs at the very edge of the plants and hoping her resulting young are strong enough to survive.

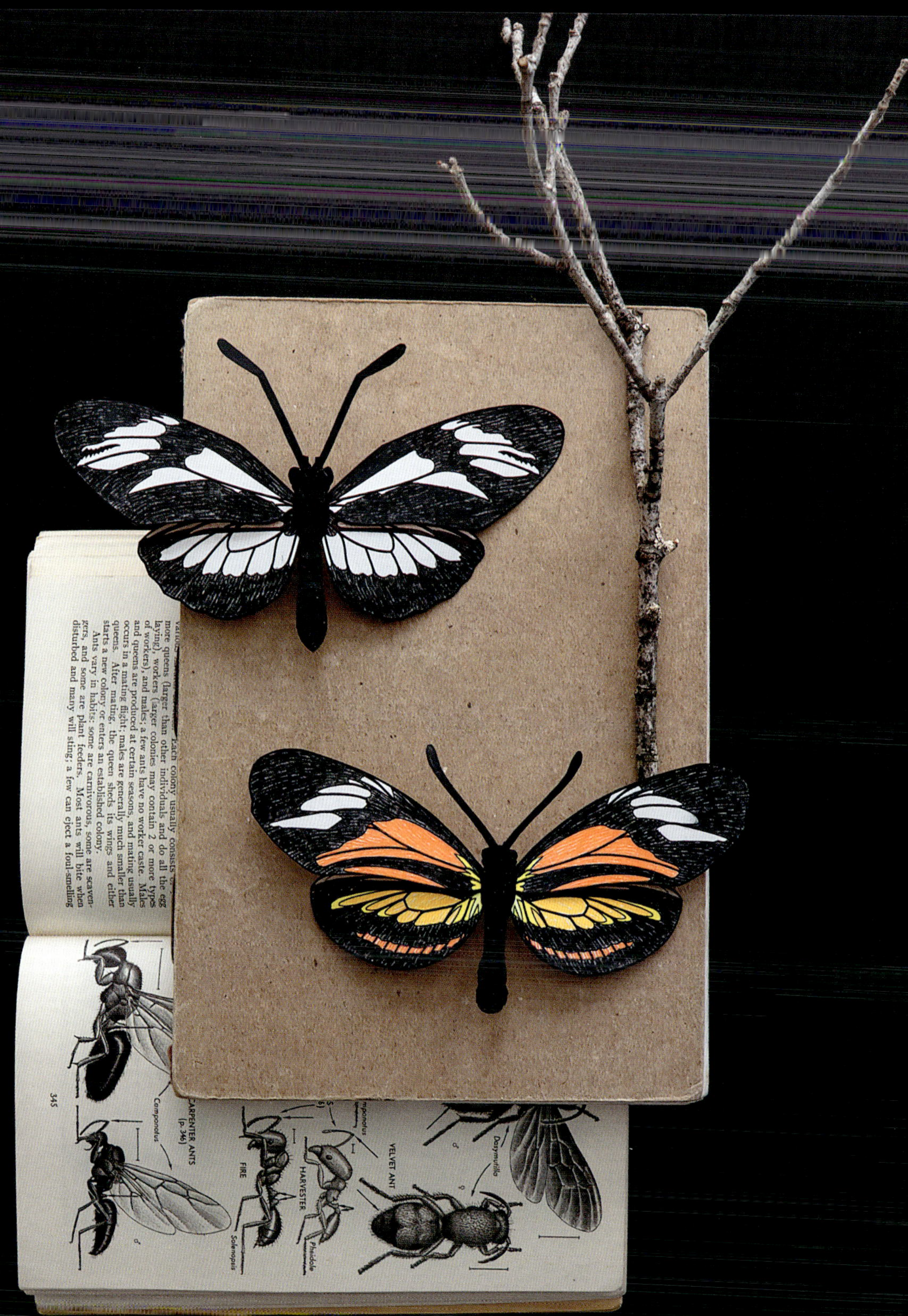

CARPENTER ANTS (p. 346)
Camponotus
FIRE
Solenopsis
HARVESTER
Pheidole
VELVET ANT
Dasymutilla

NATTERER'S LONGWING BUTTERFLY (MALE) COLOR GUIDE

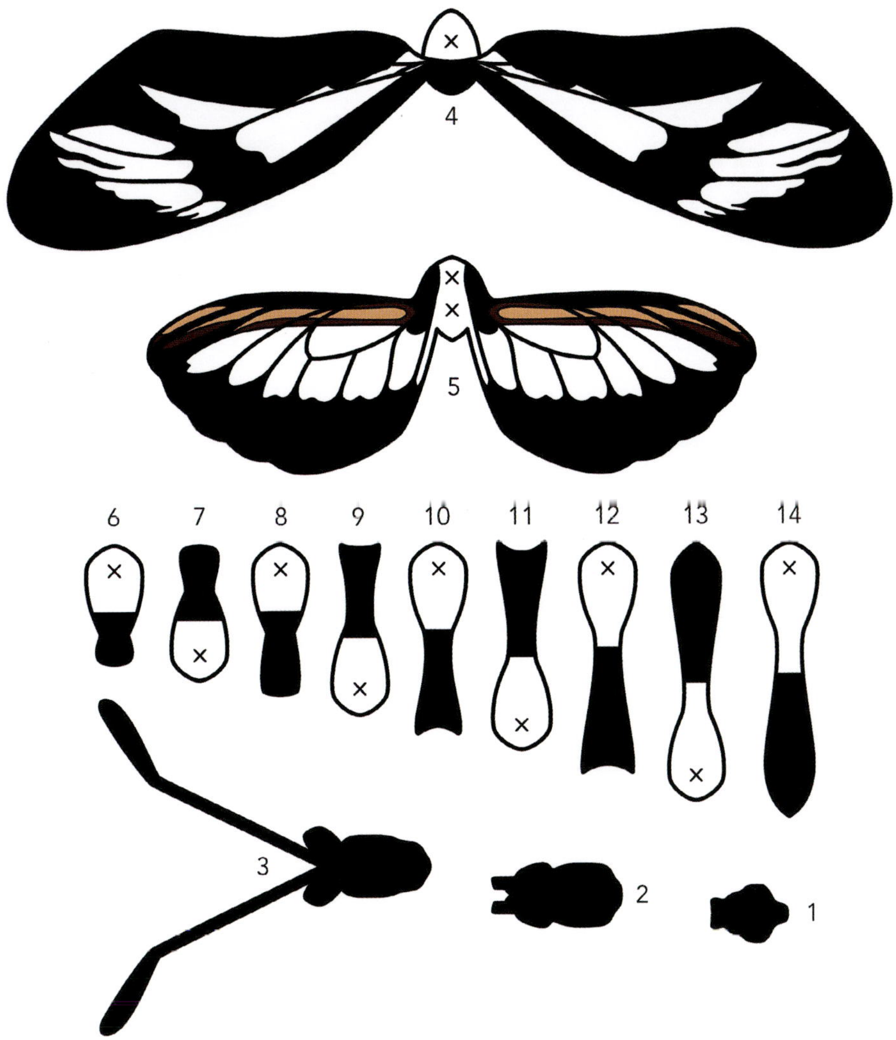

Colors Needed

- Black
- Dark umber
- Beige sienna

NATTERER'S LONGWING BUTTERFLY (MALE) ASSEMBLY

1

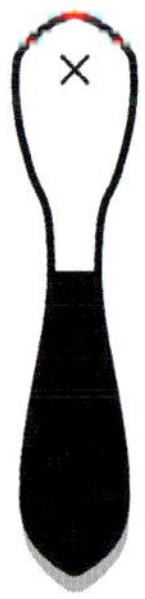

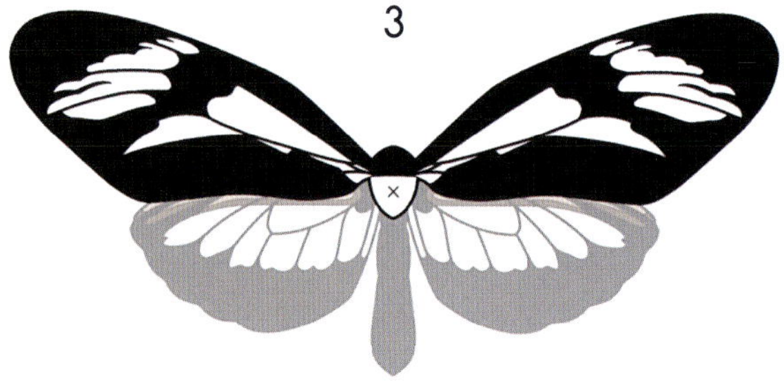

3

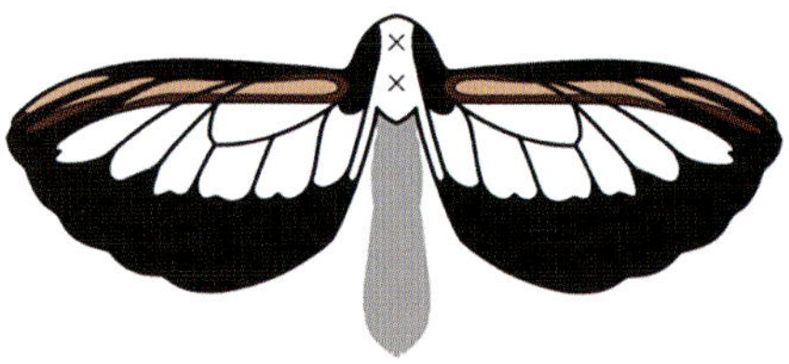

2

Note: There are two variants of this project available in this book. This project is for the Male, smaller than the female but stunning with his stark black-and-white markings.

Remove the template for this project (page 155), and using the color guide on page 85, color in the template. (You can refer to the Papercraft Tips and Tricks on page 11 for suggestions on coloring.) Once you are finished coloring, carefully cut out the template pieces along their solid black outer borders. Now it's time to assemble!

We start with the **abdomen**. Like a real lepidopteran, this paper specimen of yours has nine segments in its abdomen. Stack them in ascending order: Begin by adding glue with a toothpick or small paintbrush to the *X* mark on piece **14** and set piece **13** on top, aligning the curved top edges as shown in image 1.

Apply glue to the *X* mark on piece **13** and set piece **12** on top. Continue this way until pieces **6** through **14** are all assembled. Set your completed abdomen aside to dry for 2 to 5 minutes.

Now for the **wings**. Apply some glue to the *X* mark on piece **6**, and set piece **5**, the **hindwings**, on top, aligning as shown in image 2.

Apply glue to the *X* marks on piece **5**, and set piece **4**, the **forewings**, on top, aligning as shown in image 3.

4

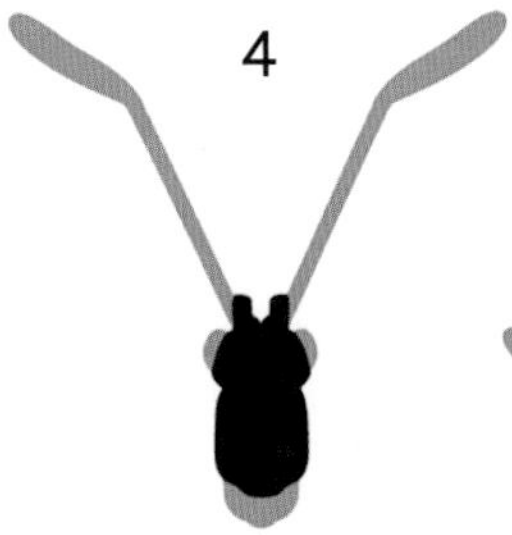

5

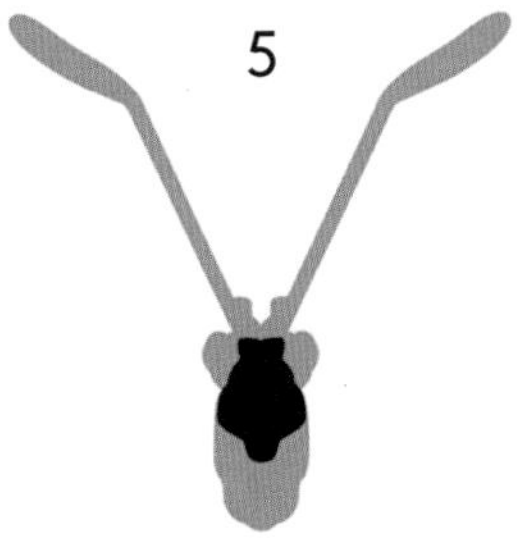

6

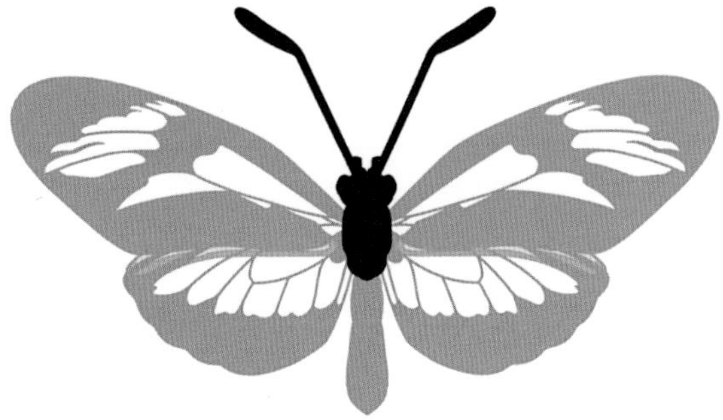

Let the wings and abdomen dry together for 2 to 5 minutes. Finally, let's assemble the **head**. Apply glue to the *X* mark on piece **3**, and set piece **2** on top, aligning as shown in image 4.

Apply glue to the *X* mark on piece **2**, and place piece **1** onto joined pieces **2** and **3** as shown in image 5.

Set the completed head aside to dry for 2 to 5 minutes, then add glue to the *X* marks on piece **4**, and set the head on top, aligning as shown in image 6. You're done!

For a final touch of dimension to your paper specimen, gently bend the forewings up with your fingers, and the hindwings down. If you'd like suggestions on how to display your completed butterfly, check out Mounting and Displaying Your Papercraft Specimens (page 109).

NATTERER'S LONGWING BUTTERFLY (FEMALE) COLOR GUIDE

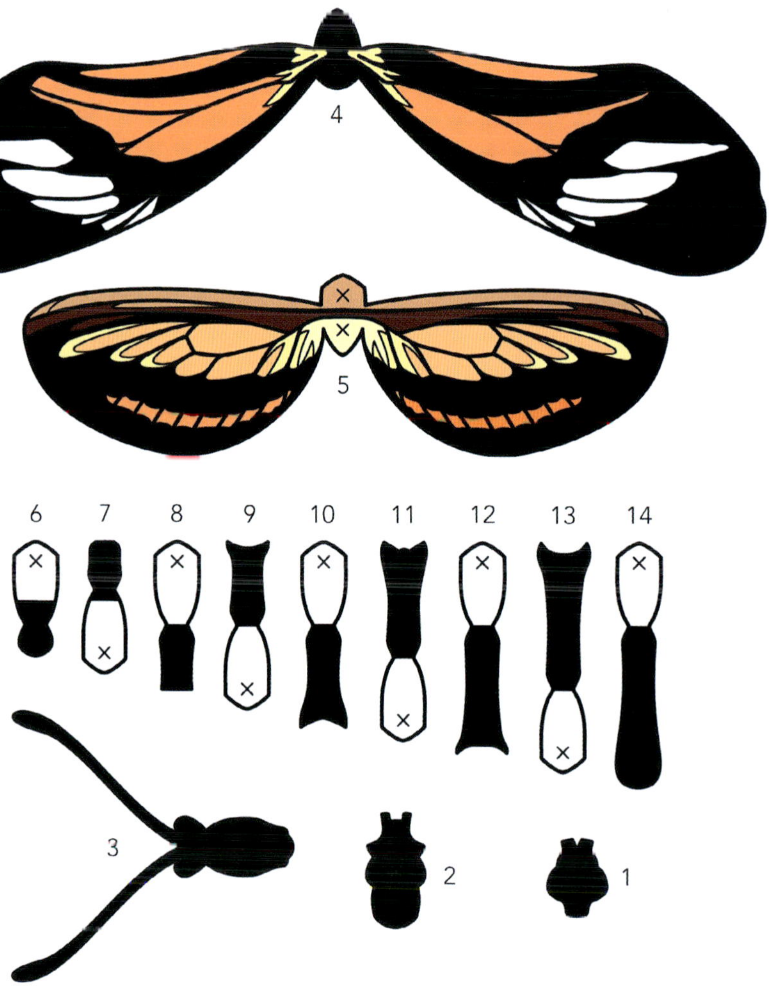

Colors Needed

- Black
- Dark umber
- Beige sienna
- Spanish orange
- Orange
- Lemon yellow
- Canary yellow

NATTERER'S LONGWING BUTTERFLY (FEMALE) ASSEMBLY

1

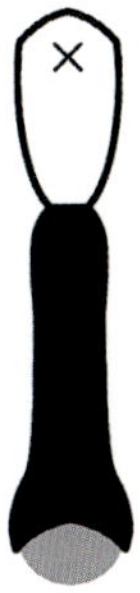

3

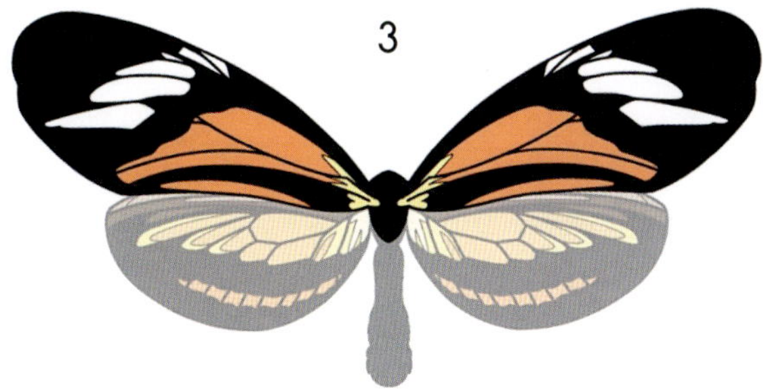

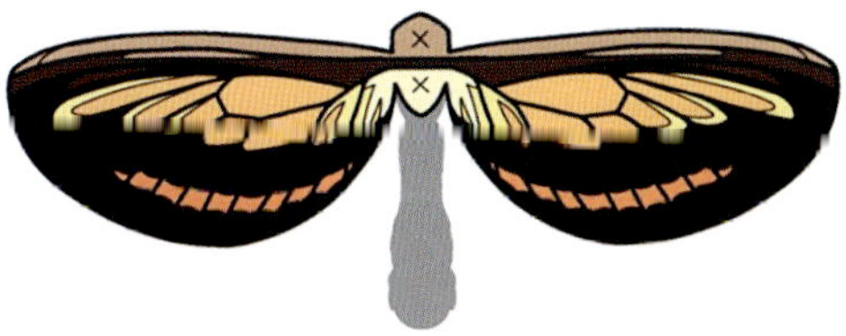

2

> **Note:** There are two variants of this project available in this book. This project is for the Female, distinguished by her smaller antennae and orange-marked wings.

Remove the template for this project (page 157), and using the color guide on the left, color in the template. (You can refer to the Papercraft Tips and Tricks on page 11 for suggestions on coloring.) Once you are finished coloring, carefully cut out the template pieces along their solid black outer borders. Now it's time to assemble!

We start with the **abdomen**. Like a real lepidopteran, this paper specimen of yours has nine segments in its abdomen. Stack them in ascending order: Begin by adding glue with a toothpick or small paintbrush to the *X* mark on piece **14** and set piece **13** on top, aligning the curved top edges as shown in image 1.

Apply glue to the *X* mark on piece **13** and set piece **12** on top. Continue this way until pieces **6** through **14** are all assembled. Set your completed abdomen aside to dry for 2 to 5 minutes.

Now for the **wings**. Apply some glue to the *X* mark on piece **6**, and set piece **5**, the **hindwings**, on top, aligning as shown in image 2.

Apply glue to the *X* marks on piece **5**, and set piece **4**, the **forewings**, on top, aligning as shown in image 3.

NATTERER'S LONGWING BUTTERFLY (FEMALE) ASSEMBLY CONTINUED

4

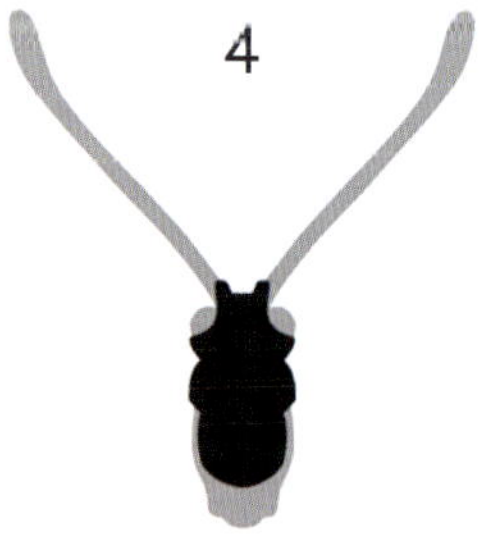

5

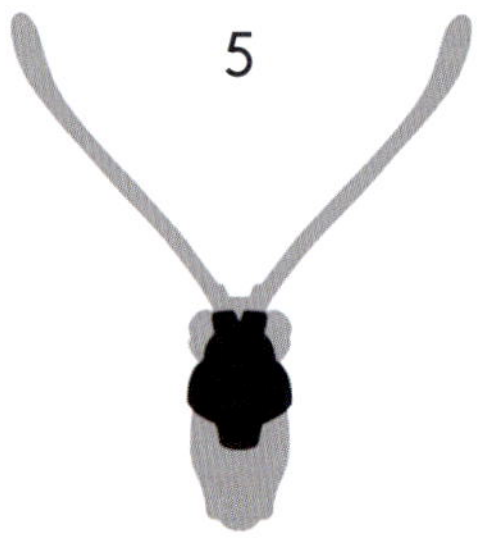

6

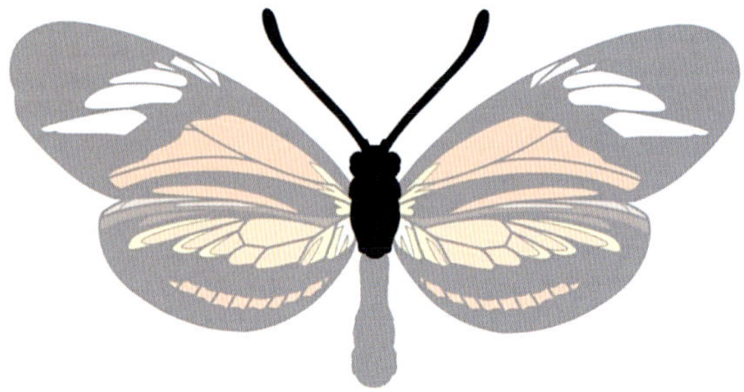

Let the wings and abdomen dry together for 2 to 5 minutes. Finally, let's assemble the **head**. Apply glue to the *X* mark on piece **3**, and set piece **2** on top, aligning as shown in image 4.

Apply glue to the *X* mark on piece **2**, and place piece **1** onto joined pieces **2** and **3** as shown in image 5.

Set the completed head aside to dry for 2 to 5 minutes, then add glue to the *X* marks on piece **4**, and set the head on top, aligning as shown in image 6. You're done!

For a final touch of dimension to your paper specimen, gently bend the forewings up with your fingers, and the hindwings down. If you'd like suggestions on how to display your completed butterfly, check out Mounting and Displaying Your Papercraft Specimens (page 109).

PUERTO RICAN HARLEQUIN BUTTERFLY

Habitat: **Subtropical Forest of Puerto Rico**

Real-life size: **Wingspan of 2½" (64 mm)**

Conservation status: **Rare; Threatened (US Endangered Species Act)**

Template: **Page 159**

Known locally as *Quebradillana* after a Northwestern area of the island it is found in, the Puerto Rican harlequin butterfly is, like many endangered and threatened species, not well known outside of its native habitat. Currently, only about 70 individual adults exist in the forests of Puerto Rico at any given time, and multiple factors of their anatomy and life-cycle contribute to their dwindling numbers.

Belonging to the Nymphalidae family of butterflies (the most numerous of any butterfly family), the Puerto Rican harlequin is what's called a brush-footed butterfly. This name comes from this family's trait of using their two foremost legs more as sensory appendages for sensing their surroundings and signaling to other butterflies. Because of this, they often hold their wings flat when perched to help with balance, revealing their bright wing patterning. This makes them easy to spot. That coupled with their slow flight makes them an easy catch for butterfly collectors. Between this, and their careful laying of only one egg on each host plant (the pricklybush, or *Oplonia spinosa*) in a country fast losing its wild forests, this species may not have long left on this earth.

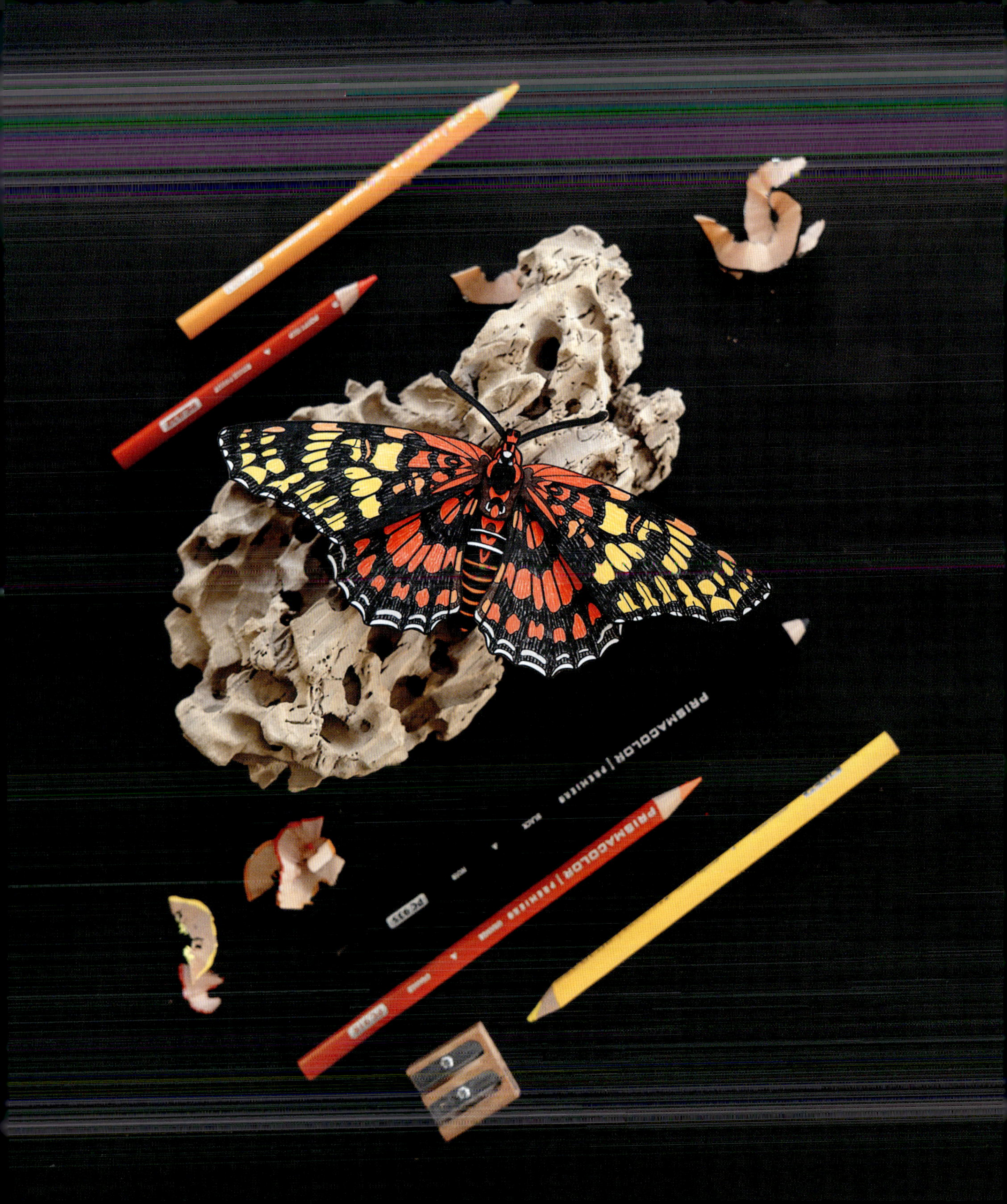
PRISMACOLOR | PREMIER
BLACK
NOIR
PC 935
PRISMACOLOR | PREMIER

PUERTO RICAN HARLEQUIN BUTTERFLY COLOR GUIDE

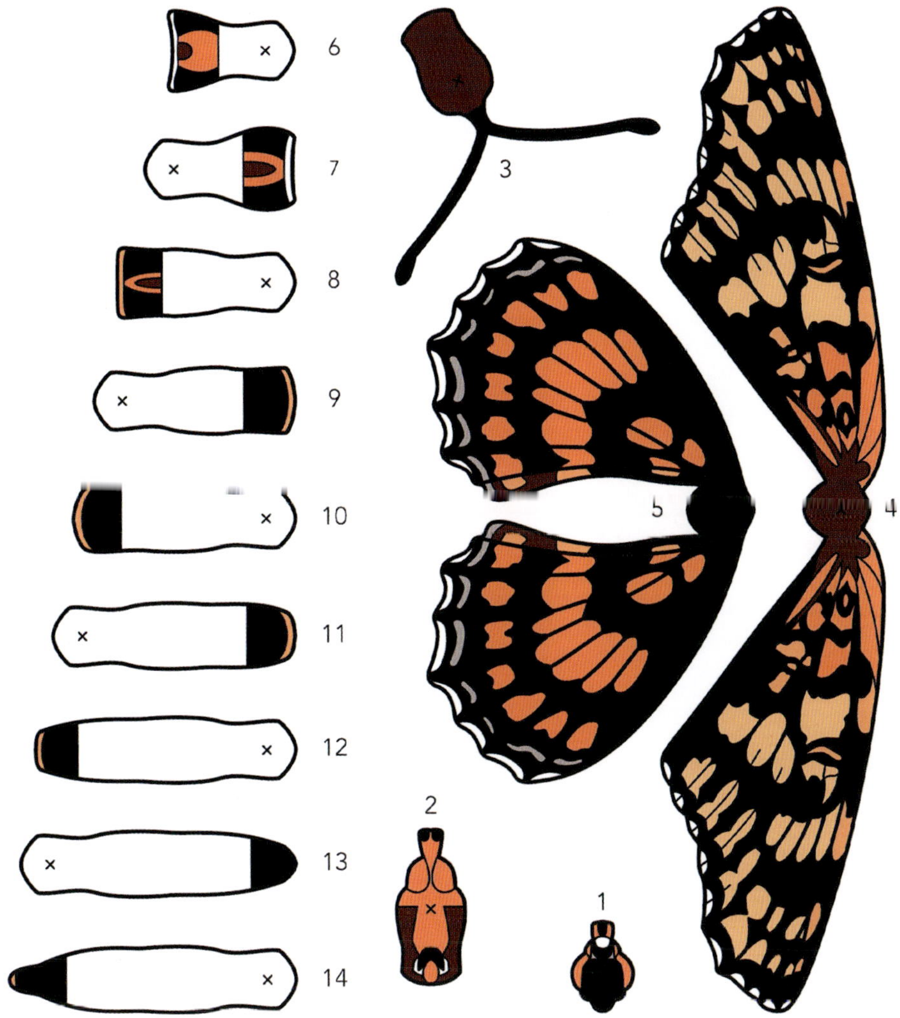

Colors Needed

- Black
- Dark umber
- Orange
- 10% warm gray
- Spanish orange
- Poppy red

PUERTO RICAN HARLEQUIN BUTTERFLY ASSEMBLY

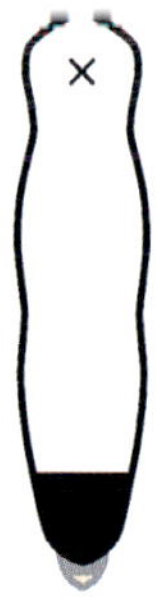

1

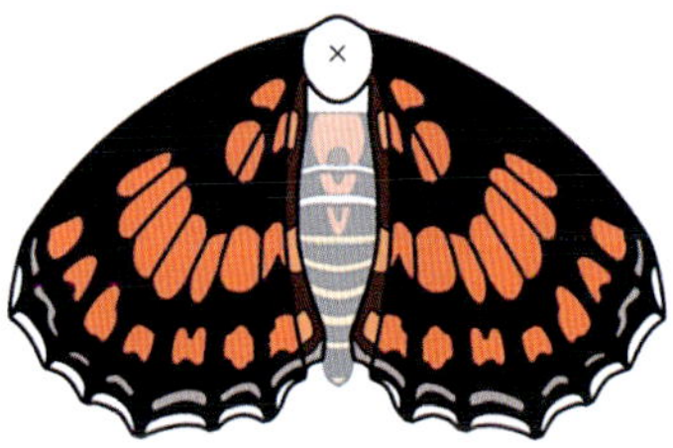

2

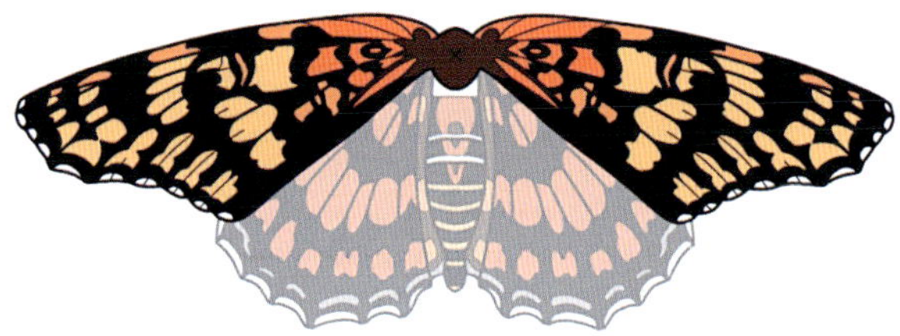

3

Remove the template for this project (page 159), and using the color guide on page 93, color in the template. (You can refer to the Papercraft Tips and Tricks on page 11 for suggestions on coloring.) Once you are finished coloring, carefully cut out the template pieces along their solid black outer borders. Now it's time to assemble!

We start with the **abdomen**. Like a real lepidopteran, this paper specimen of yours has nine segments in its abdomen. Stack them in ascending order: Begin by adding glue with a toothpick or small paintbrush to the *X* mark on piece **14** and set piece **13** on top, aligning the curved top edges as shown in image 1.

Apply glue to the *X* mark on piece **13** and set piece **12** on top. Continue this way until pieces **6** through **14** are all assembled. Set your completed abdomen aside to dry for 2 to 5 minutes. Next, mimic the curved fullness of a real butterfly's abdomen by pressing the abdomen over the barrel of one of your colored pencils with your thumb and finger, bending the edges down.

Now for the **wings**. Apply some glue to the *X* mark on piece **6**, and set piece **5**, the **hindwings**, on top, aligning as shown in image 2.

Apply glue to the *X* mark on piece **5**, and set piece **4**, the **forewings**, on top, aligning as shown in image 3.

4

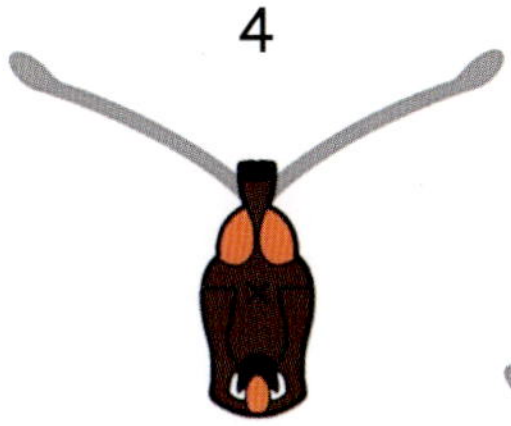

5

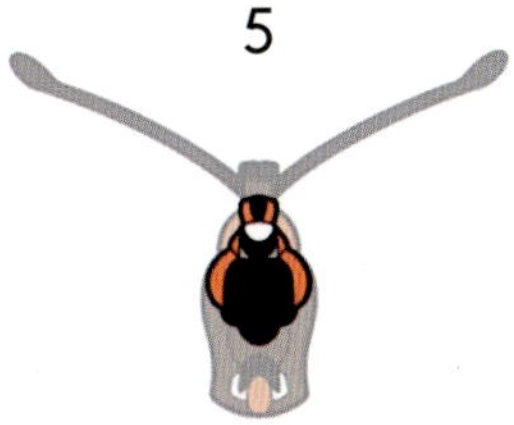

6

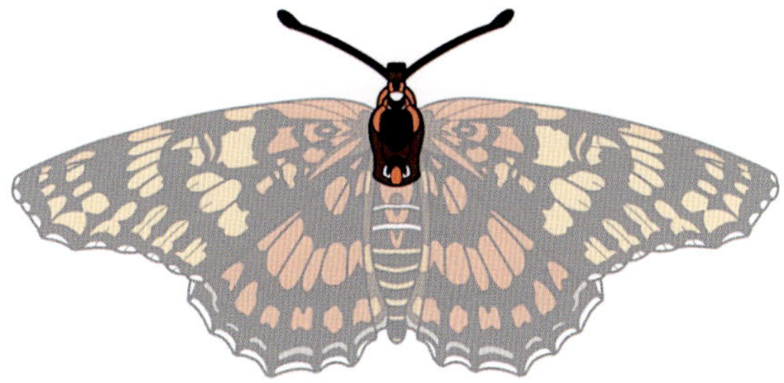

Let the wings and abdomen dry together for 2 to 5 minutes. Finally, let's assemble the **head**. Apply glue to the *X* mark on piece **3**, and set piece **2** on top, aligning as shown in image 4.

Apply glue to the *X* mark on piece **2**, and place piece **1** onto joined pieces **2** and **3** as shown in image 5.

Set the completed head aside to dry for 2 to 5 minutes, then add glue to the *X* mark on piece **4**, and set the head on top, aligning as shown in image 6. You're done!

For a final touch of dimension to your paper specimen, gently bend the forewings up with your fingers, and the hindwings down. If you'd like suggestions on how to display your completed butterfly, check out Mounting and Displaying Your Papercraft Specimens (page 109).

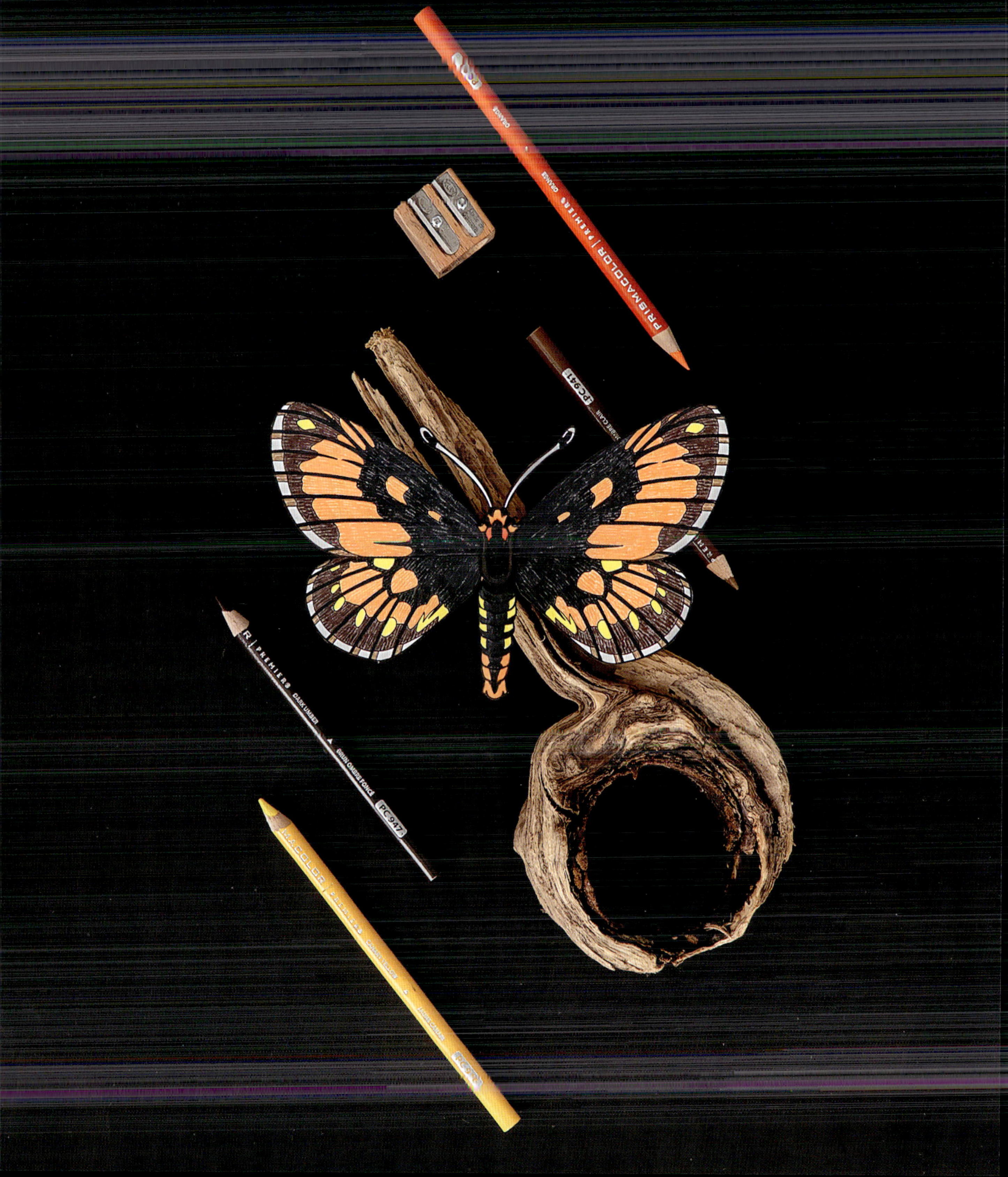
PRISMACOLOR | PREMIERS
PC941
R | PREMIERS
DARK UMBER
BRUN OMBRE FONCÉ
PC947

WOLKBERG ZULU BUTTERFLY

Scientific name: ***Alaena margaritacea***

Habitat: ***Wolkberg Mountains of South Africa***

Real-life size: ***Wingspan of 1¼" (30 mm)***

Conservation status: ***Rare; Critically Endangered (International Union for Conservation of Nature)***

Template: ***Page 161***

Included in a family of butterflies called *gossamers* for their aethereal, delicate nature, the Wolkberg Zulu is brightly patterned for a species that has a tenuous hold on its existence here on earth and a highly specific, nearly microscopic food source. Like some several hundred other species of butterflies, the Wolkberg Zulu's caterpillars eat lichen. Unlike the others, however, Wolkberg Zulu caterpillars eat only the *cyanobacteria* (blue-green algae) of lichen, a photosynthetic bacteria. But why? The only reason biologists have been able to theorize so far is that it is how they gain the toxins that will protect the caterpillars, and later on, the *imagos* (adult butterflies). But with only two colonies of the Wolkberg Zulu known to still exist in the province of Limpopo, learning more in time to save this strange, bright species will be difficult.

WOLKBERG ZULU BUTTERFLY COLOR GUIDE

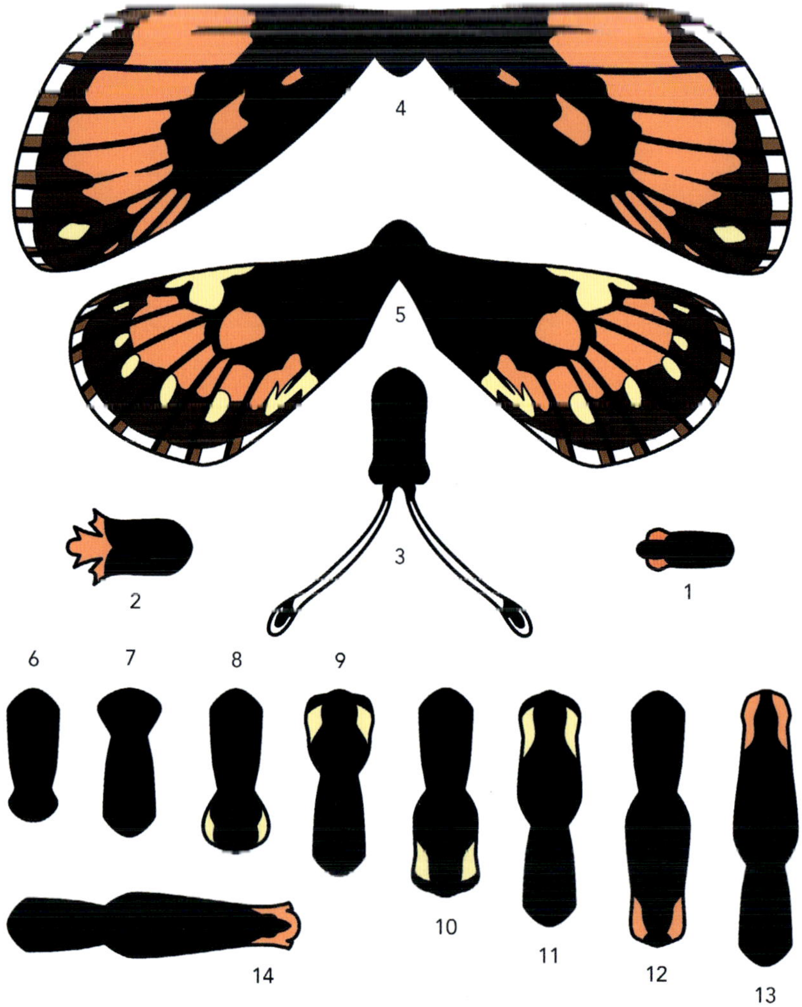

Colors Needed

- Black
- Dark umber
- Light umber
- Orange
- Canary yellow
- Poppy red

WOLKBERG ZULU BUTTERFLY ASSEMBLY

1

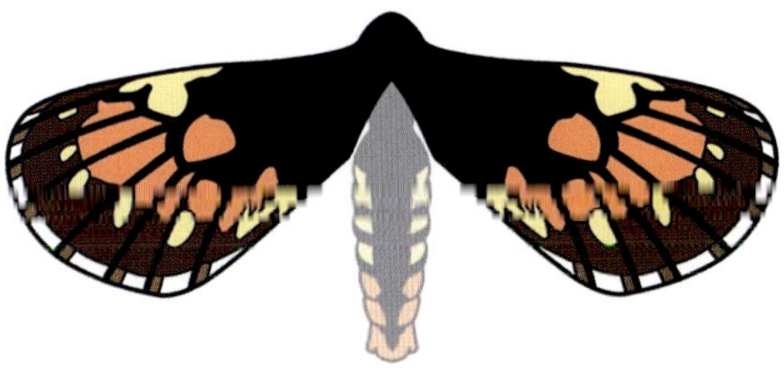

2

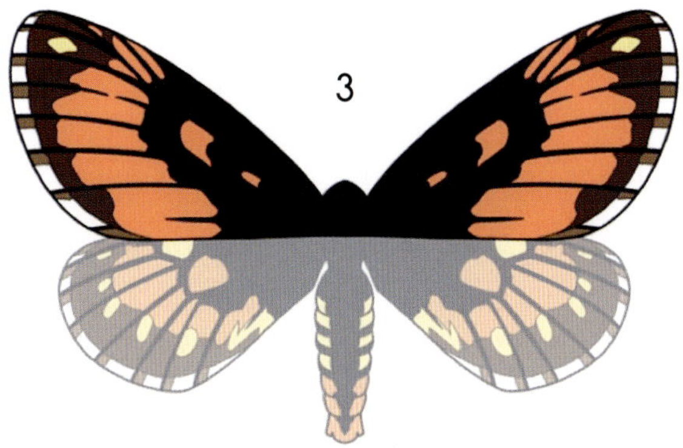

3

Remove the template for this project (page 161), and using the color guide on the left, color in the template. (You can refer to the Papercraft Tips and Tricks on page 11 for suggestions on coloring.) Once you are finished coloring, carefully cut out the template pieces along their solid black outer borders. Now it's time to assemble!

We start with the **abdomen**. Like a real lepidopteran, this paper specimen of yours has nine segments in its abdomen. Stack them in ascending order: Begin by adding glue with a toothpick or small paintbrush to the *X* mark on piece **14** and set piece **13** on top, aligning the curved top edges as shown in image 1.

Apply glue to the *X* mark on piece **13** and set piece **12** on top. Continue this way until pieces **6** through **14** are all assembled. Set your completed abdomen aside to dry for 2 to 5 minutes. Next, mimic the curved fullness of a real butterfly's abdomen by pressing the abdomen over the barrel of one of your colored pencils with your thumb and finger, bending the edges down.

Now for the **wings**. Apply some glue to the *X* mark on piece **6**, and set piece **5**, the **hindwings**, on top, aligning as shown in image 2.

Apply glue to the *X* mark on piece **5**, and set piece **4**, the **forewings**, on top, aligning as shown in image 3.

4

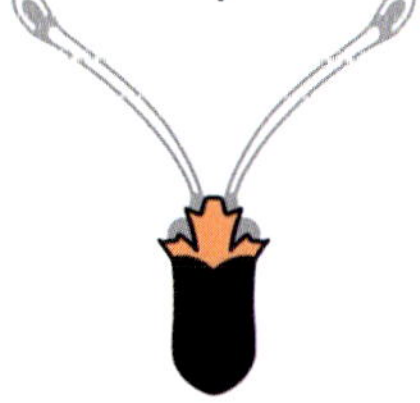

5

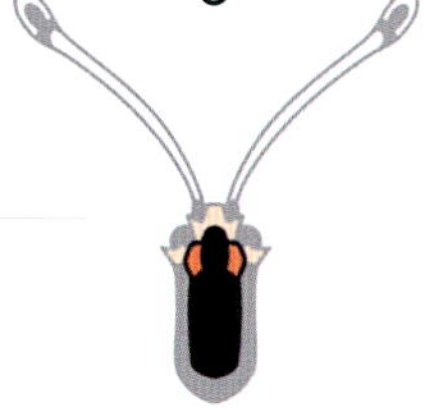

6

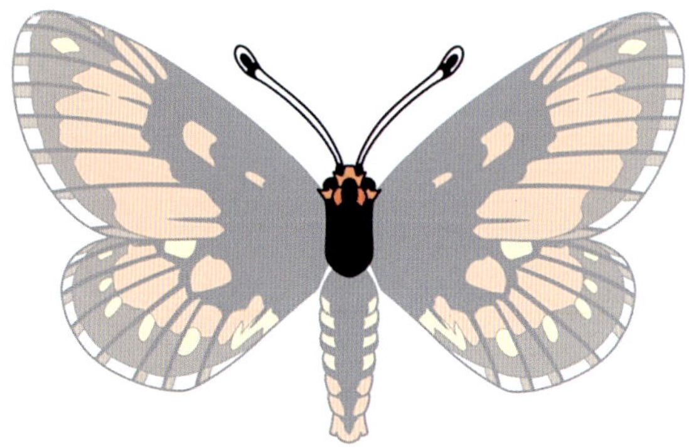

Let the wings and abdomen dry together for 2 to 5 minutes. Finally, let's assemble the **head**. Apply glue to the *X* mark on piece **3**, and set piece **2** on top, aligning as shown in image 4.

Apply glue to the *X* mark on piece **2**, and place piece **1** onto joined pieces **2** and **3** as shown in image 5.

Set the completed head aside to dry for 2 to 5 minutes, then add glue to the *X* mark on piece **4**, and set the head on top, aligning as shown in image 6. You're done!

For a final touch of dimension to your paper specimen, gently bend the forewings up with your fingers, and the hindwings down. If you'd like suggestions on how to display your completed butterfly, check out Mounting and Displaying Your Papercraft Specimens (page 109).

BATHURST COPPER BUTTERFLY

Scientific name: **Paralucia spinifera**

Habitat: **Woodlands in Southern Australia**

Real-life size: **Wingspan of 1¼" (31 mm)**

Conservation status: **Endangered (Australian Environment Protection and Biodiversity Conservation Act of 1999)**

Templates: **Pages 163 and 165**

Unlike other butterflies included in this book, the Bathurst copper has found a friend in ants, not foes. Bathurst copper caterpillars have formed a mutualistic relationship, scientifically known as *myrmecophily*, with the ant species *Anonychomyrma itinerans*. Here's how it works.

After mating, a female Bathurst copper butterfly locates a sweet bursaria plant (a flowering blackthorn shrub that is the only plant Bathurst copper caterpillars will eat) and lays her eggs on or near them. She doesn't have to be too specific because the ants are on patrol, leaving their nests among the roots of the sweet bursaria to find the baby Bathurst copper larvae as soon as they hatch. Once they do, they immediately carry the larvae back to their nest, where they keep them safe during the day, and carry them up into the sweet bursaria to feed at night. They do this until the grown caterpillar is ready to *pupate* (create a *chrysalis* and undergo *metamorphosis* into its adult form). Why? Because the whole time it's growing, the Bathurst copper caterpillar produces a sweet secretion called *honeydew* from a special gland on its back, feeding the ants in return for their protection and transportation. Once the Bathurst copper's chrysalis is complete, the ants carry it underground one last time, guarding it there until the adult butterfly emerges, and the cycle begins all over again.

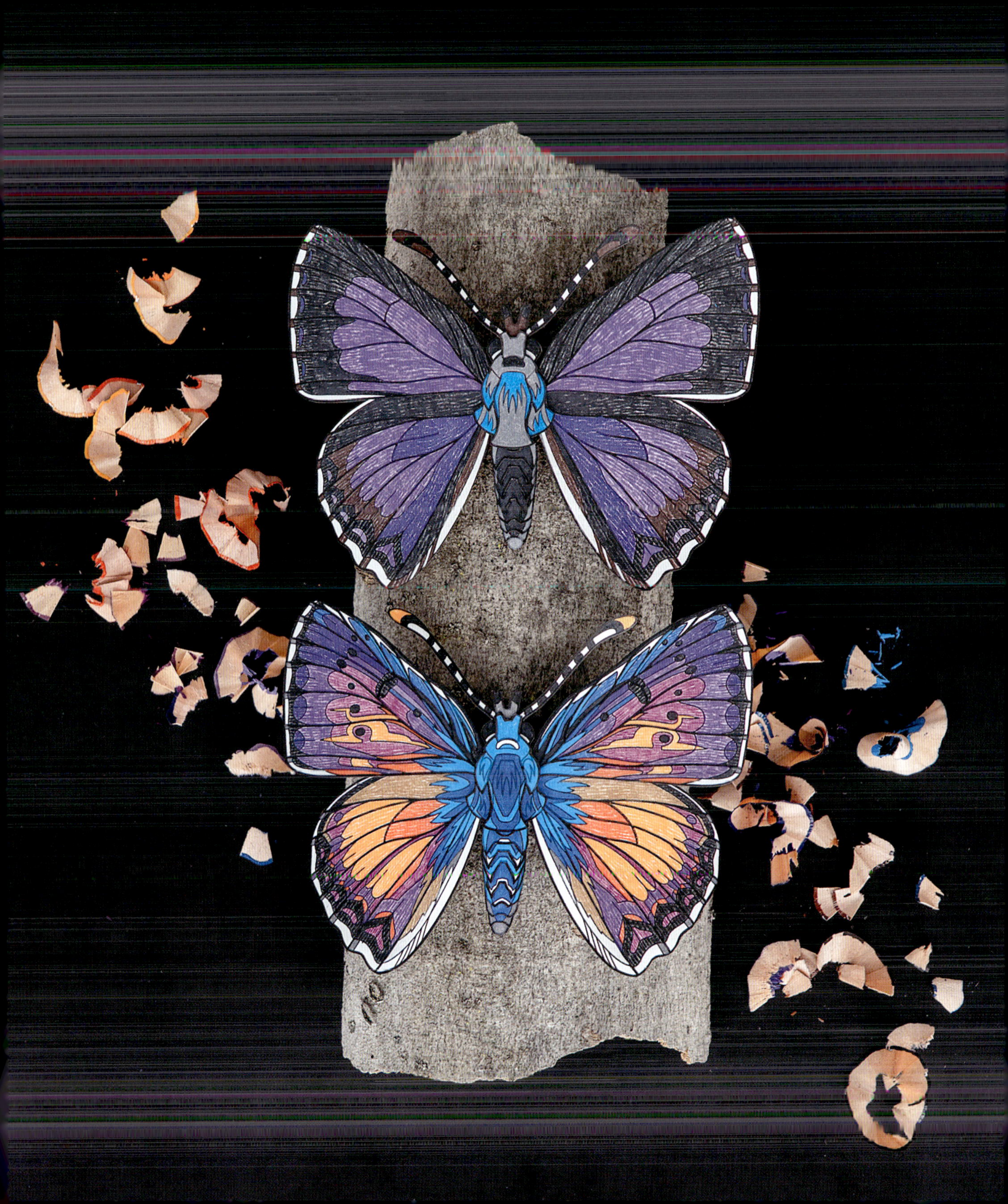

BATHURST COPPER BUTTERFLY (PURPLE VARIANT) COLOR GUIDE

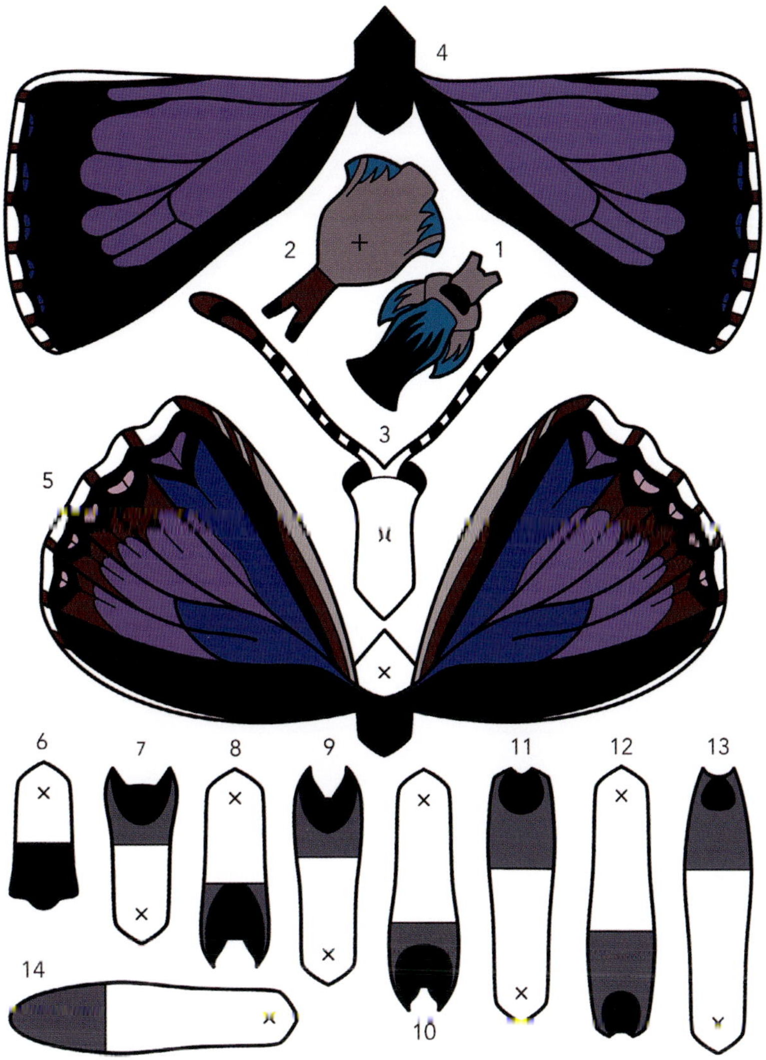

Colors Needed

- Black
- 90% warm gray
- 50% warm gray
- 10% warm gray
- Dark umber
- Peacock blue
- Parma violet
- Violet
- Dioxazine purple hue

BATHURST COPPER BUTTERFLY (IRIDESCENT VARIANT) COLOR GUIDE

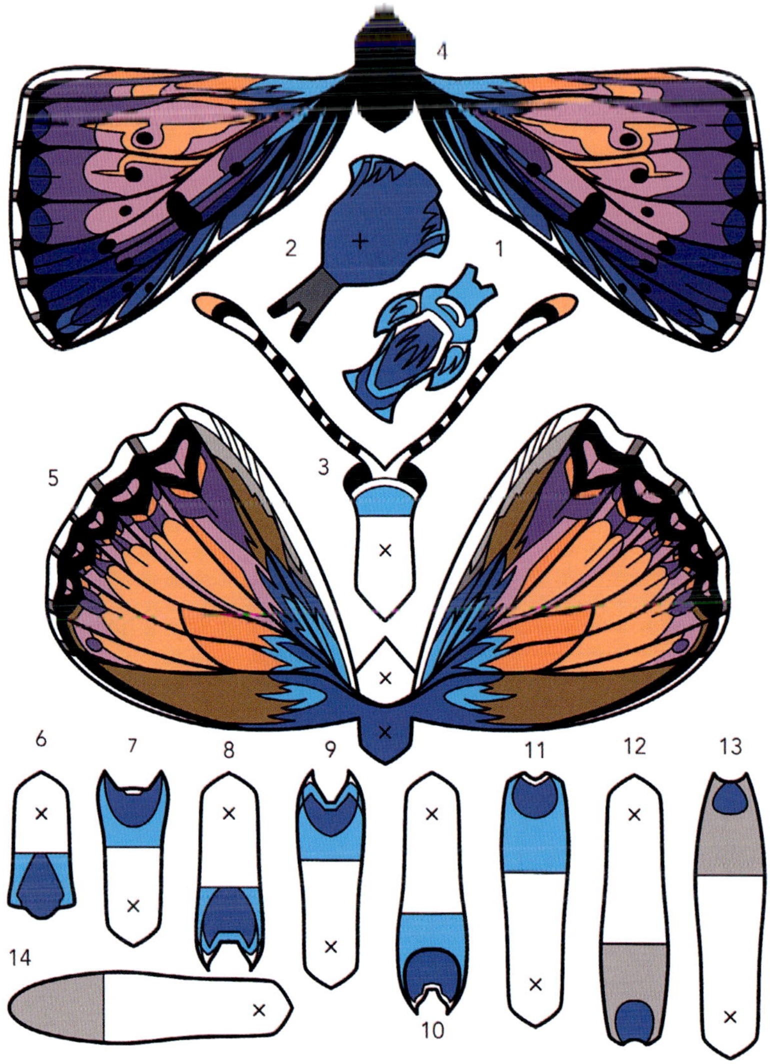

Colors Needed

- Black
- 50% warm gray
- 10% warm gray
- Light umber
- Orange
- Poppy red
- True blue
- Denim blue
- Parma violet
- Dahlia purple
- Violet
- Dioxazine purple hue

BATHURST COPPER BUTTERFLY ASSEMBLY

1

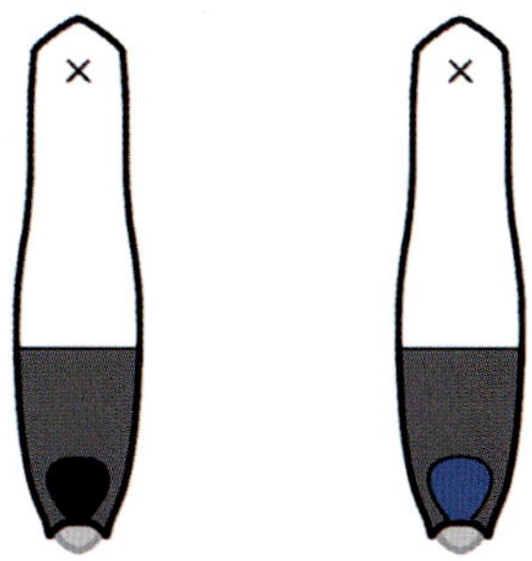

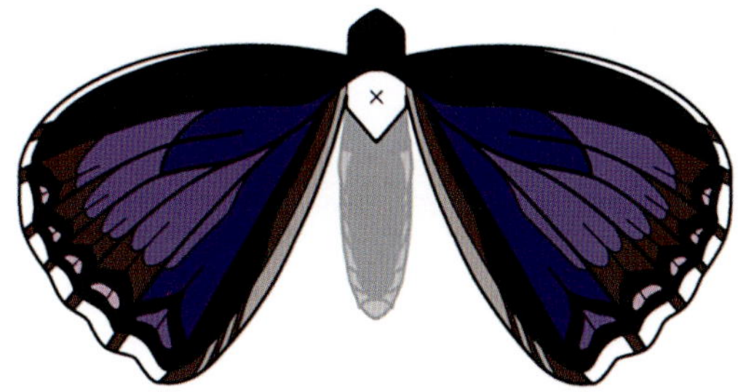

2

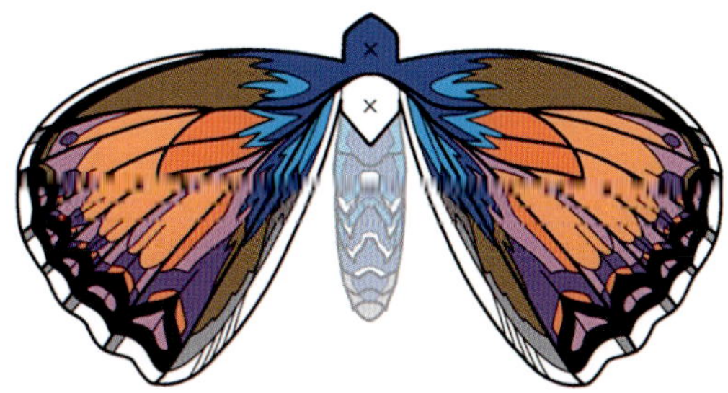

Note: There are two variants of this project available in this book: one purple and one iridescent. I included them both to showcase the color variety of the Male Bathurst copper butterfly depending on lighting and the angle you look at it from. Though each has its own template and corresponding coloring guide, the instructions below are the same for both variants.

Remove the template for this project (page 163 or 165), and using the color guides on pages 103 and 104, color in the coordinating template. (You can refer to the Papercraft Tips and Tricks on page 11 for suggestions on coloring.) Once you are finished coloring, carefully cut out the template pieces along their solid black outer borders. Now it's time to assemble!

We start with the **abdomen**. Like a real lepidopteran, this paper specimen of yours has nine segments in its abdomen. Stack them in ascending order: Begin by adding glue with a toothpick or small paintbrush to the *X* mark on piece **14** and set piece **13** on top, aligning the curved top edges as shown in image 1.

Apply glue to the *X* mark on piece **13** and set piece **12** on top. Continue this way until pieces **6** through **14** are all assembled. Set your completed abdomen aside to dry for 2 to 5 minutes. Next, mimic the curved fullness of a real butterfly's abdomen by pressing the abdomen over the barrel of one of your colored pencils with your thumb and finger, bending the edges down.

Now for the **wings**. Apply some glue to the *X* mark on piece **6**, and set piece **5**, the **hindwings**, on top, aligning as shown in image 2.

3

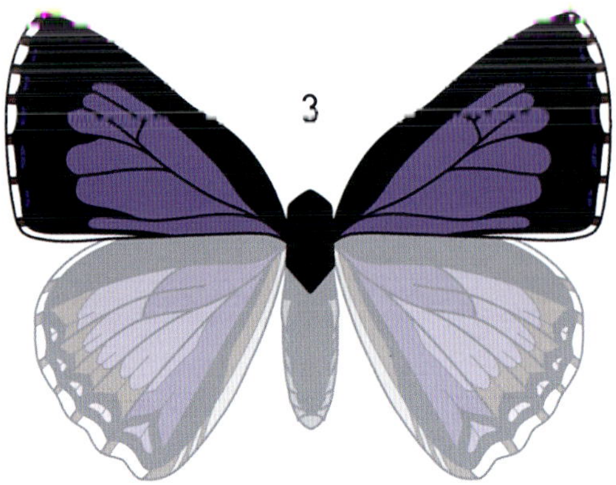

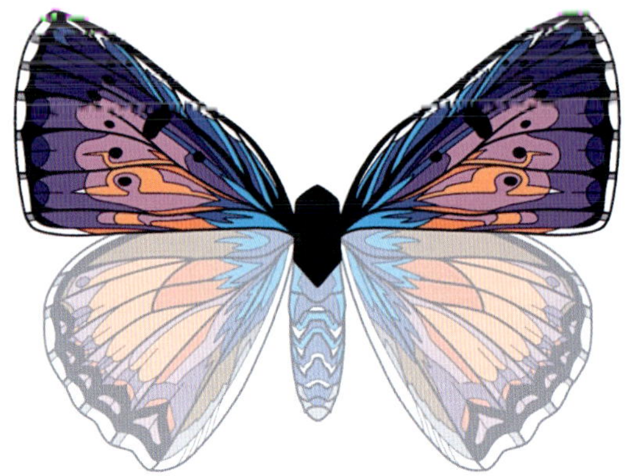

4

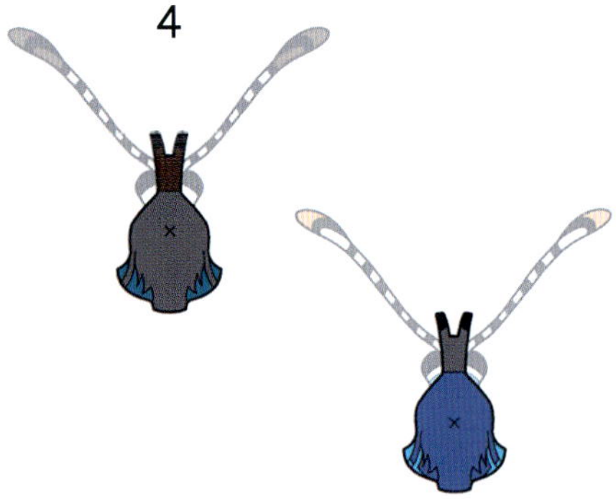

5

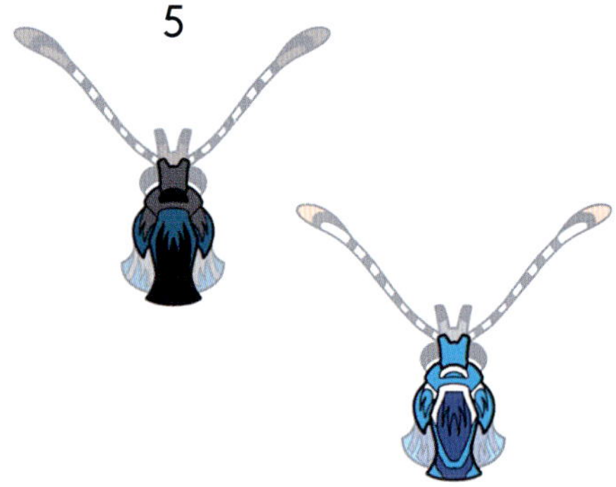

Apply glue to the *X* marks coordinating on piece **5**, and set piece **4**, the **forewings**, on top, aligning as shown in image 3.

Let the wings and abdomen dry together for 2 to 5 minutes. Finally, let's assemble the **head**. Apply glue to the *X* mark on piece **3**, and set piece **2** on top, aligning as shown in image 4.

6

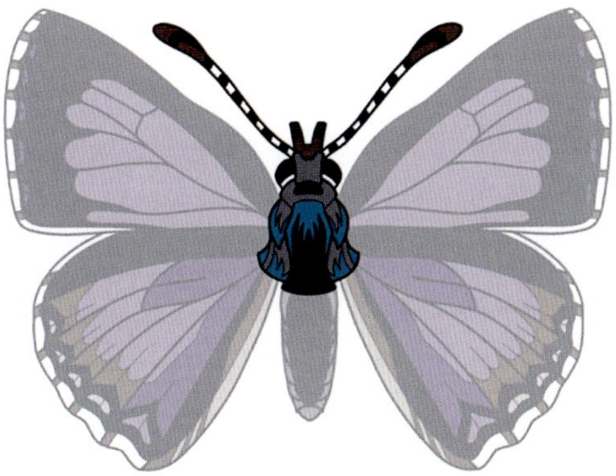

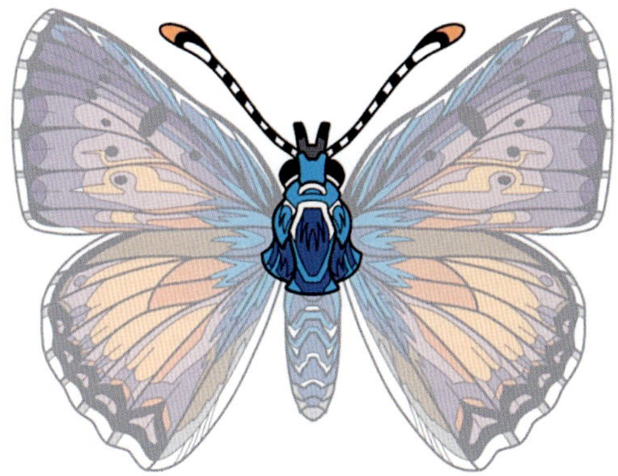

Apply glue to the *X* mark on piece **2**, and place piece **1** onto joined pieces **2** and **3** as shown in image 5.

Set the completed head aside to dry for 2 to 5 minutes, then add glue to the *X* marks on piece **4**, and set the head on top, aligning as shown in image 6. You're done!

For a final touch of dimension to your paper specimen, gently bend the forewings up with your fingers, and the hindwings down. If you'd like suggestions on how to display your completed butterfly, check out Mounting and Displaying Your Papercraft Specimens (page 109).

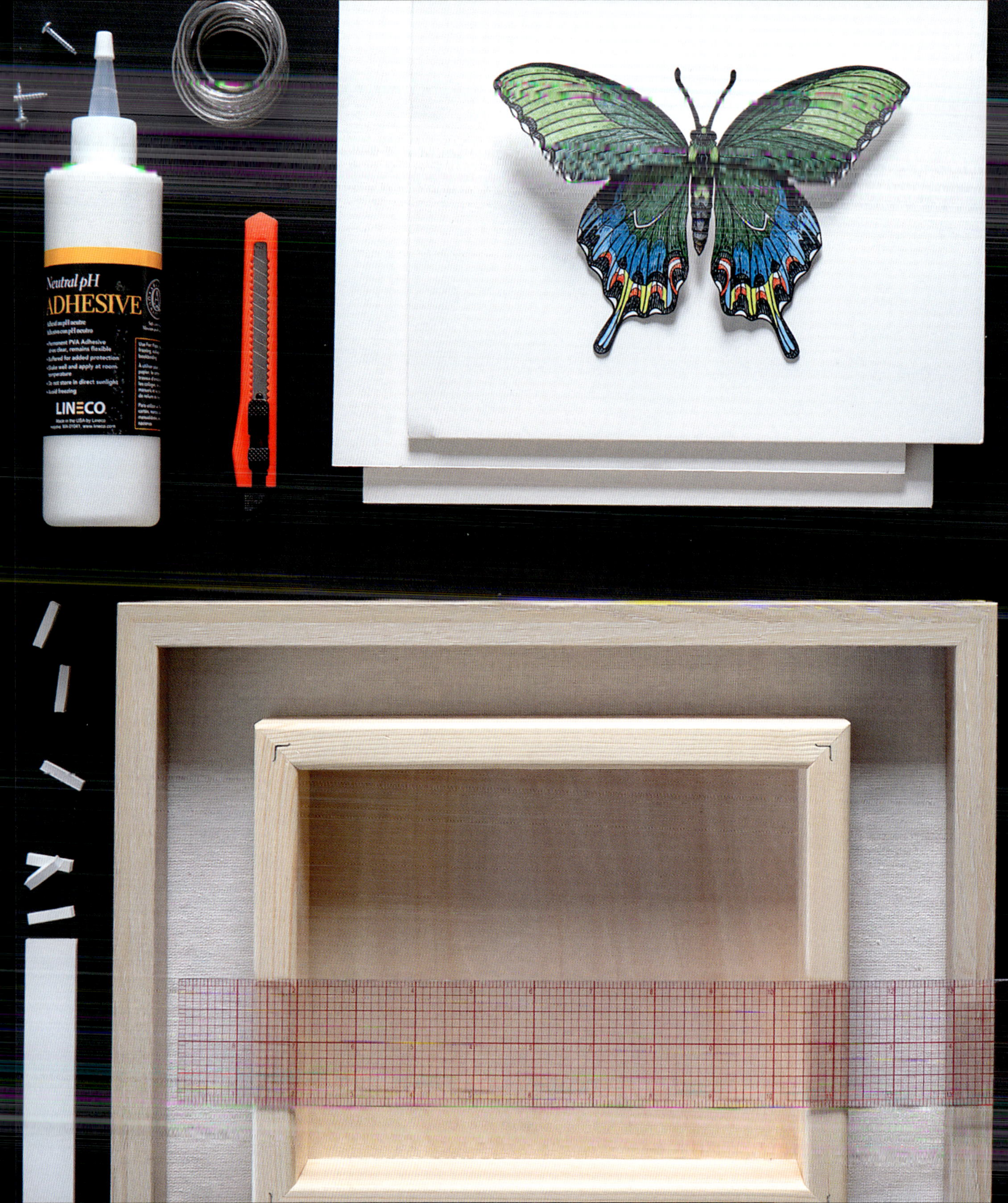
Neutral pH
ADHESIVE
LINECO

MOUNTING AND DISPLAYING YOUR PAPERCRAFT SPECIMENS

You can display your papercraft specimens any way you'd like, but here are some suggestions based on what I learned and practiced over the ten years I was a professional art framer before becoming a full-time artist.

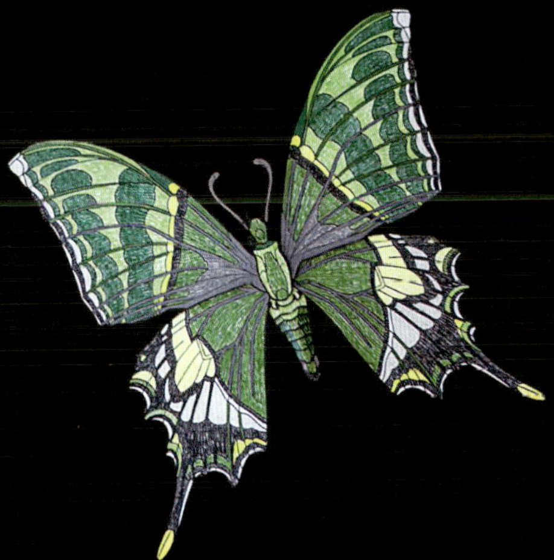

For either of these two display options, you will need the following tools and materials:

Foamcore: Also called foamboard, this material is made of a layer of dense foam between two pieces of paper or similar material, and you can find it in art or craft stores, usually in a variety of sizes and thicknesses. You don't need a lot for mounting your papercraft specimens, so a small sheet will do, and ⅕-inch (5-mm) or ½-inch (13-mm) thicknesses are common and will work best for mounting. I recommend using *acid-free* foamcore, which won't discolor itself or other materials it touches over time.

Craft knife: A fresh, sharp blade works best, both because it provides cleaner cuts and is easier to control than a duller blade.

Ruler: While any ruler will do, I recommend a *graph ruler*. This is a transparent plastic ruler with measurements displayed on it in a square grid. It is very useful for making precise cuts and trimming, as you can look through the ruler itself to check your measurements, not just along its edge. You can find graph rulers in the bookbinding or drafting sections of art stores.

Glue: The PVA glue mentioned in Papercraft Tips and Tricks (page 11) works best for mounting and display.

Hanging hardware (optional): If you're using a frame, most off-the-shelf (ready-made) frames come with hanging hardware already installed. For the Wood Panel display option (page 113), you will need to attach it yourself if you want to hang your papercraft specimens on the wall.

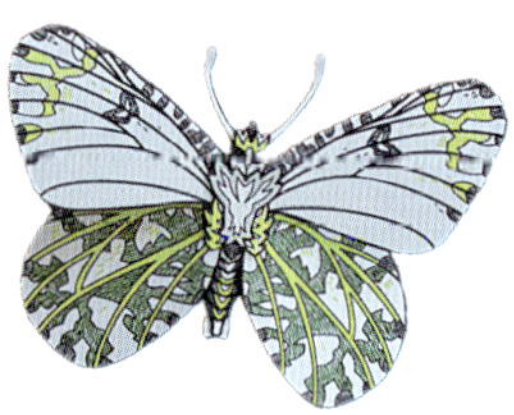

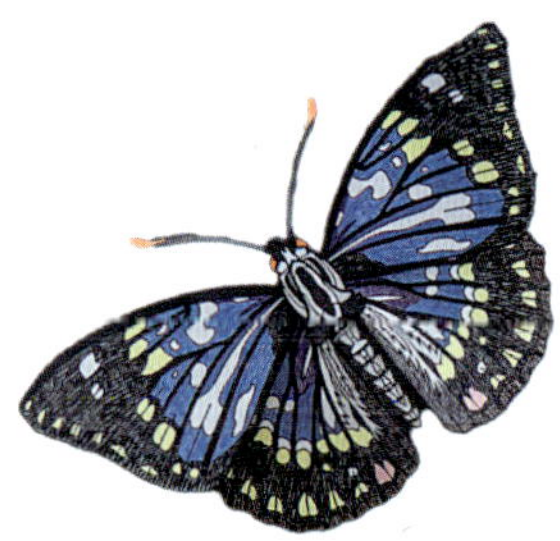

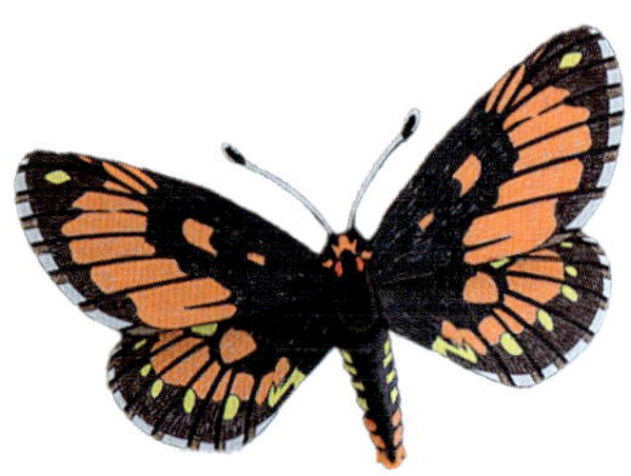

SHADOWBOX FRAME DISPLAY

Many art, craft, and framing stores sell off-the-shelf (ready-made) frames constructed for displaying dimensional items or art like your papercraft specimens, and these are called *shadowboxes*. Shadowbox frames come in a variety of sizes. Common sizes that will fit the finished projects from this book will be 5 x 7 inches, 8 x 10 inches, and 11 x 14 inches, depending on how much room you want around your papercraft specimen when displayed. In countries that use the metric system of measurement, common frame sizes will be A5 (148 x 210 mm), A4 (210 x 297 mm), and A3 (297 x 420 mm). Some shadowbox frames open from the front with hinges, like a cabinet, and some open by moving tabs on the back. Either option is fine for mounting your completed projects.

1. To mount your paper specimen, cut a thin strip from your foamcore—I recommend ¼ inch (6 mm) wide or similar. From this strip, cut a piece somewhat smaller than the length of your papercraft specimen's body using your ruler and craft knife. (If you find the foamcore hard to cut, don't try to cut through it in one go; use lighter pressure to create repeated, shallow cuts to gradually cut through the board.) If you'd like a more dimensional, floating look for your display, cut a second piece of foamcore the same length as the first, and glue them together, stacking the paper sides, not the foam sides, together. Let the glue dry for 2 to 5 minutes before proceeding.

2. Attach your short piece of foamcore to the blank underside of your papercraft specimen's body with glue, and let it dry for 2 to 5 minutes. Once dry, add glue to the free side of the foamcore piece, and set your paper specimen onto the backing board of your frame.

3. Use your ruler to make sure your papercraft specimen is centered how you'd like it on the board, working quickly to adjust as needed before the glue sets. Once the papercraft specimen is located where you'd like it, let the glue dry completely (10 minutes), then reassemble or close your frame, and your papercraft specimen is ready for display!

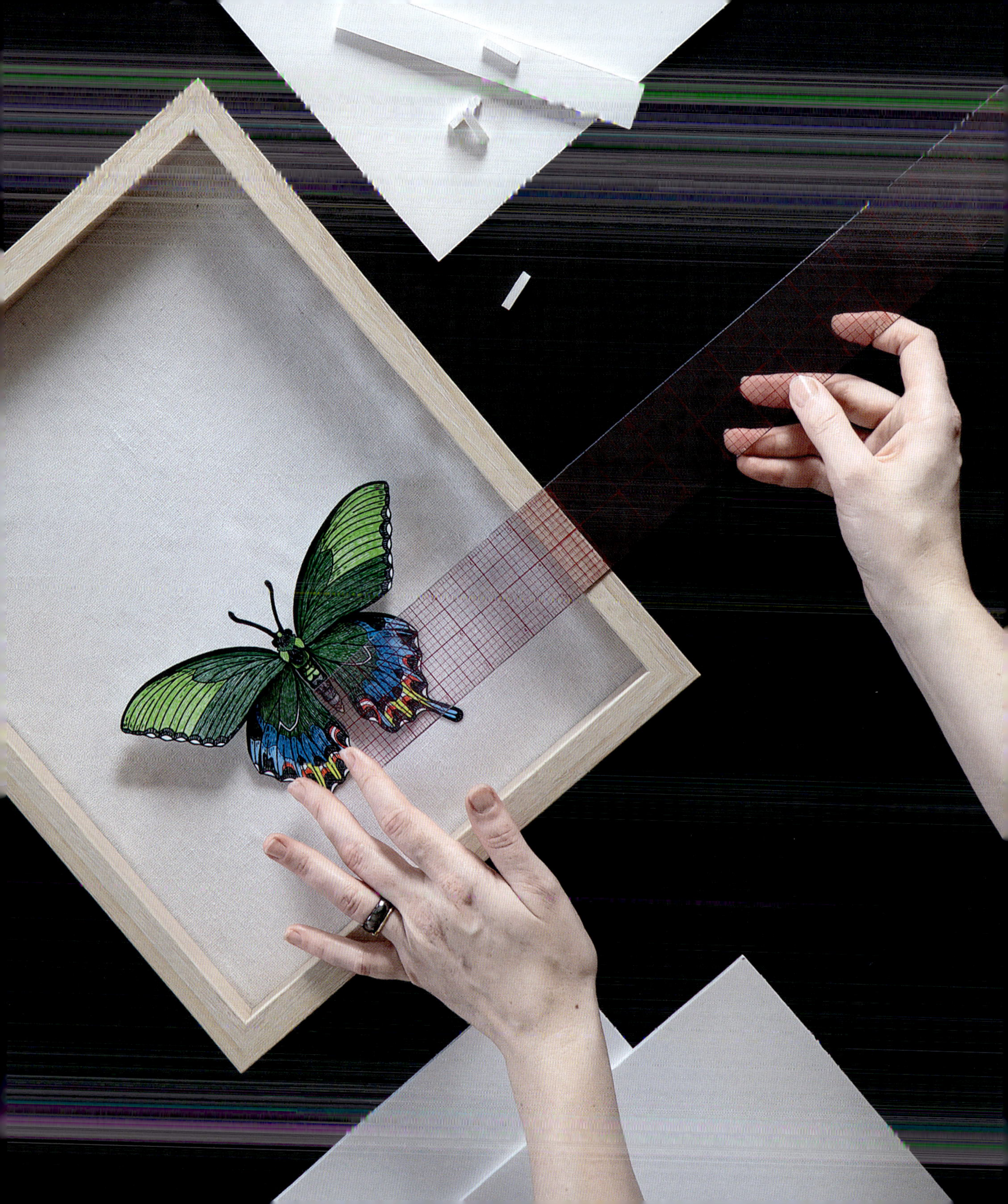

WOOD PANEL DISPLAY

This is a cheaper and more hands-on method of making a display for your papercraft specimens. Without glass like a real frame, it is easier to see all the details of your finished projects, but this also means it doesn't provide as much protection for them, either. So, keep that in mind, and don't use this display method if you want to hang your completed projects somewhere that could be damp (like a kitchen or bathroom, or near a window), or in areas they may be bumped into easily.

Get a *wooden cradled panel* (a board that has an attached wooden frame on the back for support) from a craft or art store. Panels with cradles that are ¾ to 1 inch (19 to 25 mm) wide work best. These cradled boards are designed for their flat front surface to be used for painting or other art techniques, but by flipping them around, the cradle becomes an open-faced frame for your papercraft specimen.

Cradled panels come in a variety of sizes, and you can easily pick which ones suit your needs by bringing your papercraft specimens to an art or frame store and checking how your specimen looks against the cradled side of the panels. Here in the US, common sizes that will fit your papercraft specimens from this book will be 5 x 5 inches, 8 x 8 inches, 8 x 10 inches, and 11 x 14 inches, depending on how much room you want around your papercraft specimen when displayed. In countries that use the metric system of measurement, common cradled panel sizes will be A5 (148 x 210 mm), A4 (210 x 297 mm), and A3 (297 x 420 mm).

1. Before mounting your papercraft specimen in this wooden frame, attach a hanger to the back (originally the front of the panel) if you intend to hang your papercraft specimen on a wall. If you do, make sure to place any screws or nails along the edge of the panel, where they will go into the cradle and not through the panel into the area that your papercraft specimen will be displayed in.

2. Once you've attached your hanger (if needed), cut a thin strip from your foamcore—I recommend ¼ inch (6 mm) wide or similar. From this strip, cut a piece somewhat smaller than the length of your papercraft specimen's body using your ruler and craft knife. (If you find the foamcore hard to cut, don't try to cut through it in one go; use lighter pressure to create repeated, shallow cuts that gradually cut through the board.) If you'd like a more dimensional, floating look for your display, cut a second piece of foamcore the same length as the first, and glue them together, stacking the paper sides, not the foam sides, together. Let the glue dry for 2 to 5 minutes before proceeding.

3. Attach your short piece of foamcore to the blank underside of your papercraft specimen's body with glue, and let it dry for 2 to 5 minutes. Once dry, add glue to the free side of the foamcore piece, and set your paper specimen onto the wood panel, the cradle facing up to create a frame around your papercraft specimen.

4. Use your ruler to make sure your papercraft specimen is centered how you'd like it on the board, working quickly to adjust as needed before the glue sets. Once the papercraft specimen is located where you'd like it on the panel, let it dry completely (10 minutes). Now your papercraft specimen is ready for display!

RESOURCES

Butterflies of the World by Rod and Ken Preston-Mafham

Butterflies of the World by Valerio Sbordoni and Saverio Forestiero

Life History of the Rare Boreal Tiger Moth Arctia menetriesii (Eversmann, 1846) (Lepidoptera, Erebidae, Arctiinae) *in the Russian Far East* by Evgeny S. Koshkin, Nota Lepidopterologica

The Lives of Moths: A Natural History of Our Planet's Moth Life by Andrei Sourakov and Rachen Warren Chadd

"Secrets of the Butterfly Hunter" by Kate Campbell, Swarthmore College Bulletin, Fall 2022 Issue

"Wallace Golden Birdwing Butterfly" by Keri Murrell, Bournemouth Natural Science Society: bnss.org.uk/sections/entomology/wallace-golden-birdwing-butterfly

International Union for Conservation of Nature: iucnredlist.org

New South Wales Government Office of Environment and Heritage:
threatenedspecies.bionet.nsw.gov.au
environment.nsw.gov.au

Royal Entomological Society: resjournals.onlinelibrary.wiley.com

The United States Fish and Wildlife Service: fws.gov/species

The United States National Park Service: www.nps.gov/subjects/rareandendangered/index.htm

The Xerces Society: xerces.org

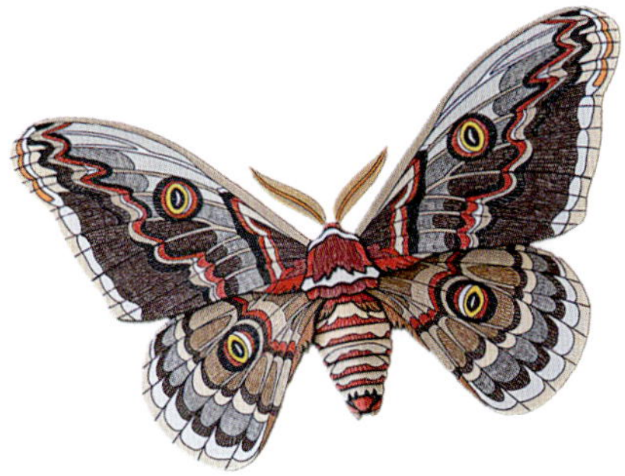

ACKNOWLEDGMENTS

This book wouldn't have happened without so many good people. Thank you to my grandparents, for teaching me how to notice and to care; to my niece and nephew for helping me rediscover wonder; to my final semester art professor Liz, for encouraging me to pursue the art I wanted to make and not what others told me I should; to my husband, for listening to all my nature fact recitations, shouldering workloads so I could take on creating this book, and believing in me from the first day we met; and to the remarkably kind and supportive team at Page Street Publishing, for seeing my paper art as good book material while that idea was still just a someday dream in my own mind, and being a delight to work with to make that dream a reality.

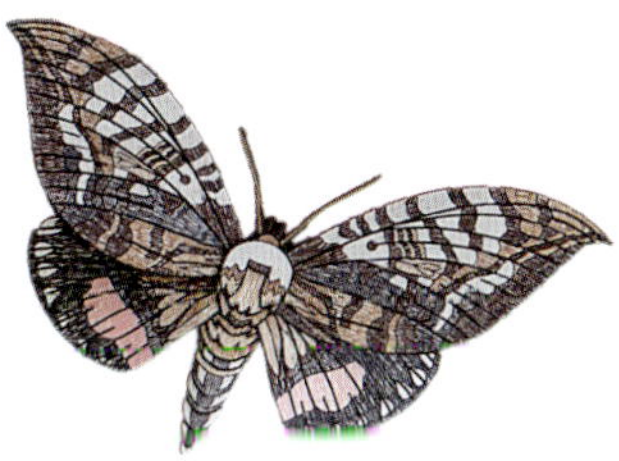

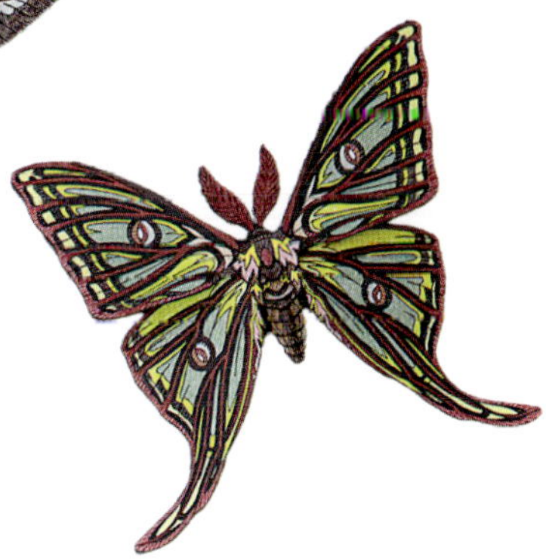

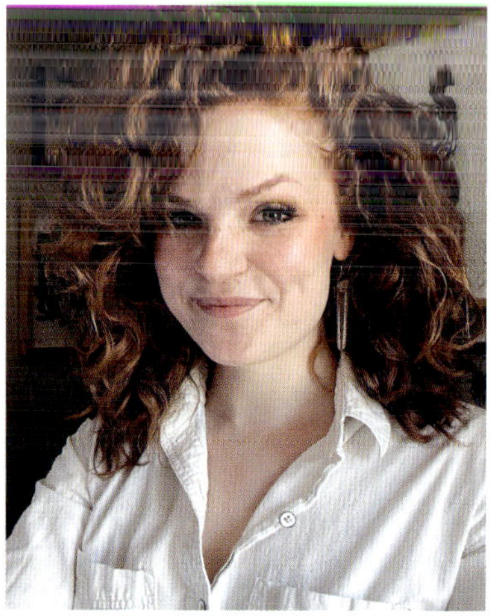

ABOUT THE AUTHOR

Working under the studio name Beastie and Bone, Stacia is a multi-disciplinary artist most known for her unique paper art. Her layered, dimensional technique blends her background in illustration, bookbinding, and fine art framing with her childhood love of the wild and her experience with various ecosystems throughout the United States.

Though raised in the Midwest, she completed a certificate program through the Rhode Island School of Design in 2017, and later launched her art career in the Pacific Northwest, where she lived in Seattle for six years. Now, she works from her tiny home studio near the Smoky Mountains amongst an ever-growing collection of nature curio. Her original works have a growing international collector base and have been shown throughout the United States, including in exhibits in museums like the Witte Museum (San Antonio, TX), the North Museum of Nature and Science (Lancaster, PA), and the National Museum of Wildlife Art (Jackson, WY).

You can learn more about her art process and shop available original works, prints, and linocuts at www.beastieandbone.com, or say hi via social media at @beastieandbone.

INDEX

TEMPLATES

BLACKBURN'S SPHINX MOTH TEMPLATE

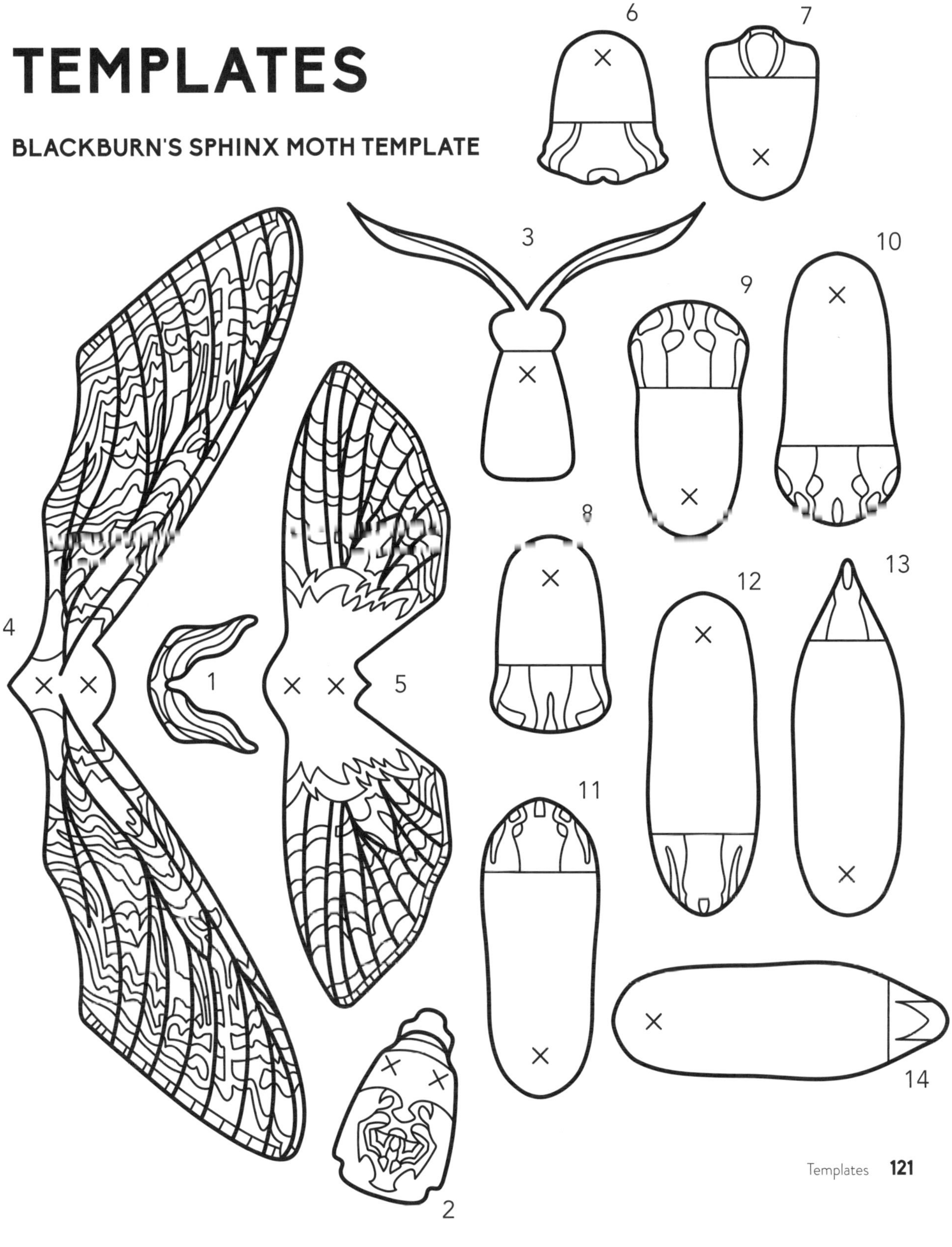

BOG BUCK MOTH TEMPLATE

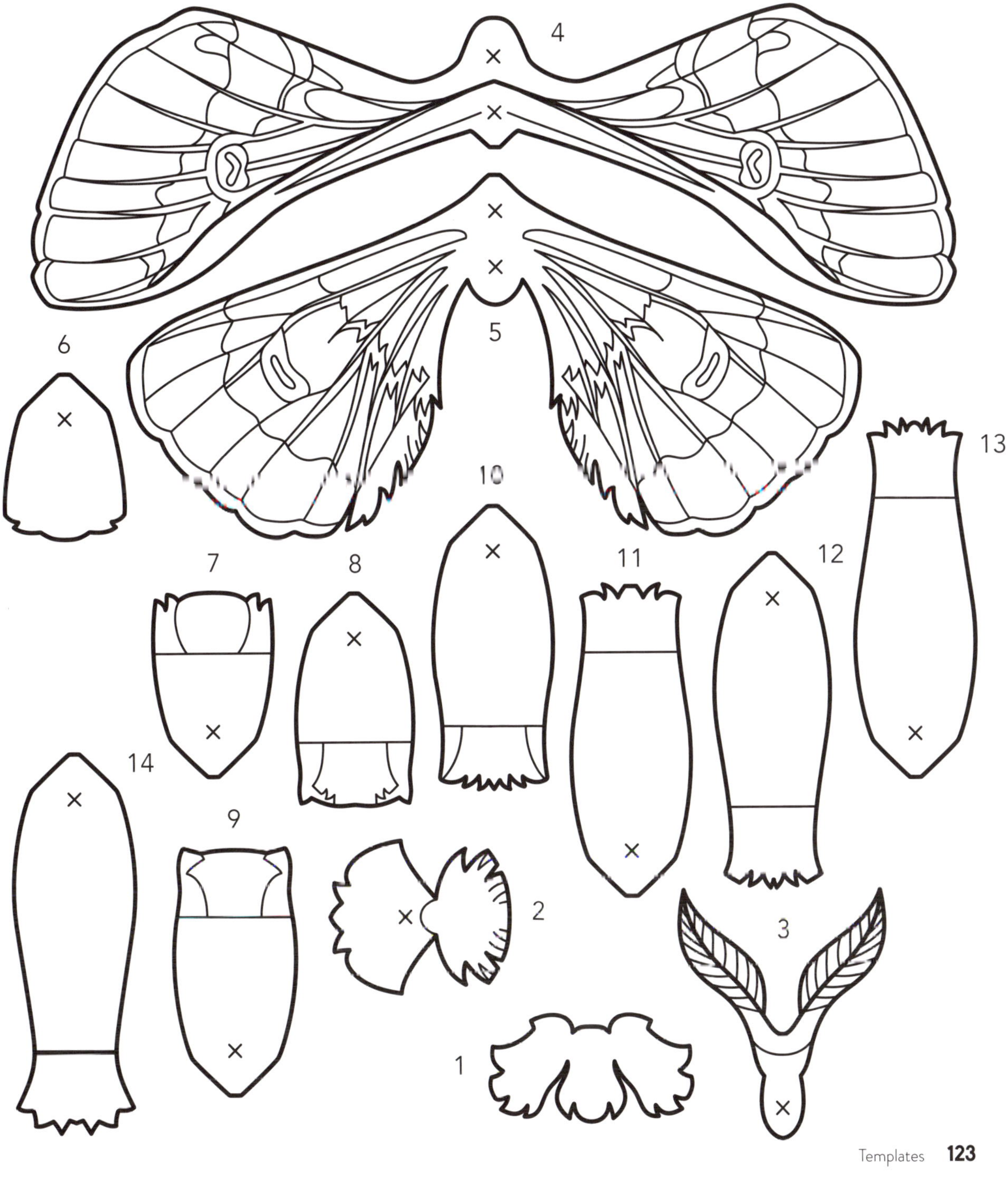

MENETRIES' TIGER MOTH TEMPLATE

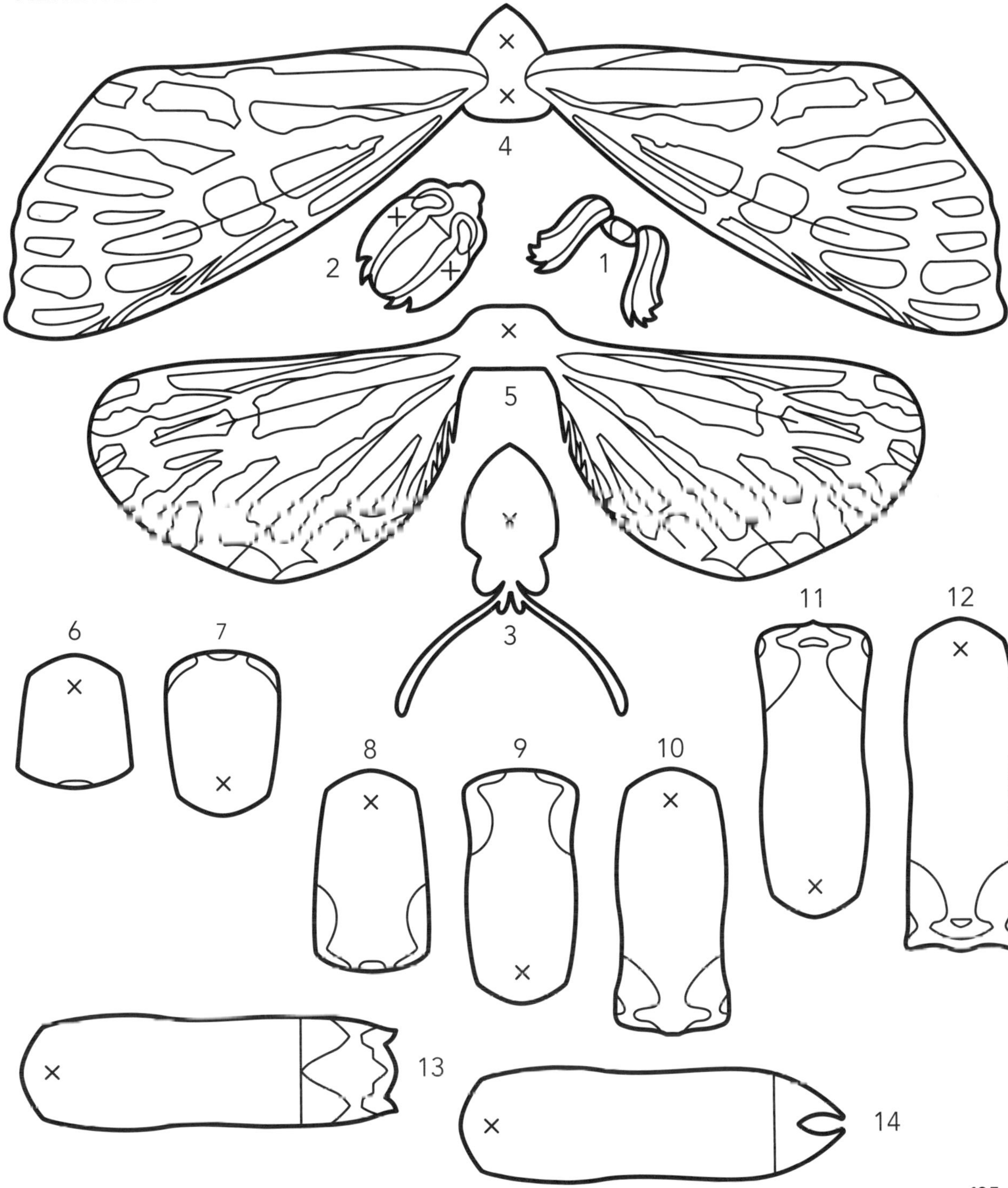

SPANISH MOON MOTH *MALE* TEMPLATE

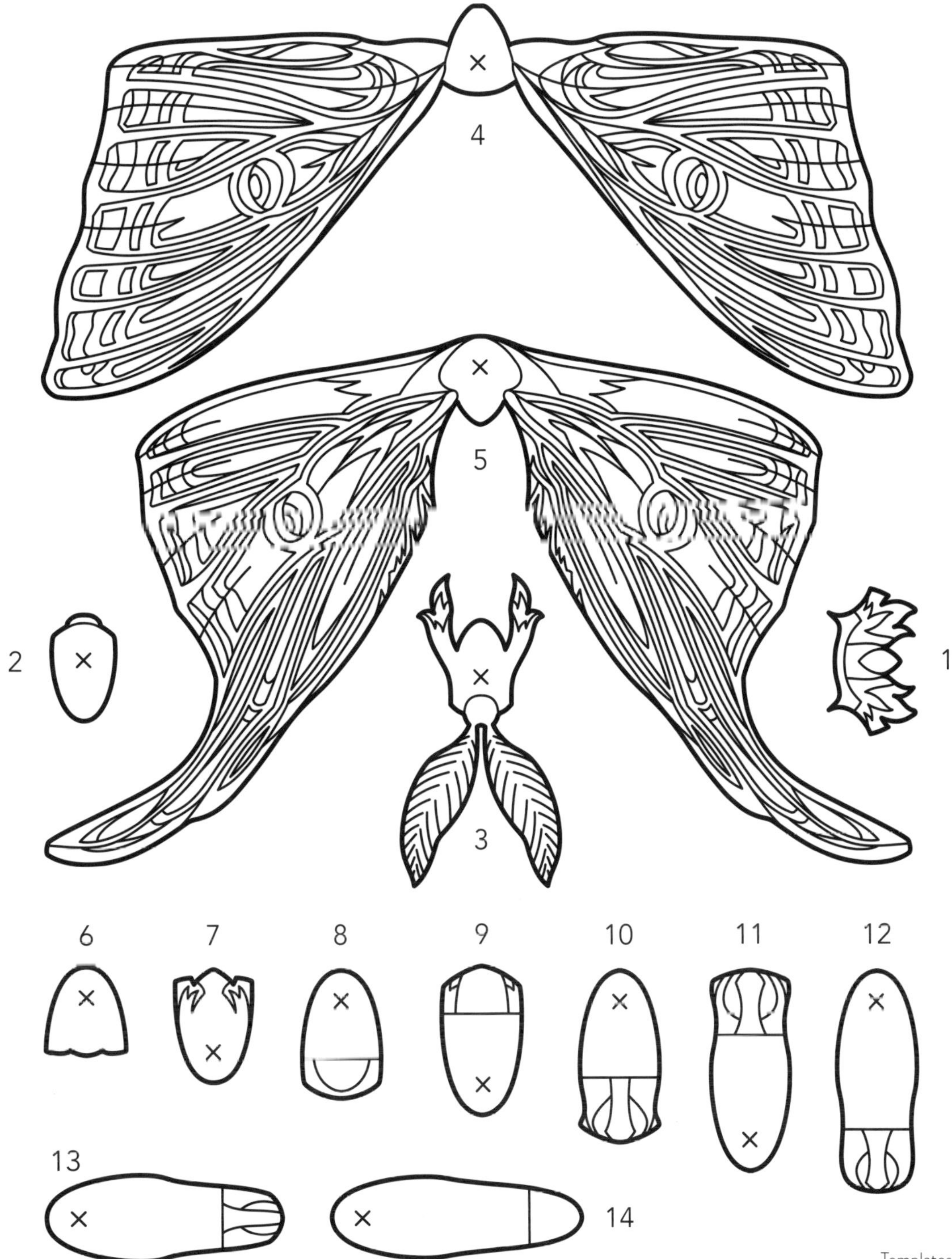

SPANISH MOON MOTH *FEMALE* TEMPLATE

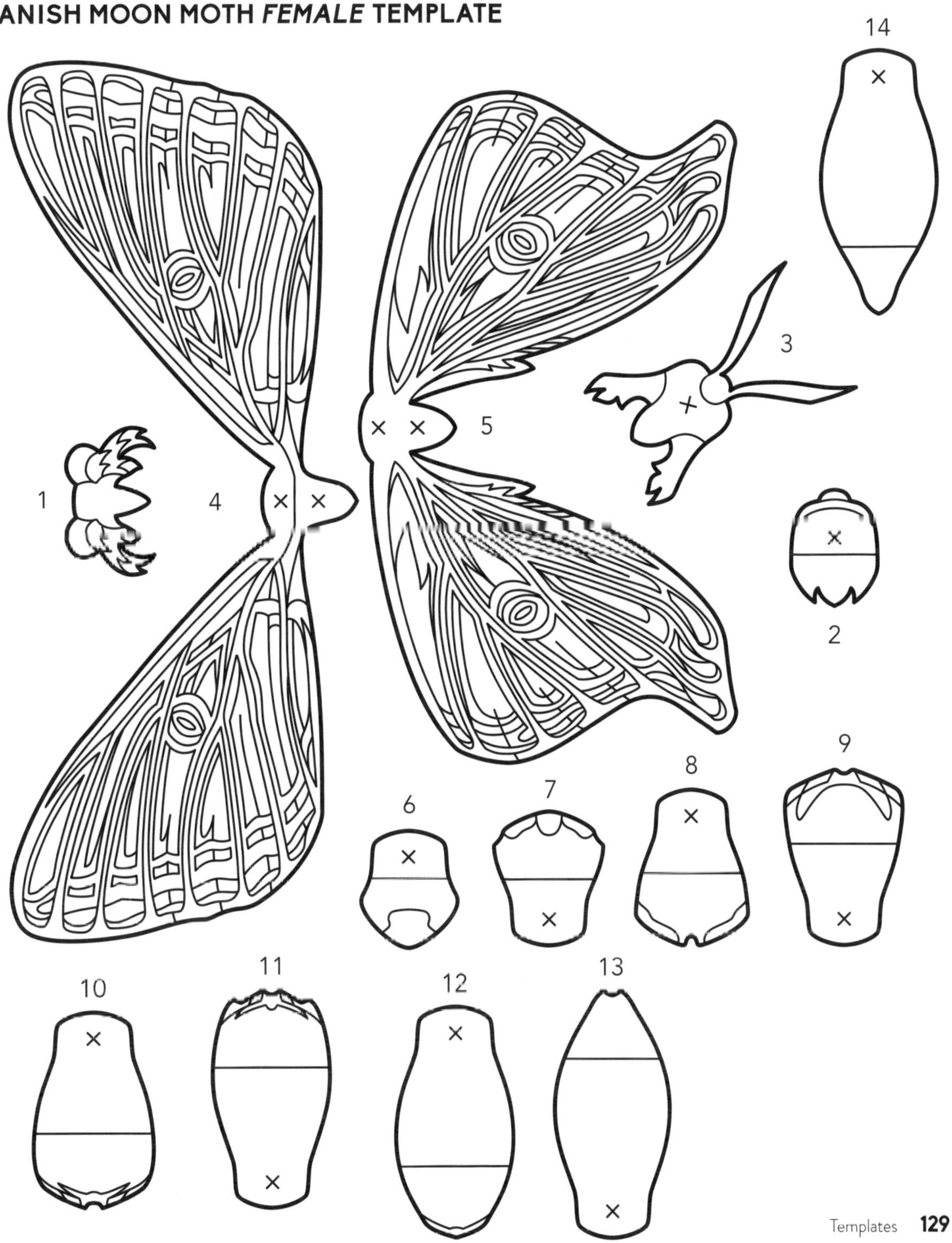

GIANT PEACOCK MOTH TEMPLATE

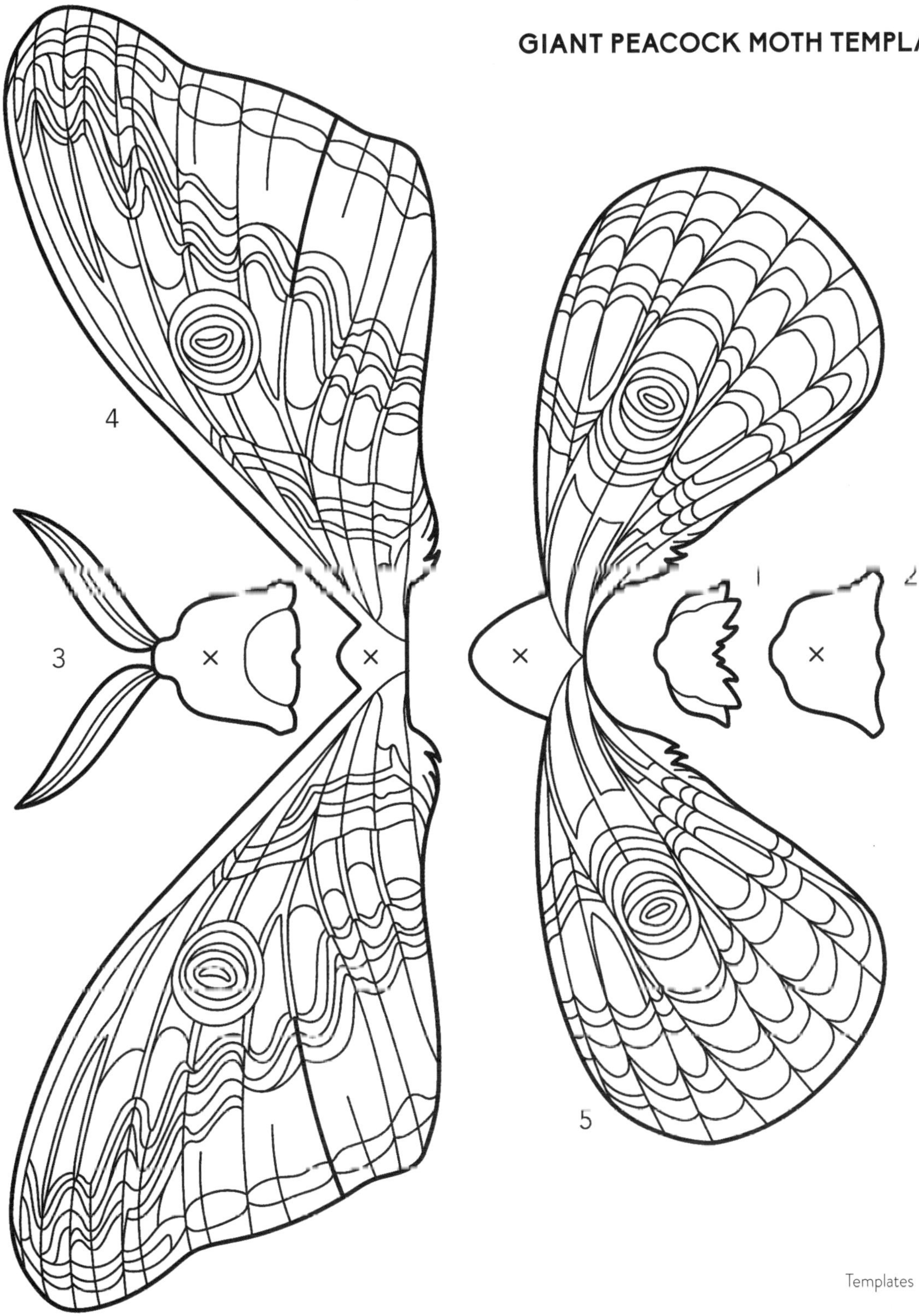

GIANT PEACOCK MOTH TEMPLATE (CONTINUED)

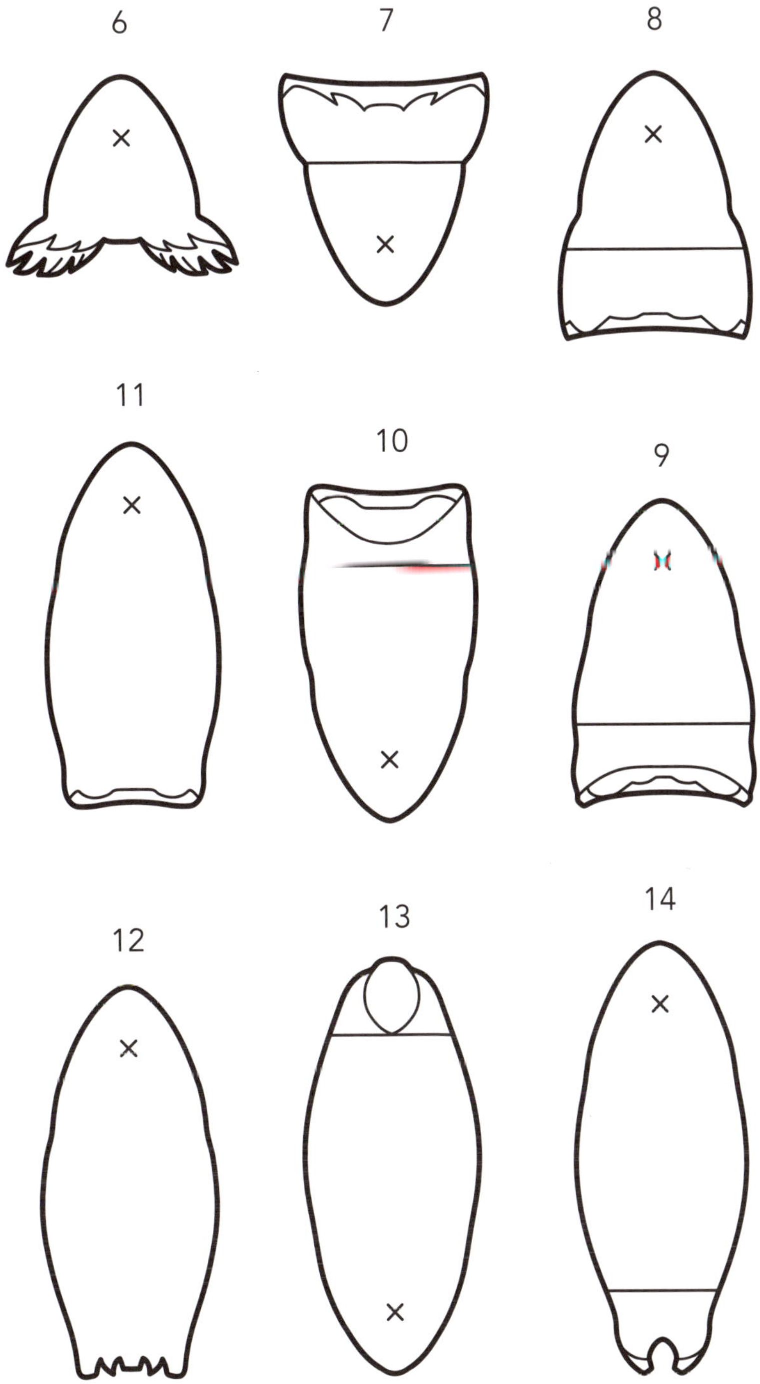

SOUTHERN PINK UNDERWING MOTH TEMPLATE

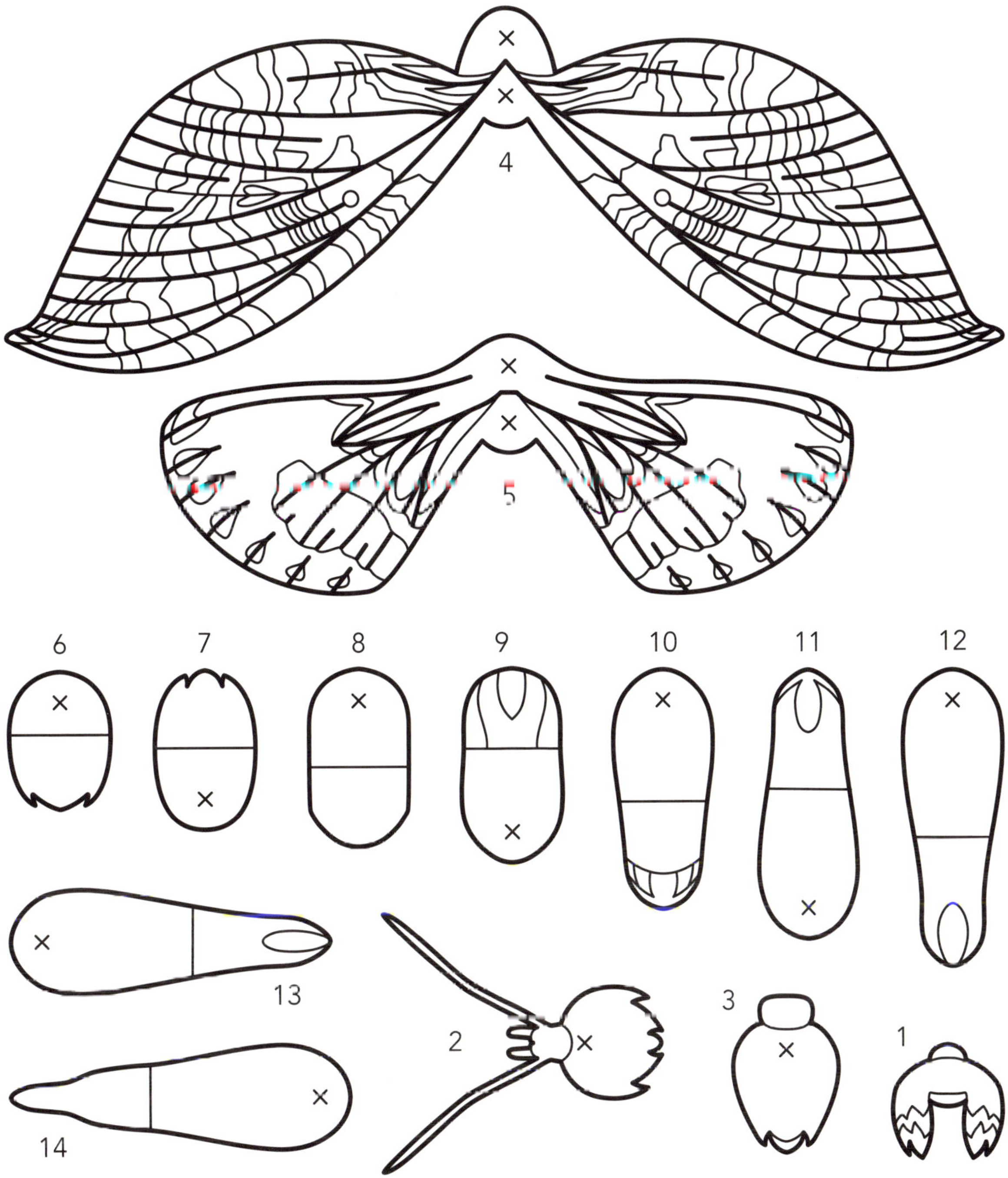

ISLAND MARBLE BUTTERFLY TEMPLATE

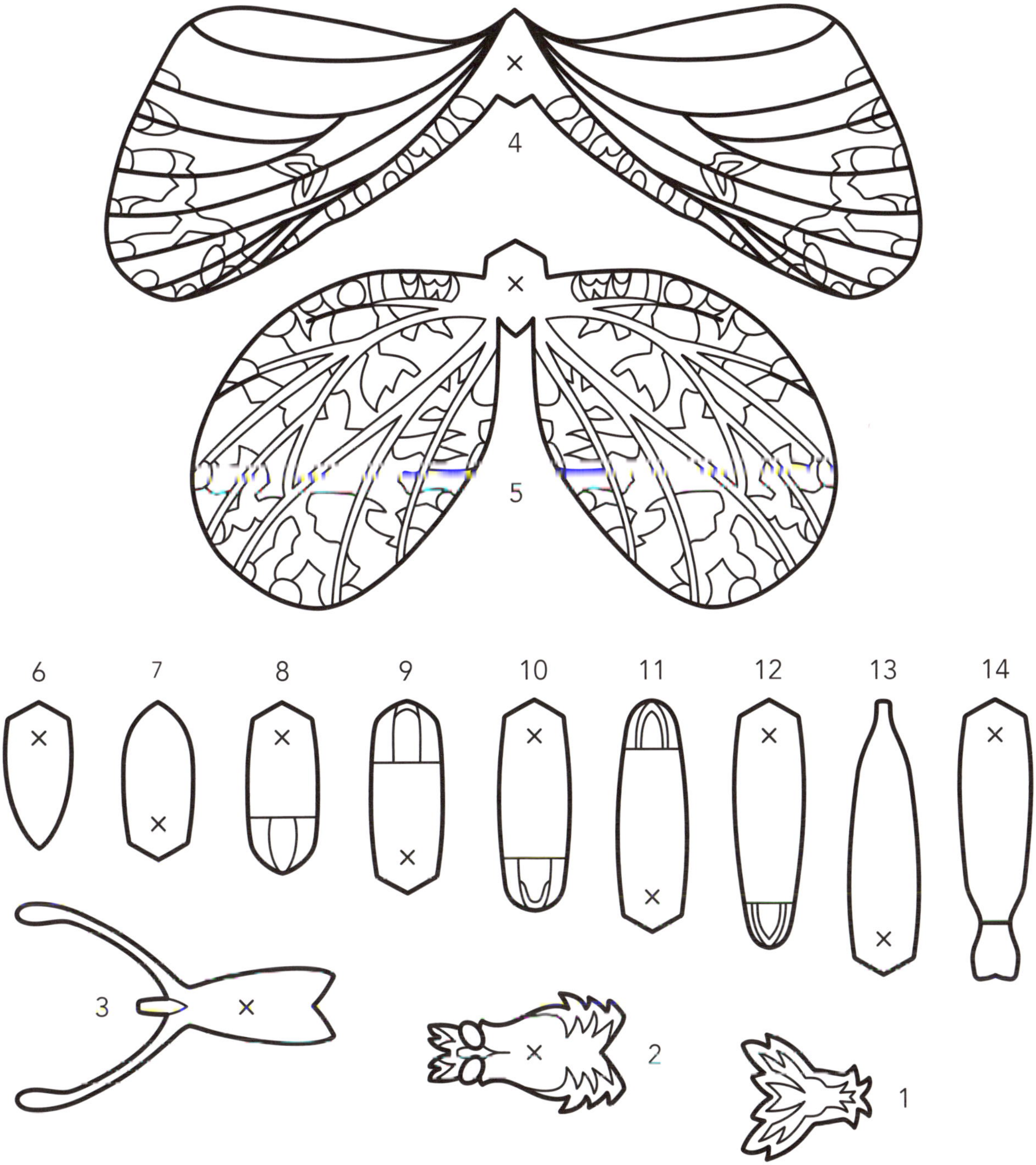

LUZON PEACOCK SWALLOWTAIL BUTTERFLY TEMPLATE

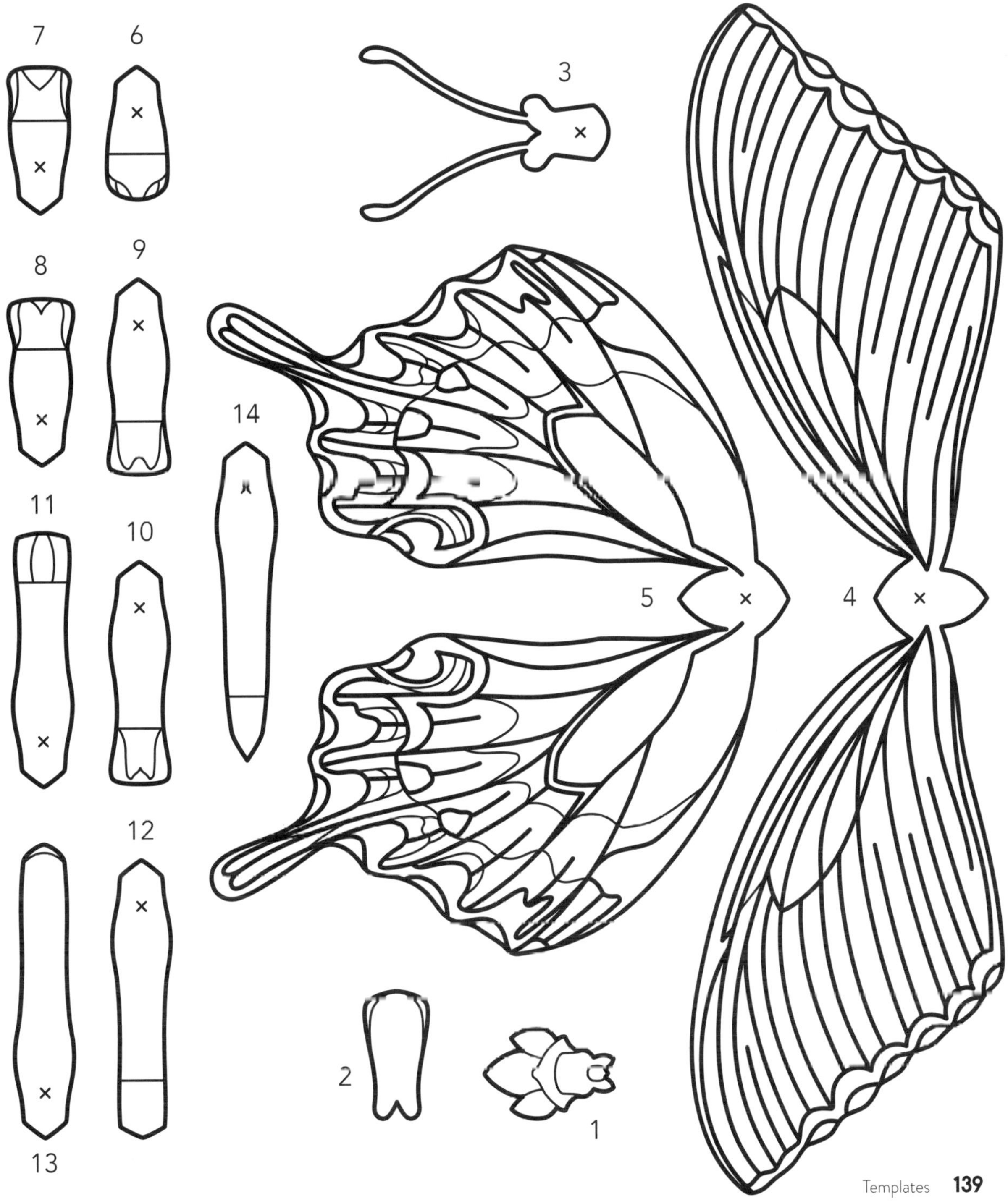

GOLDEN KAISER-I-HIND BUTTERFLY TEMPLATE

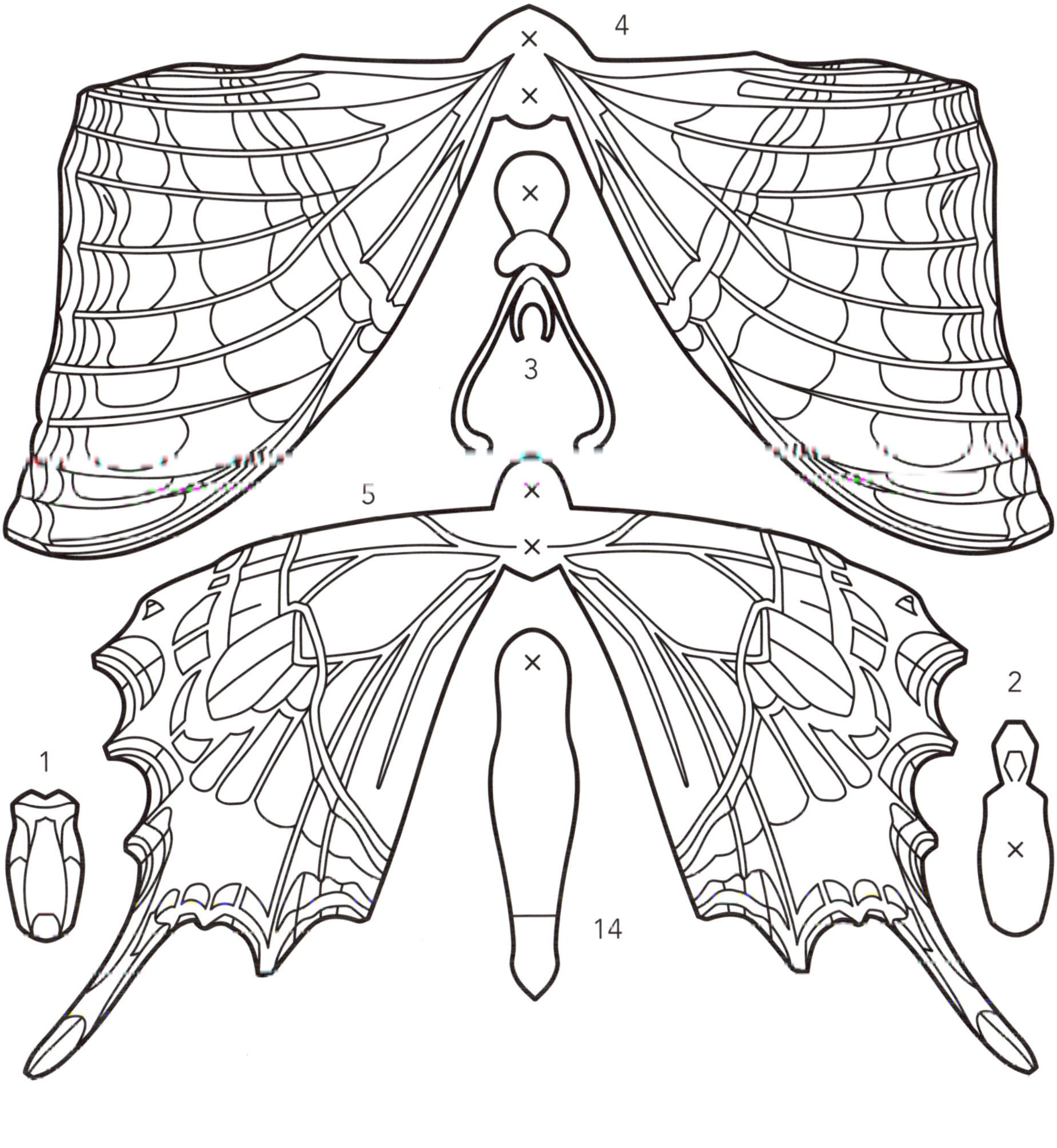

GOLDEN KAISER-I-HIND BUTTERFLY TEMPLATE (CONTINUED)

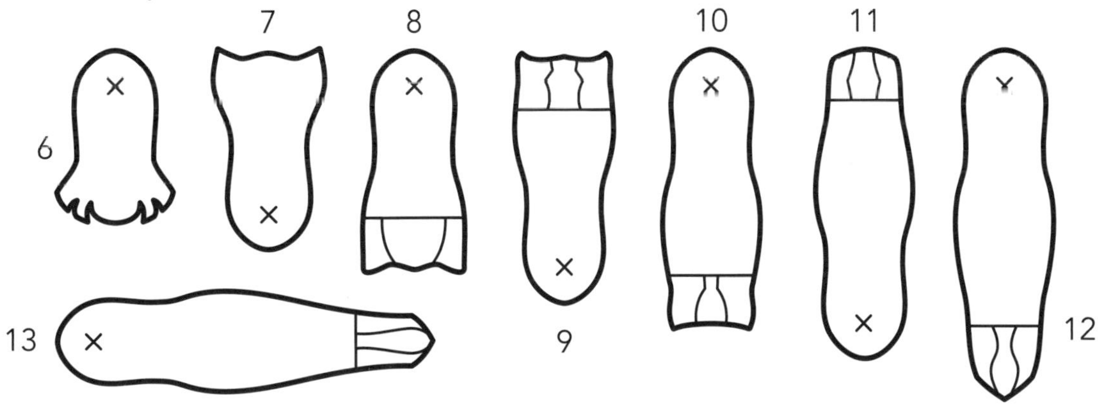

GREAT PURPLE EMPEROR BUTTERFLY *MALE* TEMPLATE

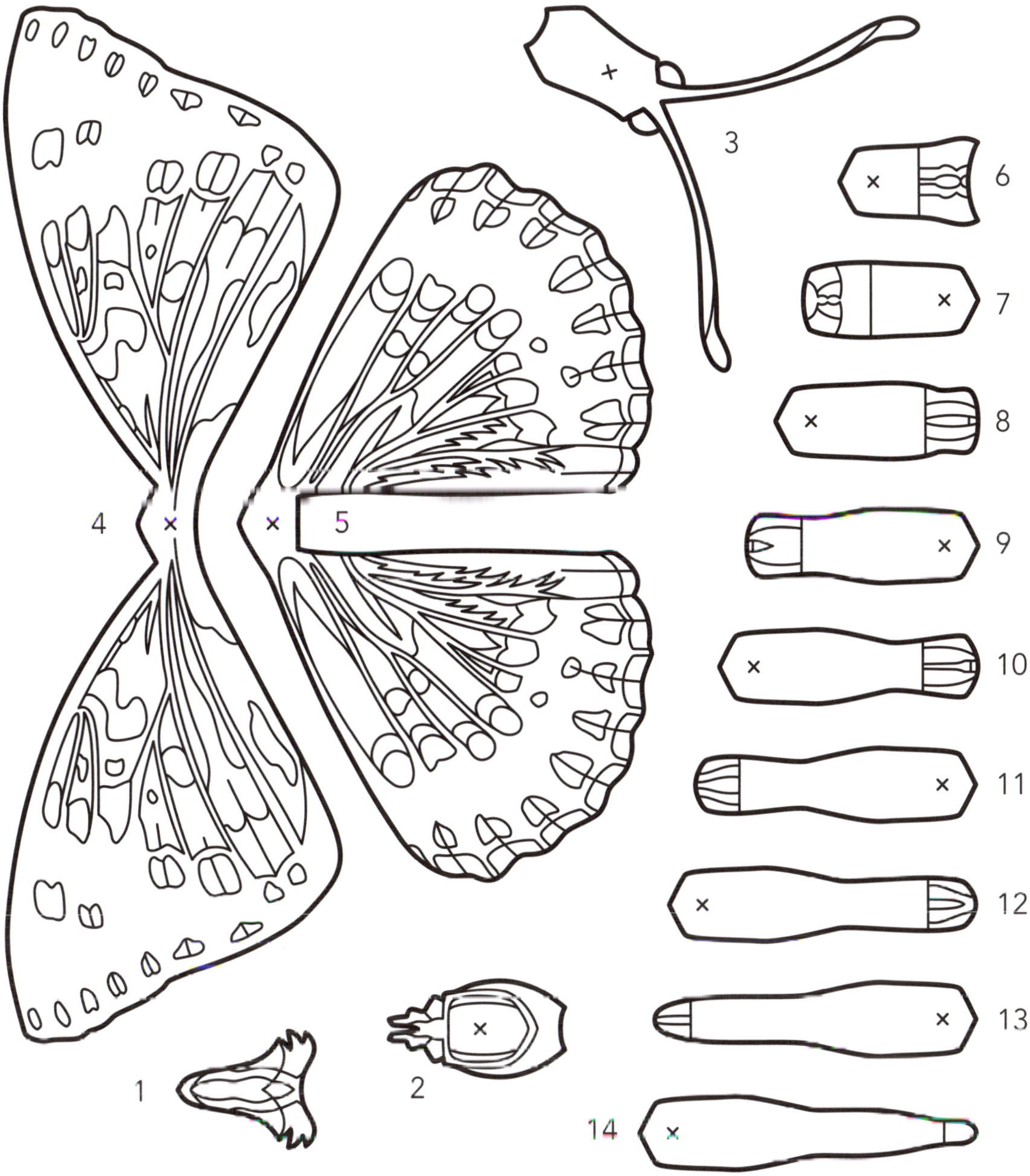

GREAT PURPLE EMPEROR BUTTERFLY *FEMALE* TEMPLATE

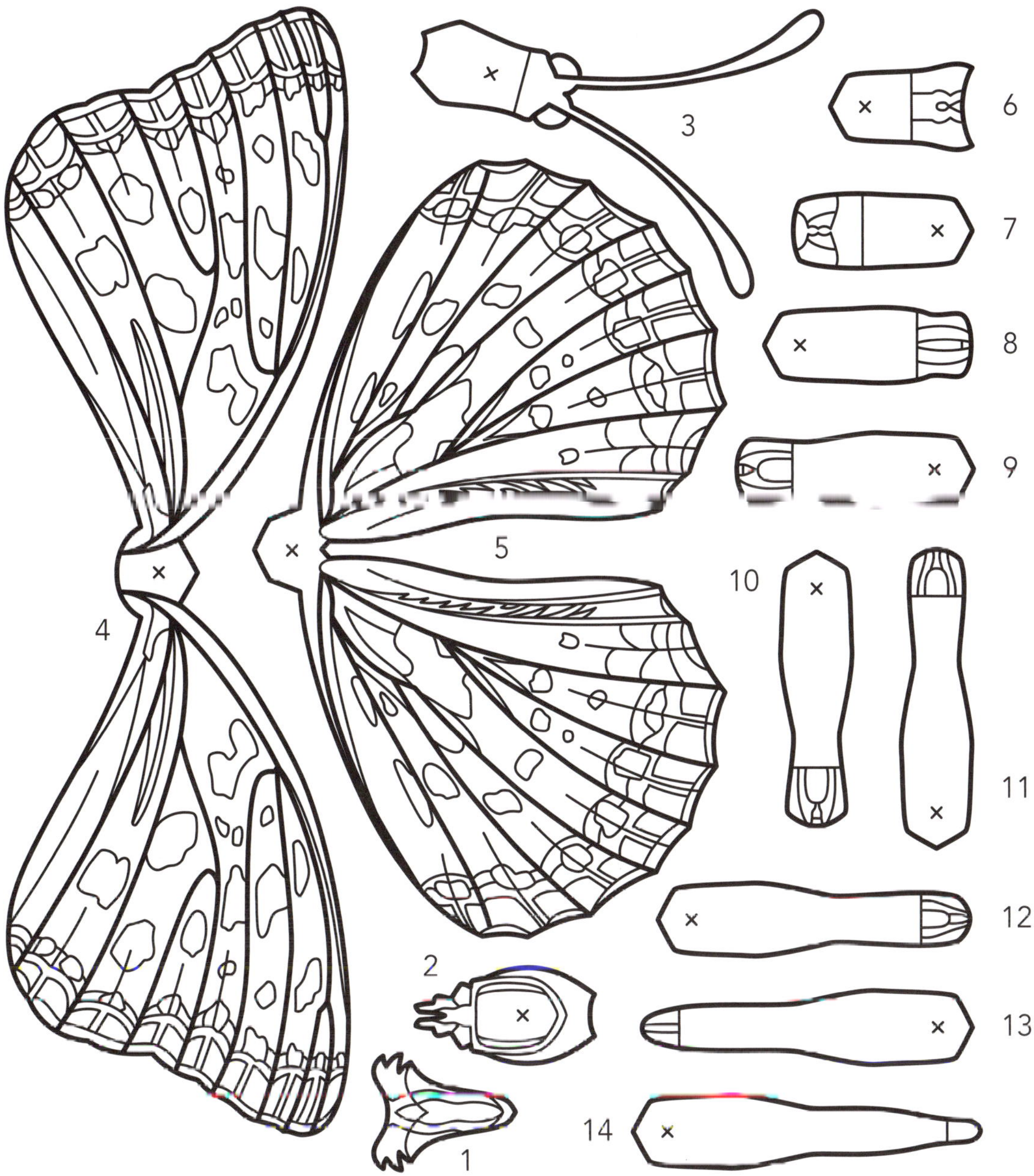

WALLACE'S GOLDEN BIRDWING *MALE* TEMPLATE

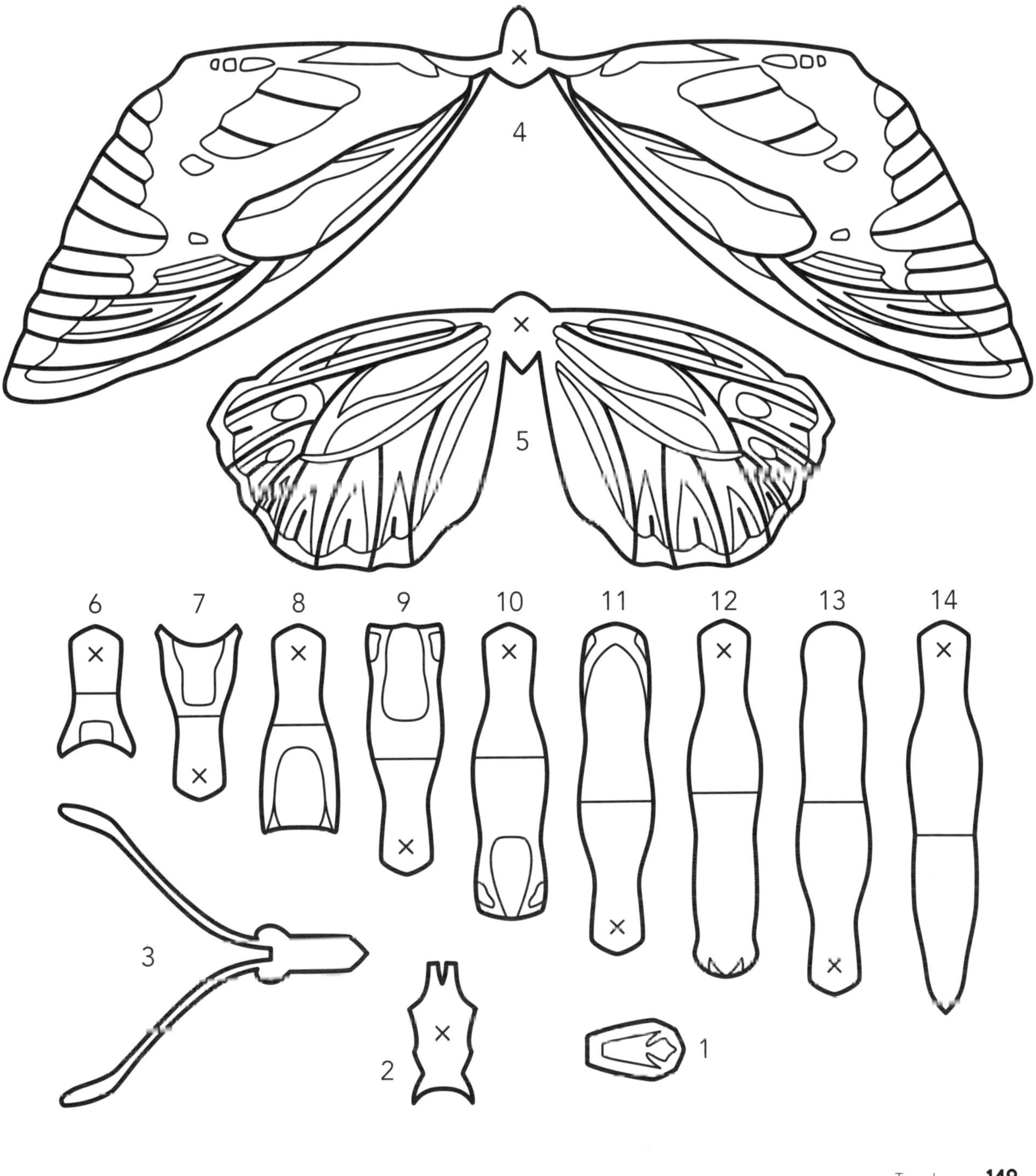

WALLACE'S GOLDEN BIRDWING *FEMALE* TEMPLATE

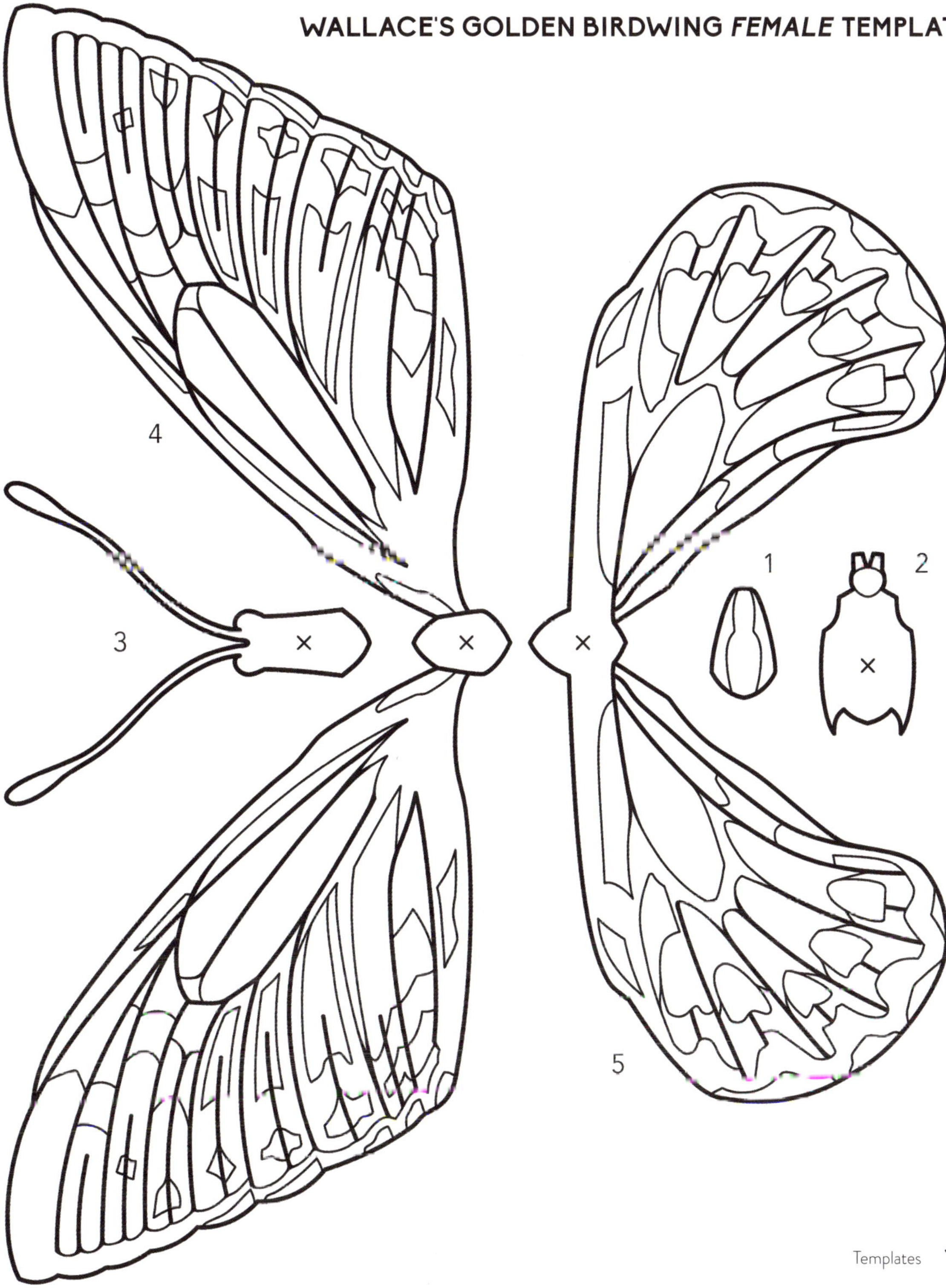

WALLACE'S GOLDEN BIRDWING *FEMALE* TEMPLATE (CONTINUED)

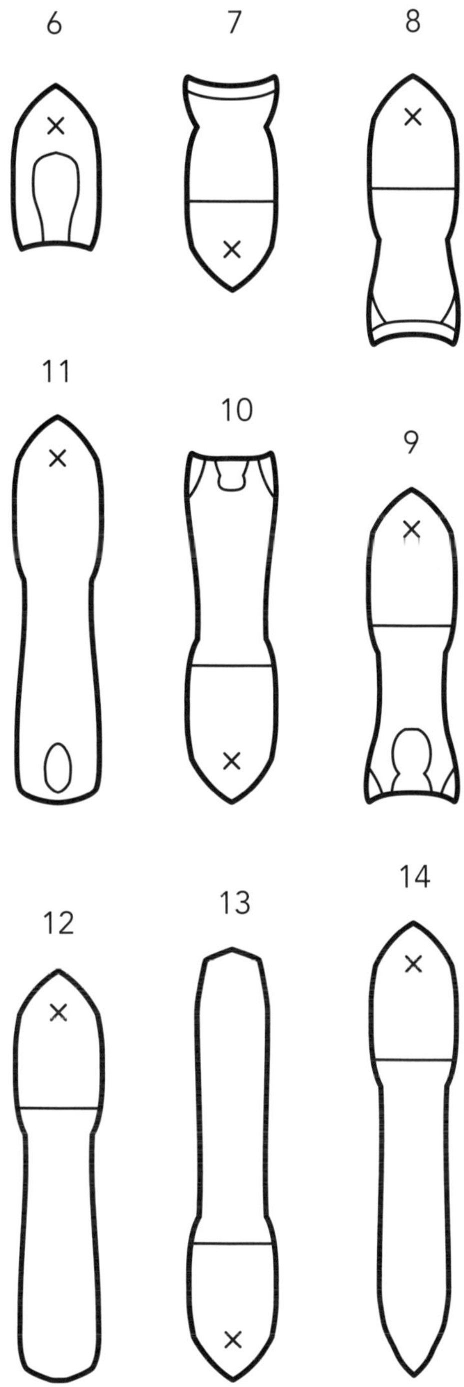

NATTERER'S LONGWING BUTTERFLY *MALE* TEMPLATE

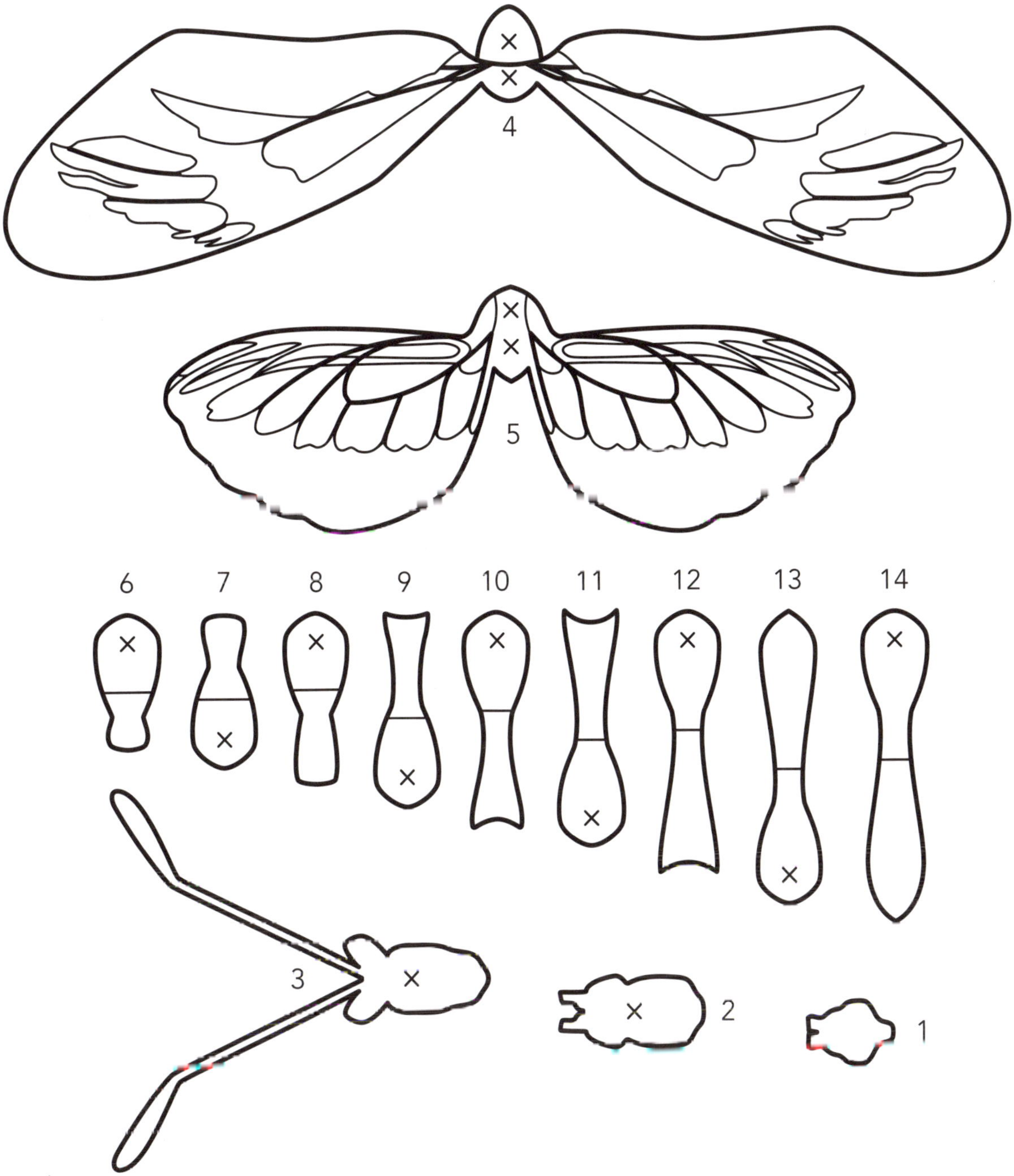

NATTERER'S LONGWING BUTTERFLY *FEMALE* TEMPLATE

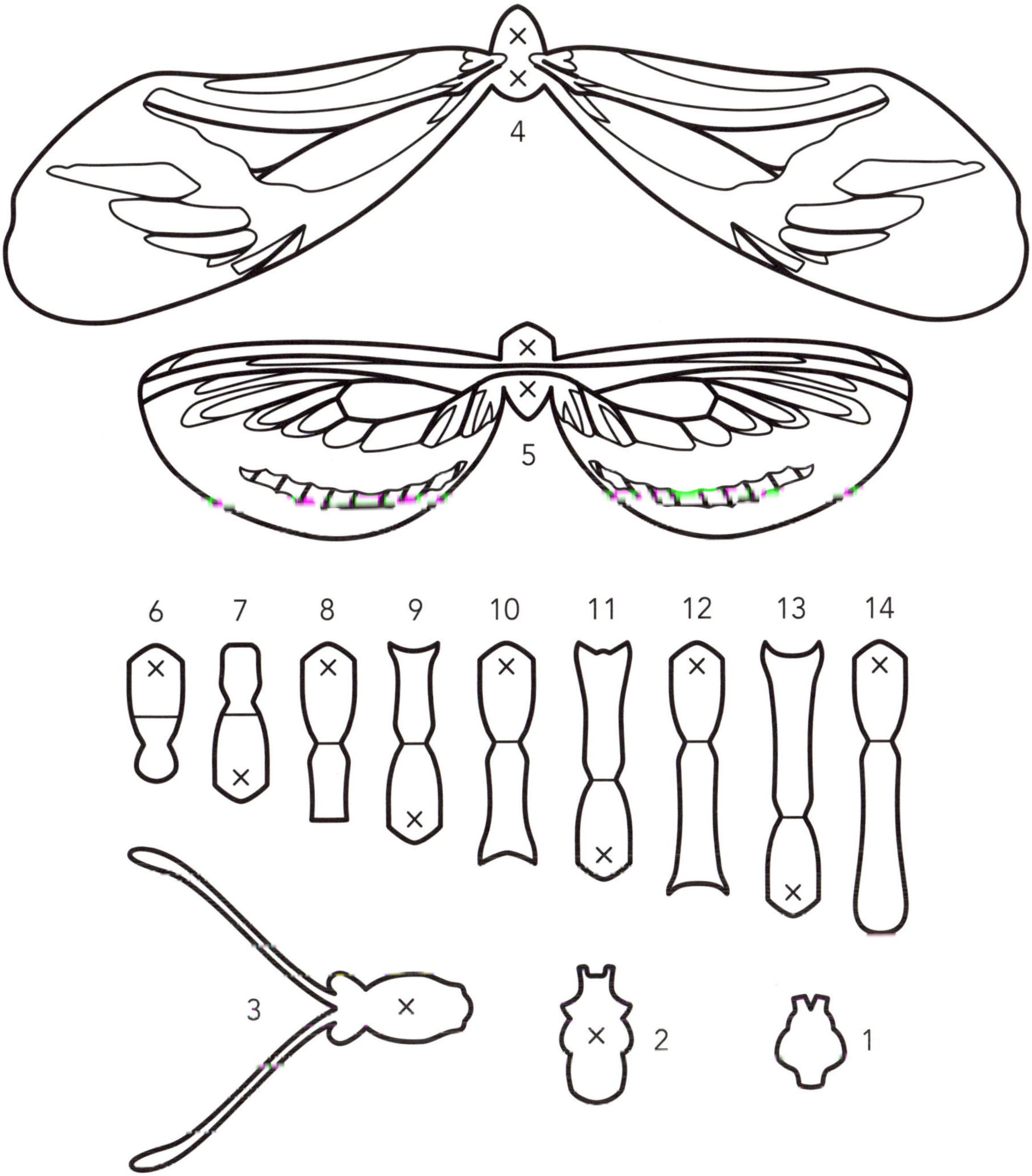

PUERTO RICAN HARLEQUIN BUTTERFLY TEMPLATE

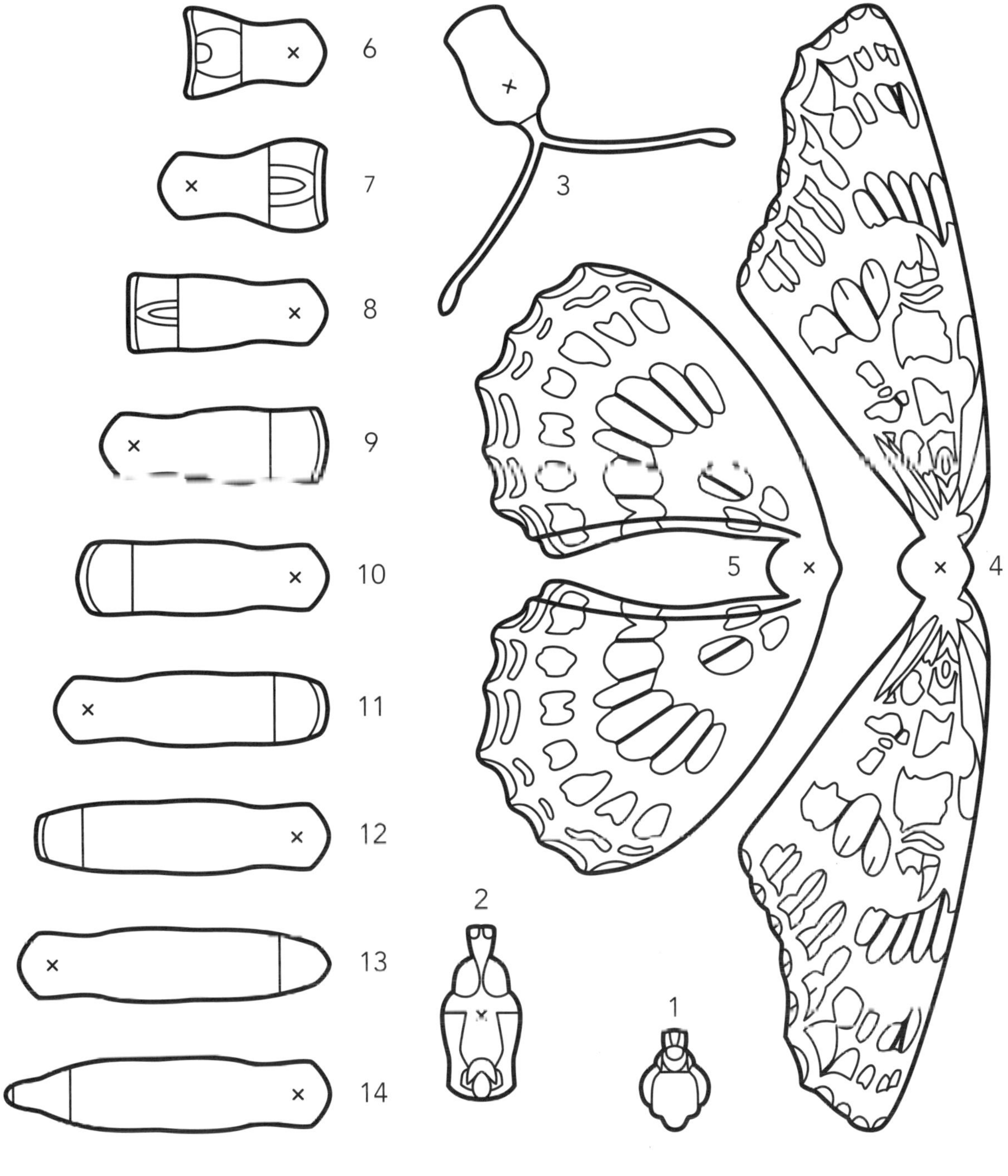

WOLKBERG ZULU BUTTERFLY TEMPLATE

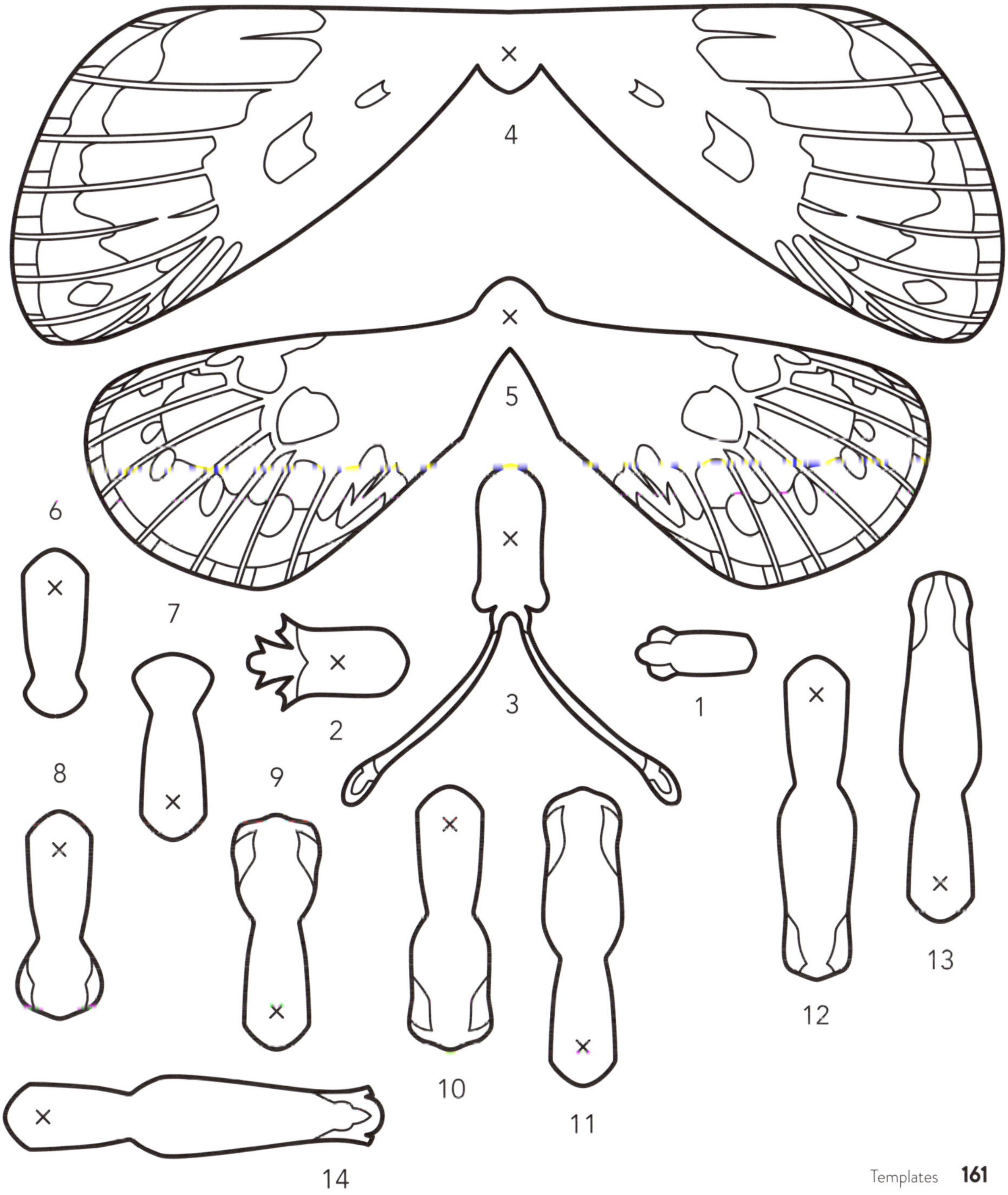

BATHURST COPPER BUTTERFLY *PURPLE* TEMPLATE

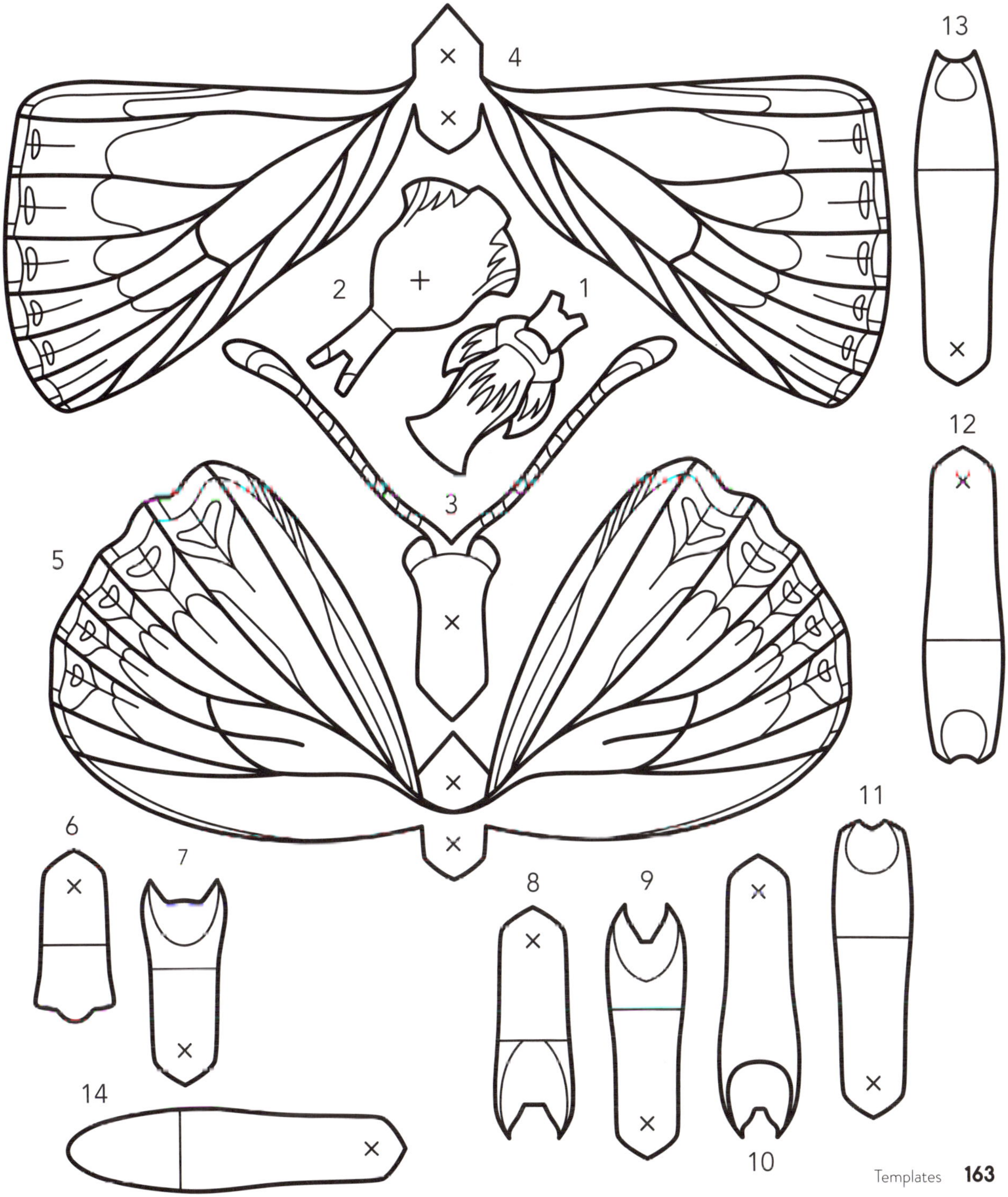

BATHURST COPPER BUTTERFLY *IRIDESCENT* TEMPLATE

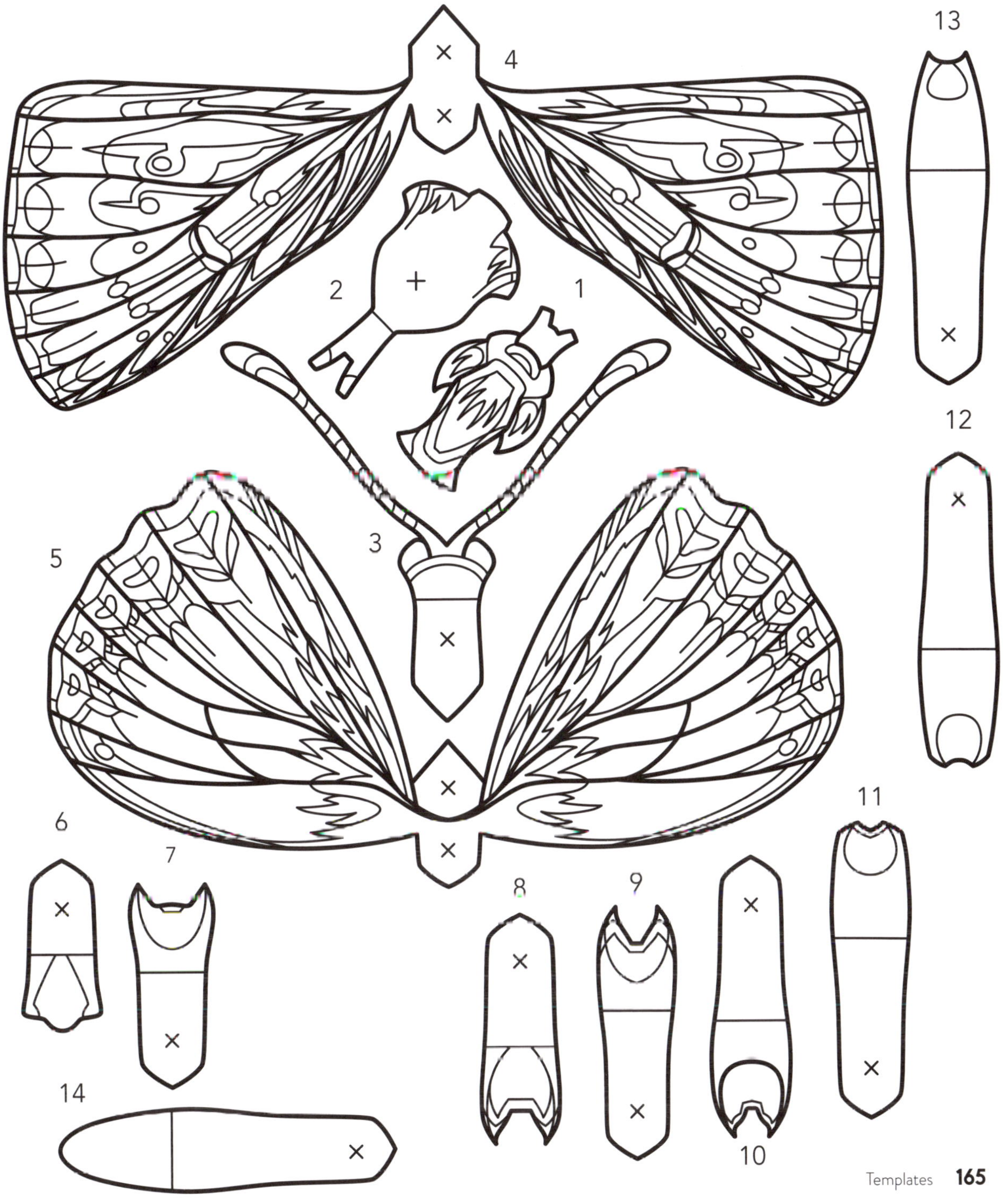